Marquee Series

MICROSOFT®

WINDOWS 8

Nita Rutkosky
Pierce College at Puyallup,
Puyallup, Washington

Denise Seguin
Fanshawe College,
London, Ontario

Audrey Roggenkamp
Pierce College at Puyallup,
Puyallup, Washington

Ian Rutkosky
Pierce College at Puyallup,
Puyallup, Washington

Paradigm
PUBLISHING

St. Paul

Contents

Managing Editor	Christine Hurney
Director of Production	Timothy W. Larson
Production Editor	Sarah Kearin
Cover and Text Designer	Leslie Anderson
Copy Editor	Sid Korpi, Proof Positive Editing
Design and Production Specialists	Jack Ross and Sara Schmidt Boldon
Testers	Desiree Carvel; Ann E. Mills, Ivy Tech Community College of Indiana, Indianapolis, IN; Brienna McWade
Indexer	Terry Casey
VP & Director of Digital Projects	Chuck Bratton
Digital Project Manager	Tom Modl

Windows® SECTION 1

Exploring Windows 8

Skills

- Navigate the Windows 8 Start screen
- Navigate the Windows 8 desktop
- Perform actions using the mouse, such as point, click, double-click, and drag
- Start and close a program
- Open and close a window
- Shut down Windows 8
- Move a window
- Minimize, maximize, and restore a window
- Stack and cascade windows
- Use the snap feature to position windows on the desktop
- Change the date and time
- Use components of a dialog box
- Adjust the volume using the Speaker slider bar
- Customize the Taskbar
- Use the Help and Support feature
- Turn on the display of file extensions

Projects Overview

Your department at Worldwide Enterprises has received new computers with the Windows 8 operating system. You will explore the Windows 8 Start screen and desktop; open, close, and manipulate windows; open a program; customize the Taskbar; explore the online help for Windows 8; and turn on the display of file extensions.

Activity 1.1

Exploring the Windows 8 Start Sceen

When you turn on your computer, the Windows 8 operating system loads and the Windows 8 Start screen displays on your monitor. The Windows 8 Start screen contains tiles you can use to open programs or access features within Windows 8. By default, the Windows 8 Start screen displays tiles for the most commonly used applications and features. Display all of the applications installed on your computer by right-clicking a blank area of the Start screen and then clicking the All apps icon that displays in the lower right corner of the screen. Windows 8 includes a Charm bar containing five buttons you can use to perform tasks such as searching apps, sharing apps, and shutting down the computer. Display the Charm bar by hovering the mouse over the upper or lower right corner of the screen.

Project

Tutorial 1.1
Exploring the
Windows 8 Start
Screen

Your department has received new computers with Windows 8 installed. You decide to take some time to explore the Windows 8 Start sceen to familiarize yourself with this new operating system.

1. Complete the step(s) needed to display the Windows 8 Start screen.

    Check with your instructor to determine the specific step(s) required to display the Windows 8 Start screen on your computer. If you are at school, you may need a user name and password to log on to the computer system. When Windows 8 starts, you will see a Start screen similar to the one shown in Figure 1.1. Your Start screen may contain additional tiles or have a different background than the one shown in Figure 1.1.

2. Move your mouse and notice how the corresponding pointer moves in the Windows 8 Start screen.

    The *mouse* is a device that controls the pointer that identifies your location on the screen. Move the mouse on your desk (preferably on a mouse pad) and the pointer moves on the screen. For information on mouse terms, refer to Table 1.1 and for information on mouse icons, refer to Table 1.2.

FIGURE 1.1 Windows 8 Start Screen

TABLE 1.1 Mouse Terms and Actions

Term	Action
point	Position the mouse pointer on the desired item.
click	Quickly tap the left button on the mouse once.
right-click	Quickly tap the right button on the mouse once.
double-click	Tap the left mouse button twice in quick succession.
drag	Press and hold down the left mouse button, move the mouse pointer to a specific location, and then release the mouse button.

TABLE 1.2 Mouse Icons

Icon	Description
I	The mouse appears as an I-beam pointer in a program screen in which you enter text (such as Microsoft Word) and also in text boxes. You can use the I-beam pointer to move the insertion point or select text.
↖	The mouse pointer appears as an arrow pointing up and to the left (called the *arrow pointer*) on the Windows desktop and also in other program title bars, menu bars, and toolbars.
↙↗ ↕↔	The mouse pointer becomes a double-headed arrow (either pointing left and right, up and down, or diagonally) when performing certain functions, such as changing the size of a window.
✥	Select an object in a program, such as a picture or image, and the mouse pointer displays with a four-headed arrow attached. Use this four-headed arrow pointer to move the object left, right, up, or down.
↖	When you position the mouse pointer inside selected text in a document (such as a Microsoft Word document) and then drag the selected text to a new location in the document, the pointer displays with a gray box attached, indicating that you are moving the text.
↖○	When a request is being processed or a program is being loaded, the mouse pointer may display with a moving circle icon beside it. The moving circle means "please wait." When the process is completed, the moving circle disappears.
👆	When you position the mouse pointer on certain icons or hyperlinks, it turns into a hand with a pointing index finger. This image indicates that clicking the icon or hyperlink will display additional information.

3 Click the Desktop tile in the Start screen.

The desktop is the main screen in Windows 8. Different tools and applications can be opened on the desktop, similar to how different tools, documents, and items can be placed on a desk.

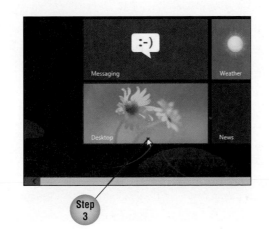

Step 3

continues

4 Position the mouse in the upper right corner of the desktop screen until the Charm bar displays.

> The Charm bar contains five buttons you can use to access different features and tools in Windows 8.

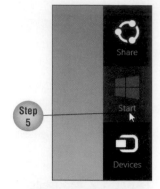

5 With the Charm bar displayed, click the Start button to return to the Start screen.

> Alternatively, you can return to the Start screen by positioning the mouse pointer in the lower left corner of the desktop until a Start screen thumbnail displays and then clicking the left mouse button.

Step 5

6 Right-click in a blank area of the Start screen and then click the All apps icon that appears in the lower right corner of the screen.

> The Windows 8 Start screen displays the most commonly used applications and features. Display all applications (grouped in categories) in the Start screen if you cannot find a desired application.

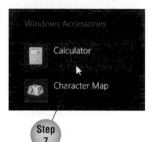

Step 6

7 Click the Calculator tile that displays in the *Windows Accessories* section.

> Clicking the Calculator tile causes the Calculator tool to open and display on the desktop.

8 Close the Calculator by clicking the Close button ✕ that displays in the upper right corner of the program.

Step 7

Step 8

9 Complete Steps 4 and 5 to return to the Start screen.

10 Click the Internet Explorer tile.

> Certain applications, such as Internet Explorer, can be opened in the Start screen as well as on the desktop. Applications opened in the Start screen have been optimized to be used on touch devices.

Step 10

11 Close Internet Explorer by positioning the mouse pointer at the top of the screen until the pointer turns into a hand, holding down the left mouse button, dragging the mouse pointer to the bottom of the screen, and then releasing the left mouse button.

> Closing applications in the Windows 8 Start screen is different than closing applications on the desktop. Dragging an application down to the bottom of the screen closes it, while dragging an application to the left or right portion of the screen resizes the application and positions it on the side to which it was dragged.

In Brief

Start Program
1. Display Windows 8 Start screen.
2. Click desired program tile.

Shut Down Windows
1. Display Charm bar.
2. Click Settings button.
3. Click Power tile.
4. Click *Shut down*.

12 Display the Charm bar by positioning the mouse in the upper right corner of the screen and then click the Settings button on the Charm bar.

> The Settings button contains options for changing Windows 8 settings. It also contains the controls to shut down the computer.

13 Click the Power tile located toward the bottom of the Settings panel.

14 Click the *Shut down* option at the pop-up list that displays.

> The Power tile contains three options. The *Sleep* option turns off the monitor and hard drives to conserve power. The *Shut down* option turns off the computer, and the *Restart* option turns off the computer and then restarts it.

Step 13

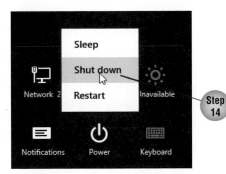

Step 14

Need Help?

Check with your instructor before shutting down Windows 8. If you are working in a computer lab at your school, a shared computer lab policy may prevent you from shutting down the computer. In this case, proceed to the next activity.

In Addition

Putting the Computer to Sleep

In Windows 8, Sleep mode saves all of your work and places the computer in a low power state by turning off the monitor and hard drive. A light on the outside of the computer case blinks or turns a different color to indicate Sleep mode is active. Wake up the computer by pressing the Power button on the front of the computer case, or by moving the mouse. After you log on, the screen will display exactly as you left it when you activated Sleep mode. Sleep mode causes Windows to automatically save your work, whereas shutting down does not.

Activity
1.2

Exploring the Windows 8 Desktop

The Windows 8 desktop can be compared to the top of a desk in an office. A person places necessary tools—such as pencils, pens, paper, files, or a calculator—on his or her desktop to perform functions. Similarly, the Windows 8 desktop contains tools for operating the computer. These tools are logically grouped and placed in dialog boxes or windows that can be accessed using the icons located on the desktop. The desktop is the most common screen in Windows 8 and is the screen in which most applications and tools will open and run.

Project You decide to take some time to explore the Windows 8 desktop to familiarize yourself with this important screen of the operating system.

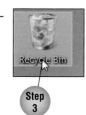

Tutorial 1.2
Exploring the
Windows 8 Desktop

1. If necessary, turn on the power to your computer to start Windows. At the Windows 8 Start screen, click the Desktop tile.

    When the Windows 8 Start screen is displayed, you will see a screen similar to the one in Figure 1.1 on page 2. When your Windows desktop displays, it may contain additional icons or have a different background than the desktop shown in Figure 1.2 below.

2. Move the mouse pointer to the bottom right corner of the desktop where the current day and time display at the right side of the Taskbar. After approximately one second, a pop-up box appears with the current day of the week as well as the current date.

    To identify the location of the Taskbar, refer to Figure 1.2.

3. Position the mouse pointer on the Recycle Bin icon and then double-click the left mouse button.

    Icons provide an easy method for opening programs or documents. Double-clicking the *Recycle Bin* icon displays the Recycle Bin window. When you open a program, a defined work area, referred to as a ***window***, appears on the screen.

FIGURE 1.2 Windows 8 Desktop

Recycle
Bin icon

Position the
mouse pointer
here to access
the Start screen.

Taskbar

4 Close the Recycle Bin window by clicking the Close button that displays in the upper right corner of the window.

In Brief
Display Windows 8 Desktop
Click Desktop tile.

5 Position the mouse pointer in the lower left corner of the screen until the Start screen thumbnail displays and then click the right mouse button.

When you right-click the Start screen thumbnail, a pop-up list displays with various options. You can use these options to access computer and operating system management features such as the Control Panel, Task Manager, and Device Manager.

6 Click the *System* option in the pop-up list to display information about your computer in a new window.

Your computer's information will appear in the System window. This information can be useful when determining if your computer is capable of running advanced software, or when you want to upgrade hardware such as RAM or a processor.

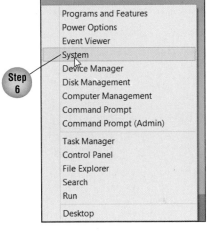

Step 6

7 Close the System window by clicking the Close button that displays in the upper right corner of the window.

8 Right-click in a blank area of the desktop (not on an icon or the Taskbar).

A shortcut menu will display with various options you can use to manage files and/or change the way the desktop appears on your monitor.

9 Click the *Personalize* option at the shortcut menu.

The Personalization window contains options such as the Desktop Background, Color, Sounds, and Screen Saver, which you can customize.

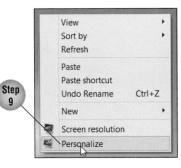

Step 9

10 Close the Personalization window by clicking the Close button in the upper right corner of the window.

In Addition

Changing the Appearance of Windows 8

You can change the appearance of Windows 8 with options that display when you right-click a blank area of the desktop. Click the *Personalize* option at the shortcut menu if you want to change the Windows theme, desktop background, color, sounds, or screen saver. You can also change how the desktop icons and mouse pointers display. Click the *Screen resolution* option at the shortcut menu if you want to change the screen resolution, the monitor orientation, or the size of text or other items. The Screen Resolution window also contains controls for setting up multiple displays. Customizing how Windows 8 appears on your monitor by increasing the size of certain elements or changing certain colors can make Windows easier to use.

Activity 1.3

Opening and Manipulating Windows

When you open a program, a defined work area, referred to as a *window*, appears on the screen. You can move a window on the desktop and change the size of a window. The top of a window is called the Title bar and generally contains buttons at the right side for closing, minimizing, maximizing, and/or restoring the size of the window. More than one window can be open at a time, and open windows can be cascaded or stacked. When a window is moved to the left or right side of the screen, the Snap feature in Windows 8 causes it to "stick" to the edge of the screen. When the window is moved to the top of the screen, the window is automatically maximized, and when a maximized window is dragged down, the window is automatically restored down.

Project

You decide to continue your exploration of the Windows 8 desktop by opening and manipulating windows.

Tutorial 1.3
Opening and Using Windows

1. At the Windows 8 desktop, double-click the Recycle Bin icon.

   This opens the Recycle Bin window on the desktop. If the Recycle Bin window fills the entire desktop, click the Restore Down button, which is the second button from the right (immediately left of the Close button) in the upper right corner of the window.

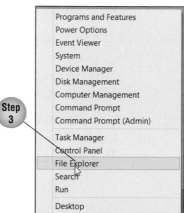

Step 1

2. Move the window on the desktop. To do this, position the mouse pointer on the window's Title bar (the bar along the top of the window), hold down the left mouse button, drag the window to a different location on the desktop, and then release the mouse button.

3. Position the mouse pointer in the lower left corner of the desktop to display the Start screen thumbnail, click the right mouse button, and then click the *File Explorer* option in the pop-up list.

   If the Computer window fills the entire desktop, click the Restore Down button in the upper right corner of the window. You now have two windows open on the desktop—Computer and Recycle Bin.

```
Programs and Features
Power Options
Event Viewer
System
Device Manager
Disk Management
Computer Management
Command Prompt
Command Prompt (Admin)

Task Manager
Control Panel
File Explorer
Search
Run

Desktop
```

Step 3

4. Make sure the Title bar of the Recycle Bin window is visible (if not, move the Computer window) and then click the Recycle Bin Title bar.

   Clicking the Recycle Bin Title bar makes the Recycle Bin window active and moves it in front of the Computer window.

5. Minimize the Recycle Bin window to the Taskbar by clicking the Minimize button (located toward the right side of the Recycle Bin Title bar).

   The minimized Recycle Bin window is positioned behind the File Explorer button (displays as a group of file folders) on the Taskbar. Notice the File Explorer button now appears with another button stacked behind it.

Step 5

6. Minimize the Computer window to the Taskbar (behind the File Explorer button) by clicking the Minimize button located at the right side of the Title bar.

7 Move the pointer over the File Explorer button at the left side of the Taskbar.

> The two minimized windows are stacked behind the File Explorer button. Resting the pointer on the File Explorer button causes a thumbnail preview of each window to display.

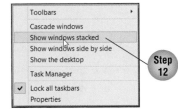

Step 7

Step 8

In Brief

Move Window
1. Position mouse pointer on window Title bar.
2. Hold down left mouse button.
3. Drag window to desired position.
4. Release mouse button.

Stack Windows
1. Right-click an unused section of Taskbar.
2. Click *Show windows stacked* at shortcut menu.

Cascade Windows
1. Right-click an unused section of Taskbar.
2. Click *Cascade windows* at shortcut menu.

8 Click the thumbnail preview for the Computer window to redisplay the window on the desktop.

9 Rest the pointer over the File Explorer button on the Taskbar and then click the thumbnail preview for the Recycle Bin window.

10 Drag the Title bar for the Recycle Bin window to the top of the desktop and then release the mouse button.

> Dragging a window to the top of the desktop causes the window to automatically maximize when you release the mouse button. The Snap feature allows you to resize a window by dragging the window to the edge of a screen. You can also maximize the window by clicking the Maximize button ▭ adjacent to the Close button at the right side of the Title bar.

11 Drag the Title bar for the Recycle Bin window down from the top of the desktop to restore the window to its previous size before it was maximized.

12 Right-click a blank, unused section of the Taskbar and then click *Show windows stacked* at the shortcut menu.

> The Taskbar shortcut menu provides three options to display windows: *Cascade windows,* which places the windows in a fanned, single stack with the title bar of each open window visible; *stacked,* which places windows in a horizontal stack with a portion of each window visible; or *side by side,* which places open windows next to each other.

| Toolbars ▸ |
| Cascade windows |
| Show windows stacked |
| Show windows side by side |
| Show the desktop |
| Task Manager |
| ✓ Lock all taskbars |
| Properties |

Step 12

13 Drag the Recycle Bin window off the right edge of the screen and then release the mouse button. When you release the mouse button, the window resizes to fill one-half the width of the screen.

14 Drag the Computer window off the left edge of the screen and then release the mouse button. When you release the mouse button, the window resizes to fill the remaining width of the screen.

15 Close each of the two windows by clicking the Close button ✕ located at the right side of the Title bar.

In Addition

Sizing a Window

Using the mouse, you can increase or decrease the size of a window. To change the width, position the mouse pointer on the border at the right or left side of the window until the mouse turns into a left-and-right-pointing arrow. Hold down the left mouse button, drag the border to the right or left, and then release the mouse button. Complete similar steps to increase or decrease the height of the window using the top or bottom borders. To change the width and height of the window at the same time, position the mouse pointer at the left or right corner of the window until the pointer turns into a diagonally pointing, double-headed arrow and then drag in the desired direction to change the size.

Activity 1.4

Exploring the Taskbar, Charm Bar, and Dialog Box Components

The bar that displays at the bottom of the desktop is called the **Taskbar** and it is divided into three sections: the Start screen area, the task button area, and the notification area. Position the mouse in the Start screen area to display the Start screen thumbnail. Open programs display as task buttons in the task button area of the Taskbar. The notification area displays at the right side of the Taskbar and contains a clock and the program icons for programs that run in the background on your computer. You can right-click a blank, unused portion of the Taskbar to display a shortcut menu with options for customizing the Taskbar. The bar that displays at the right side of the desktop when the mouse pointer is positioned in the upper or lower right corner of the desktop is called the *Charm bar*. Click buttons in the Charm bar to access common operating system features. Some settings are changed in a window called a *dialog box*. Dialog boxes contain similar features such as tabs, text boxes, and option buttons that you can use to change settings.

Project

Tutorial 1.4
Exploring the Taskbar and the Charm Bar

As you continue exploring Windows 8, you want to learn more about the features available on the Taskbar.

1. At the Windows 8 desktop, click the current time that displays at the far right side of the Taskbar and then click the <u>Change date and time settings</u> hyperlink in the pop-up box.

   Figure 1.3 identifies the components of the Taskbar. Clicking the current time and then clicking the <u>Change date and time settings</u> hyperlink causes the Date and Time dialog box to display. Refer to Table 1.3 on the next page for information on dialog box components. Each listed component will not be present in every dialog box.

2. Check to make sure the correct date and time display in the Date and Time dialog box.

   If the date is incorrect, click the Change date and time button. At the Date and Time Settings dialog box, click the correct date in the calendar box. If necessary, use the left- or right-pointing arrows to change the calendar display to a different month. To change the time, double-click the hour, minutes, or seconds and then type the correct entry or use the up- or down-pointing arrows to adjust the time. Click OK when finished.

3. Click the Additional Clocks tab located toward the top of the Date and Time dialog box.

   At this tab, you can add the ability to show a second clock when you hover over or click the current time in the Taskbar. For example, you could show the current time for Cairo, Egypt, in addition to the current time for your time zone.

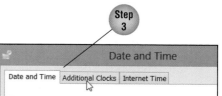

FIGURE 1.3 Taskbar

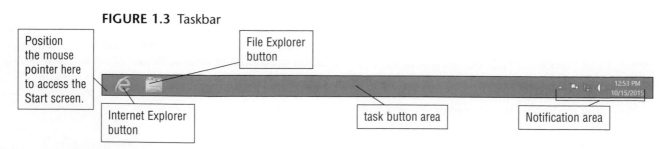

Position the mouse pointer here to access the Start screen.

File Explorer button

Internet Explorer button

task button area

Notification area

TABLE 1.3 Possible Dialog Box Components

Name	Image	Function
tabs	Date and Time | Additional Clocks | Internet Time	Click a dialog box tab and the dialog box options change.
text box	Search Computer 🔍	Type or edit text in a text box. A text box may contain up- or down-pointing arrows to allow you to choose a number or an option instead of typing it.
drop-down list box	M/d/yyyy M/d/yyyy M/d/yy MM/dd/yy MM/dd/yyyy yy/MM/dd yyyy-MM-dd dd-MMM-yy	Click the down-pointing arrow at the right side of an option box and a drop-down list displays.
list box	Windows Asterisk Calendar Reminder Close Program Critical Battery Alarm Critical Stop	A list box displays a list of options.
check boxes	Desktop icons ☐ Computer ☑ Recycle Bin ☐ User's Files ☐ Control Panel ☐ Network	If a check box contains a check mark, the option is active; if the check box is empty, the option is inactive. In some cases, any number of check boxes may be active.
option buttons	○ Smaller - 100% (default) ◉ Medium - 125% ○ Larger - 150%	Only one option button in a dialog box section can be selected at once. An active option button contains a dark or colored circle.
command buttons	OK Cancel Apply	Click a command button to execute or cancel a command. If a command button name is followed by an ellipsis (...), clicking the button will open another dialog box.
slider bar	Slow ———▽——— Fast	Using the mouse, drag a slider button on a slider bar to increase or decrease the number, speed, or percentage of the option.
scroll bar	(UTC-12:00) International Date Line West (UTC-11:00) Coordinated Universal Time-11 (UTC-10:00) Hawaii (UTC-09:00) Alaska (UTC-08:00) Baja California (UTC-08:00) Pacific Time (US & Canada) (UTC-07:00) Arizona (UTC-07:00) Chihuahua, La Paz, Mazatlan (UTC-07:00) Mountain Time (US & Canada) (UTC-06:00) Central America (UTC-06:00) Central Time (US & Canada)	A scroll bar displays when the amount of information in a list is larger than can fit in a single window.

continues

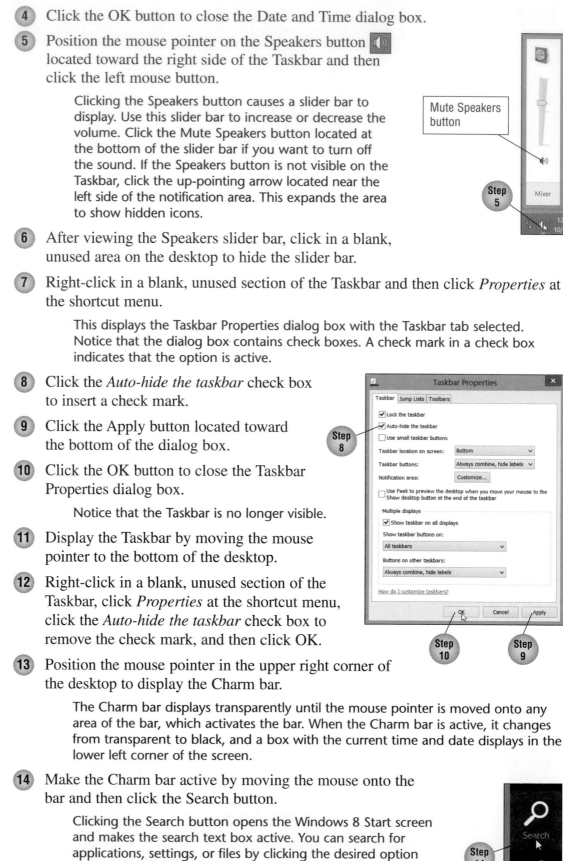

4 Click the OK button to close the Date and Time dialog box.

5 Position the mouse pointer on the Speakers button located toward the right side of the Taskbar and then click the left mouse button.

> Clicking the Speakers button causes a slider bar to display. Use this slider bar to increase or decrease the volume. Click the Mute Speakers button located at the bottom of the slider bar if you want to turn off the sound. If the Speakers button is not visible on the Taskbar, click the up-pointing arrow located near the left side of the notification area. This expands the area to show hidden icons.

6 After viewing the Speakers slider bar, click in a blank, unused area on the desktop to hide the slider bar.

7 Right-click in a blank, unused section of the Taskbar and then click *Properties* at the shortcut menu.

> This displays the Taskbar Properties dialog box with the Taskbar tab selected. Notice that the dialog box contains check boxes. A check mark in a check box indicates that the option is active.

8 Click the *Auto-hide the taskbar* check box to insert a check mark.

9 Click the Apply button located toward the bottom of the dialog box.

10 Click the OK button to close the Taskbar Properties dialog box.

> Notice that the Taskbar is no longer visible.

11 Display the Taskbar by moving the mouse pointer to the bottom of the desktop.

12 Right-click in a blank, unused section of the Taskbar, click *Properties* at the shortcut menu, click the *Auto-hide the taskbar* check box to remove the check mark, and then click OK.

13 Position the mouse pointer in the upper right corner of the desktop to display the Charm bar.

> The Charm bar displays transparently until the mouse pointer is moved onto any area of the bar, which activates the bar. When the Charm bar is active, it changes from transparent to black, and a box with the current time and date displays in the lower left corner of the screen.

14 Make the Charm bar active by moving the mouse onto the bar and then click the Search button.

> Clicking the Search button opens the Windows 8 Start screen and makes the search text box active. You can search for applications, settings, or files by clicking the desired option below the search text box.

15 Type **snipping tool** in the search text box.

> Notice that Windows 8 actively narrows the search results in the *Apps* section of the screen as you type.

16 Press the Enter key on the keyboard.

> Pressing the Enter key opens the Snipping Tool in a new window on the desktop. If the search does not return a match for what you typed in the text box, a list of possible results will display.

Step 15

In Brief

Display Date and Time Dialog Box
1. Click current time at right side of Taskbar.
2. Click Change date and time settings.

Display Speakers Slider Bar
Click Speakers button on Taskbar.

Display Taskbar Properties Dialog Box
1. Right-click an unused section on Taskbar.
2. Click *Properties* at shortcut menu.

17 Close the Snipping Tool window by clicking the Close button in the upper right corner of the window.

18 Make the Charm bar active and then click the Settings button.

19 At the Settings panel, click the *Change PC settings* option located at the bottom of the panel.

> When you click the *Change PC settings* option in the Settings panel, the PC settings screen displays. This screen contains a variety of options for changing the settings of your computer. These options are grouped into categories that display at the left side of the PC settings screen.

Step 19

20 Close the PC settings screen by positioning the mouse pointer at the top of the screen until it turns into a hand, holding down the left mouse button, dragging the PC settings screen to the bottom of the screen until it dims, and then releasing the left mouse button.

> In Windows 8, certain applications and tools open in the Start screen instead of in a window on the desktop. To close applications or tools that open in the Start screen, drag the top of the screen to the bottom of the screen until it becomes dim and then release the mouse button.

In Addition

Managing Devices Using the Charm Bar

The Charm bar contains the Devices button ▣, which you can use to manage devices plugged into your computer. Click the Devices button on the Charm bar and the Devices panel displays at the right side of the screen. Devices plugged into your computer display as a list in the Devices panel.

Click a device in the Devices list to display options for a particular device. Devices that are commonly listed in the Devices panel are monitors, projectors, and other peripheral devices that may be plugged into your computer.

Activity 1.5

Getting Help in Windows; Displaying File Extensions

Windows 8 includes an on-screen reference guide, called Windows Help and Support, that provides information, explanations, and interactive help on learning Windows features. The Windows Help and Support feature contains complex files with hypertext that can be clicked to display additional information. Display the Windows Help and Support window by right-clicking a blank area of the Start screen, clicking the All apps icon and then clicking the Help and Support tile in the Windows System section. You can also press F1 at the desktop and the Windows Help and Support window will display with information on your current task. At the Windows Help and Support window, you can perform such actions as choosing a specific help topic, searching for a keyword, and displaying a list of help topics.

Project You decide to use the Windows Help and Support feature to learn how to pin an application to the Taskbar. You also want to find out how to turn on the display of file extensions.

Worldwide Enterprises

SNAP

Tutorial 1.5
Getting Help
in Windows 8

1. Display the Windows 8 Start screen, right-click a blank area of the screen, and then click the All apps icon.

2. Use the horizontal scroll bar at the bottom of the screen to display the *Windows System* section and then click the Help and Support tile.

3. At the Windows Help and Support window with the insertion point positioned in the search text box, type **taskbar** and press Enter.

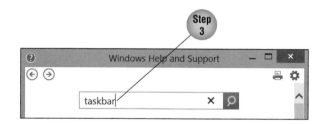

4. Click the How to use the taskbar hyperlink in the search results list.

5. Scroll down the Windows Help and Support window and then read the information under the heading *Pin an app to the taskbar*.

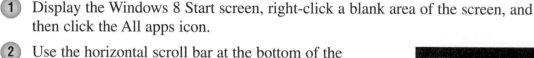

You will open and then pin the Snipping Tool application to the Taskbar in the following steps.

6. Open the Snipping Tool from the Windows 8 Start screen or by using the Charm bar to conduct a search for the Snipping Tool application.

7. Return to the Windows Help and Support window by clicking the Windows Help and Support button on the Taskbar.

8. Follow the instructions in the *Pin an app to the taskbar* section of the Windows

Help and Support window to pin the Snipping Tool to the Taskbar.

When you pin an application to the Taskbar, the button for the application will be added to and remain on the Taskbar until it is unpinned (even if you restart the computer). Pinning applications you use often to the Taskbar reduces the steps required to open them.

In Brief

Display Help and Support Window
1. Open Start screen.
2. Right-click blank area of Start screen.
3. Click All apps icon.
4. Click Help and Support tile.

9 Read information in the *Pin an app to the taskbar* section of the Windows Help and Support Window on how to remove a pinned application from the Taskbar and then unpin the Snipping Tool.

Note that unpinning the Snipping Tool application while the application is still open will unpin the button, but the button will display on the taskbar until the Snipping Tool application is closed.

10 Close the Windows Help and Support window and the Snipping Tool application by clicking the Close button located in the upper right corner of each window.

Worldwide Enterprises requires that employees work with the display of file extensions turned on. This practice helps employees identify source applications associated with files and can prevent employees from accidentally opening email attachments that contain harmful data. In the next steps, you will turn on the display of file extensions.

11 Click the File Explorer button on the Taskbar.

12 Click the View tab on the ribbon.

Windows 8 File Explorer contains a ribbon with four tabs: File, Home, Share, and View. These tabs contain options and buttons to change File Explorer settings and manage folders and files.

13 Click the *File name extensions* check box in the Show/hide group to insert a check mark. ***Note: If the check box appears with a check mark in it, then file extensions are already turned on—click the Cancel button.***

Inserting a check mark in a check box makes the option active.

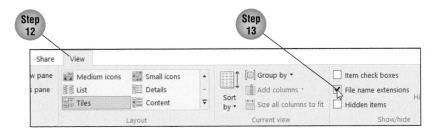

14 Close the File Explorer window by clicking the Close button located at the right side of the Title bar.

In Addition

Browsing the Windows Help and Support Window by Topic Lists

You can locate Help information by browsing the Contents list of topics instead of typing key words in the search text box. Click the Browse help button (located below the search text box) in the Windows Help and Support window. This displays the Windows Help topics list. Click the hyperlink to a topic category in the Windows Help topics list and then continue clicking hyperlinks until you find the information you need.

Features Summary

Feature	Button	Action
close window	✕	Click Close button on Title bar.
Computer window		Right-click Start screen thumbnail, click *File Explorer*.
Date and Time dialog box		Click time on Taskbar, click <u>Change date and time settings</u>.
maximize window	▭	Drag window to top of screen or click Maximize button on Title bar.
minimize window	▬	Click Minimize button on Title bar.
move window on desktop		Drag window Title bar.
restore window	▣	Drag maximized window down or click Restore Down button on Title bar.
shut down computer		Click Settings button on Charm bar, click Power, click *Shut down*.
Start screen		Click Start screen area on Taskbar.
Taskbar and Start Menu Properties dialog box		Right-click unused section of Taskbar, click *Properties* at shortcut menu.
Taskbar shortcut menu		Right-click unused section of Taskbar.
Speakers slider bar	🔊	Click Speakers button on Taskbar.
Windows Help and Support window		Open Start screen, right-click blank area, click All apps icon, click *Help and Support*.

Knowledge Check

Completion: In the space provided at the right, indicate the correct term, command, or option.

1. This mouse term refers to tapping the left mouse button twice in quick succession. _____

2. Click this button on a window Title bar to reduce the window to a task button on the Taskbar. _____

3. Click this button on a window Title bar to expand the window so it fills the entire screen. _____

4. Click the time located at the right side of the Taskbar and then click this option to open the Date and Time dialog box. _____

5. This is the name of a bar you can display on the desktop for quick access to a variety of Windows 8 features. _____

6. Windows Help and Support is accessed from this screen. _____

Skills Review

Review 1 Opening and Manipulating Windows

1. At the Windows 8 desktop, click the File Explorer button on the Taskbar. (If the Libraries window fills the desktop, drag the window down from the top of the screen or click the Restore Down button located in the upper right corner of the window.)
2. Double-click the Recycle Bin icon on the desktop. (If the Recycle Bin window fills the desktop, drag the window down from the top of the screen or click the Restore Down button.)
3. Position the mouse pointer on the Recycle Bin Title bar, hold down the left mouse button, and then drag the Recycle Bin window so the Libraries Title bar is visible.
4. Click the Libraries Title bar to make the window active.
5. Right-click in a blank, unused section of the Taskbar and then click *Cascade windows* at the shortcut menu.
6. Click the Minimize button (located toward the right side of the Title bar) on the Libraries Title bar to reduce the window to a task button behind the File Explorer button on the Taskbar.
7. Click the Minimize button on the Recycle Bin window to reduce the window to a task button behind the File Explorer button on the Taskbar.
8. Point to the File Explorer button on the Taskbar and then click the thumbnail preview for the Recycle Bin window to restore the Recycle Bin window on the desktop.
9. Point to the File Explorer button on the Taskbar and then click the thumbnail preview for the Libraries window to restore the Libraries window on the desktop.
10. Drag the Libraries window to the top of the screen and then release the mouse button. (The window expands to fill the entire screen.)
11. Drag the Libraries window down from the top of the screen to restore the window to its previous size and then release the mouse button.
12. Drag the Libraries window off the right edge of the screen until a transparent box displays on the right half of the screen and then release the mouse button.
13. Drag the Recycle Bin window off the left edge of the screen until a transparent box displays on the left half of the screen and then release the mouse button.
14. Close the Libraries window.
15. Close the Recycle Bin window.

Review 2 Exploring the Taskbar

1. At the Windows 8 desktop, click the time that displays in the notification area at the right side of the Taskbar and then click <u>Change date and time settings</u> hyperlink in the pop-up box.
2. At the Date and Time dialog box, click the Change date and time button.
3. At the Date and Time Settings dialog box, click the right arrow in the calendar to display the next month (from the current month).
4. Click the OK button twice.
5. Click the Start screen thumbnail, right-click in a blank area of the Start screen, click the All apps icon, and then click the Notepad tile in the *Windows Accessories* section. (Notepad is a program used for creating and editing text files.)
6. Close Notepad by clicking the Close button at the right side of the Notepad Title bar.

Skills Assessment

Assessment 1 Manipulating Windows

1. Click the File Explorer button on the Taskbar and then double-click the Pictures icon. (If the Pictures window fills the entire desktop, drag the window down from the top of the screen or click the Restore Down button.)
2. Right-click the File Explorer button on the Taskbar, click *File Explorer* in the pop-up list, and then double-click the Music icon. (If the Music window fills the entire desktop, drag the window down from the top of the screen or click the Restore Down button.)
3. Stack the two windows.
4. Make the Pictures window active and then reduce it to a task button on the Taskbar.
5. Reduce the Music window to a task button on the Taskbar.
6. Restore the Pictures window.
7. Restore the Music window.
8. Arrange the two windows side-by-side on the desktop with each window filling one-half the width of the screen.
9. Close the Music window and then close the Pictures window.

Assessment 2 Customizing the Taskbar

1. At the Windows 8 desktop, display the Date and Time dialog box.
2. Change the current hour to one hour ahead and then close the dialog box.
3. Display the Speakers slider bar, drag the slider to increase the volume, and then click the desktop outside the slider to hide the slider bar.
4. Display the Taskbar Properties dialog box, use the *Taskbar location on screen* option box to change the Taskbar location on the screen to *Top*, and then close the dialog box. (Notice that the Taskbar is now positioned along the top edge of the screen.)
5. Display the Charm bar and then click the Search button.
6. At the Search panel, type **calculator** in the text box and then press Enter.
7. Close the Calculator application.

Assessment 3 Restoring the Taskbar

1. At the Windows 8 desktop, display the Date and Time dialog box and then change the date and time to today's date and the current time.
2. Display the Speakers slider bar and then drag the slider button back to the original position.
3. Display the Taskbar Properties dialog box and change the Taskbar location so that the Taskbar displays back at the bottom of the screen.

Windows SECTION 2

Maintaining Files and Customizing Windows

Skills

- Browse the contents of storage devices
- Change folder and view options
- Create a folder
- Rename a folder or file
- Select, move, copy, and paste folders or files
- Delete files/folders to and restore files/folders from the Recycle Bin
- Explore the Control Panel
- Use search tools to find applications, folders, and/or files
- Customize the desktop
- Change screen resolution

Student Resources

Before beginning the activities in Windows Section 2, copy to your storage medium the Windows folder on the Student Resources CD. This folder contains the data files you need to complete the projects in Windows Section 2.

Projects Overview

Worldwide Enterprises

Explore options for browsing and viewing folders and files and then organize folders and files for your department at Worldwide Enterprises. This organization includes creating and renaming folders, as well as moving, copying, renaming, deleting, and restoring files. You will also search for specific files and customize your desktop to the corporate computer standard.

Performance Threads

Organize files for Performance Threads including creating folders and copying, moving, renaming, and deleting files.

First Choice TRAVEL

Organize files for First Choice Travel including creating folders and copying, moving, renaming, and deleting files. Assist your supervisor by searching for information on how to set up a computer for multiple users and how to work with libraries.

19

Activity 2.1

Browsing Storage Devices and Files in a Computer Window

Open a Computer window to view the various storage devices connected to your computer. The Content pane of the Computer window displays an icon for each hard disk drive and each removable storage medium such as a CD, DVD, or USB device. Next to each storage device icon, you can see the amount of storage space available as well as a bar with the amount of used space shaded with color. This visual cue allows you to see at a glance the proportion of space available relative to the capacity of the device. Double-click a device icon in the Content pane to show the contents stored on the device. You can display contents from another device or folder using the Navigation pane or the Computer window Address bar.

Project You decide to explore the contents of the various storage devices on the computer you are using as you become familiar with the Windows 8 environment.

Note: To complete the projects in this section, you will need to use a USB flash drive or computer hard drive rather than your SkyDrive. Before beginning the projects in this section, make sure you have copied the WindowsS2 folder from the Student Resources CD to your storage medium. If necessary, refer to the inside back cover of this textbook for instructions on how to copy a folder from the Student Resources CD to your storage medium.

Tutorial 2.1
Browsing Devices and Files

① If necessary, insert into an empty USB port the storage medium that you are using for the files in this course.

FIGURE 2.1 Computer Window

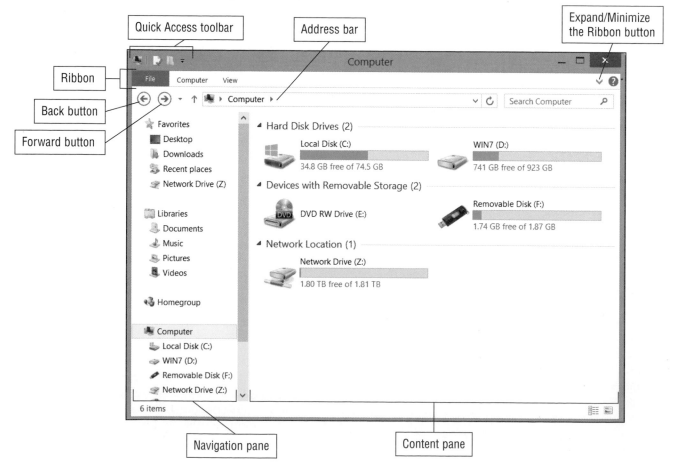

2 At the Windows desktop, position the mouse in the lower left corner of the screen to display the Start screen thumbnail, right-click the thumbnail to display a pop-up list, and then click *File Explorer*.

Step 2

> The Computer window displays. It should appear similar to the one shown in Figure 2.1.

3 Double-click the icon for the hard disk drive named *Local Disk (C:)*.

> The Computer window changes so that the Content pane displays the files and folders that are stored on the local hard disk drive assigned drive letter C:. Notice also that the Address bar in the Computer window updates to show the location where you are viewing *Local Disk (C:)* within *Computer* (your drive name may vary). You can navigate back using either the Back button or by clicking *Computer* in the Address bar.

4 Click the Back button ← to return to the Computer window.

5 Double-click the icon for the storage medium onto which you copied the WindowsS2 folder. *Note: The screens shown in this section show **Removable Disk (F:)** as the storage medium in the Computer window. Your icon label and drive letter may vary.*

Step 4

> USB flash drives are shown in the section of the Content pane labeled *Devices with Removable Storage.* Each device is assigned a drive letter

Step 5

> by Windows, usually starting at E or F and continuing through the alphabet depending on the number of removable devices that are currently in use. The label that displays next to the drive letter depends on the manufacturer of the USB flash drive. If no manufacturer label is present, Windows displays *Removable Disk.*

6 Double-click the *WindowsS2* folder to view the contents of the folder in the Content pane.

7 Look at the Address bar and notice how it displays the path to the current content list: Computer ▶ Removable Disk (F:) ▶ WindowsS2.

> You can use the Address bar to navigate to any other device or folder by clicking a drive or folder name or by clicking the right-pointing black arrow to view a drop-down list of folders or other devices.

Step 8   Step 7

8 Click *Computer* in the Address bar.

9 Click the right-pointing arrow ▶ next to *Computer* in the Address bar (the arrow becomes a down-pointing arrow when clicked) and then click the drive letter representing the removable storage device that contains the WindowsS2 folder.

Step 9

10 Click *Desktop* in the *Favorites* section of the Navigation pane.

> You can also change what displays in the Content pane by clicking the device or folder name in the Navigation pane. Click the white right-pointing arrow next to a device or folder name in the Navigation pane to expand the list and view what is stored within the item.

Step 10

11 Close the Computer window.

Activity 2.2

Changing Folder and View Options

You can change the view of the File Explorer window to show the contents of your current location (drive or folder) in various formats, including icons, tiles, or a list, among others. With the Content pane in Details view, you can click the column headings to change how the contents are sorted and whether they are sorted in ascending or descending order. You can customize a window's environment by using buttons and options on the File Explorer View tab. You can change how panes are displayed, how content is arranged in the Content pane, how content is sorted, and which features are hidden.

Project You decide to experiment with various folder and view options as you continue to become acquainted with the Windows 8 environment.

Tutorial 2.2
Changing Folder
and View Options

(1) Click the File Explorer button [ ] on the Taskbar.

> A Libraries window opens. For a description of libraries, refer to the In Addition section at the end of this activity.

(2) Click the drive letter representing your storage medium in the *Computer* section in the Navigation pane.

(3) Double-click the *WindowsS2* folder in the Content pane.

(4) Click the View tab located below the WindowsS2 Title bar.

(5) Click the *Large icons* option in the Layout group.

> After you click an option on the View tab, the View tab collapses to provide more space in the File Explorer window.

Step 2

Step 4   Step 5

(6) Click the View tab.

(7) Click the *Details* option in the Layout group.

Step 6   Step 7

(8) With folders now displayed in Details view, click the *Name* column heading to sort the list in descending order by name.

Step 8

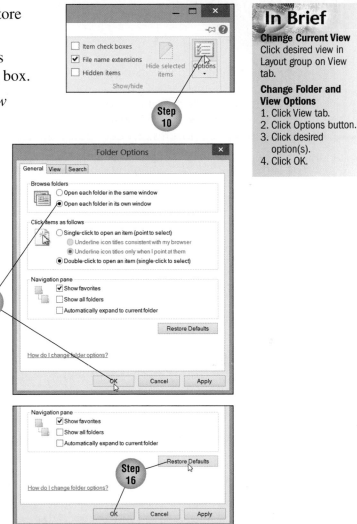

9. Click the *Name* column heading again to restore the list to ascending order by name.

10. Click the View tab and then click the Options button to open the Folder Options dialog box.

11. Click the *Open each folder in its own window* option in the *Browse folders* section on the General tab and then click OK.

12. Close the WindowsS2 window.

13. Click the File Explorer button on the Taskbar and then click the drive representing your storage medium in the *Computer* section in the Navigation pane.

14. Double-click the *WindowsS2* folder.

> Notice that this time a new window opens with the WindowsS2 content list layered on top of the original window.

15. Close the WindowsS2 folder window.

16. Click the View tab, click the Options button, click the Restore Defaults button located near the bottom of the General tab, and then click OK.

17. Close the Removable Disk (F:) window.

In Brief

Change Current View
Click desired view in Layout group on View tab.

Change Folder and View Options
1. Click View tab.
2. Click Options button.
3. Click desired option(s).
4. Click OK.

In Addition

Windows Libraries

While browsing the Computer window you may have noticed a section in the Navigation pane with the title *Libraries*. Libraries are tools you can use to keep track of and/or organize files that have something in common, regardless of where they are stored. A library does not store the actual files but instead keeps track of locations where the source files are stored. When you click the library name in the Navigation pane, the library displays all of the files in the locations that it is keeping track of associated with that library. For example, in the Pictures library, you could have Windows show you the contents of a Pictures folder on the local disk, from another folder on an external hard disk, and from a folder on a networked computer. Four default libraries are created when Windows 8 is installed: Documents, Music, Pictures, and Videos. You can create your own library and customize the locations associated with the default libraries. You will explore Libraries further in an assessment at the end of this section.

Changing the Default View for All Folders

You can set a view to display by default for all folders of a similar type (such as all disk drive folders or all documents folders). To do this, change the current view to the desired view for the type of folder that you want to set, such as a disk drive folder or a documents folder. Next, click the Options button on the View tab and then click the View tab at the Folder Options dialog box. Click the Apply to Folders button in the *Folder views* section and then click OK. Click Yes at the Folder Views message asking if you want all folders of this type to match this folder's view settings.

Activity 2.3

Creating a Folder; Renaming a Folder or File

As you begin working with programs, you will create files in which data (information) is saved. A file might be a Word document, an Excel workbook, or a PowerPoint presentation. Files can also be pictures or videos that you transfer from your digital camera to your computer. As you begin creating files, developing a system by which to organize those files becomes important so that you can easily retrieve a document or photograph when you need it. The first step in organizing your files is to create folders. Creating a folder is like creating a separate container in which you can place similar types of files. File management tasks such as creating a folder, renaming a folder or file, and copying and moving files and folders can be completed at a variety of locations, including the Computer and Documents windows.

Project

You need to organize files for your department at Worldwide Enterprises, so you decide to start by creating a folder.

Tutorial 2.3
Creating a Folder and Renaming a Folder or File

1. At the Windows desktop, position the mouse in the lower left corner of the screen to display the Start screen thumbnail, right-click the thumbnail, and then click *File Explorer* in the pop-up list.

2. Double-click the icon representing the storage medium onto which you copied the WindowsS2 folder.

3. Click the New folder button 🗀 on the Quick Access toolbar.

   A new folder icon is added to the Content pane with the text *New folder* already selected.

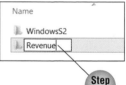

4. With the text *New folder* selected next to the folder icon, type **Revenue** and then press Enter. (As soon as you type the *R* in *Revenue*, the existing text *New folder* is immediately deleted.)

   This changes the folder name from *New folder* to *Revenue*.

5. You can also create a new folder using a shortcut menu. To begin, right-click in a blank, unused area of the Content pane, point to *New*, and then click *Folder*.

6. With the text *New folder* already selected next to the folder icon, type **Contracts** and then press Enter.

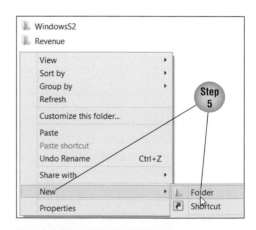

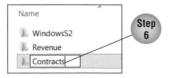

7. Click once on the *Revenue* folder to select the folder.

8. Click the Home tab and then click the Rename button in the Organize group.

9 With the text *Revenue* selected, type **Income** and then press Enter.

You can also use the shortcut menu to rename a file or folder.

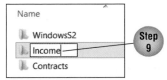

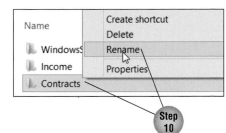
Step 9

In Brief

Create New Folder
1. Display Computer window.
2. Double-click device in which to create folder.
3. Click New folder button on Quick Access toolbar.
4. Type folder name and press Enter.

Rename Folder or File
1. Display Computer window.
2. Navigate to desired drive and/or folder.
3. Right-click file to be renamed.
4. At shortcut menu, click *Rename*.
5. Type new file name and press Enter.

10 Right-click the *Contracts* folder and then click *Rename* at the shortcut menu.

Step 10

Step 11

11 With the text *Contracts* selected, type **Administration** and then press Enter.

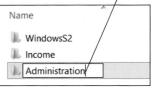

12 Double-click the *WindowsS2* folder.

13 Right-click the file **FCTExcelSalesCom.xlsx** and then click *Rename* at the shortcut menu.

14 Type **FCTSalesCommissions** and then press Enter.

Notice when you rename a file that Windows does not select the file extension. Programs such as Microsoft Word and Microsoft Excel automatically assign a file extension to each file (in this case, Word documents or Excel workbooks). These file extensions should remain intact. If you rename or remove a file extension by accident, Windows prompts you with a message that the file may no longer be usable and asks you if you are sure.

Name

- FCTBookings.xlsx
- FCTCCSkiing.docx
- FCTSalesCommissions.xlsx
- FCTHawaiianSpecials.docx
- FCTIslandFlights.docx
- FCTNorwayTour.docx

Step 14

15 Close the Computer window.

In Addition

More about Organizing Files into Folders

Think of a *folder* on the computer the same way you think of a file folder in which you would store paper documents in your filing cabinet. Generally, you put similar types of documents into the same folder. For example, all of your rent receipts might be placed inside a file folder on which you have written the label *Rent* on the folder tab. Similarly, on the computer, you could create a folder named *Rent* and store all of the electronic copies of all of your rental documents within that folder. On the computer, a folder can have another folder stored inside it. The folder within the folder is referred to as a *subfolder*. For example, you may have thousands of pictures stored on your computer. Saving all of the pictures in one folder named *Pictures* would be too cumbersome when the content list contains thousands of images. You would be scrolling a long time to locate a particular picture. Instead, consider creating subfolders in the Pictures folder so that related pictures are grouped together in one place.

Activity 2.4

Selecting and Copying Folders and Files

In addition to creating and renaming files and folders, file management activities include selecting, moving, copying, and deleting files or folders. Open a Computer or Documents window to perform file management tasks. Use options on the Home tab or at a shortcut menu. More than one file or folder can be moved, copied, or deleted at one time. Select adjacent files and folders using the Shift key, and select nonadjacent files and folders using the Ctrl key. When selecting multiple files or folders, you may want to change the view to *List* in the Computer window.

Project

As you continue to organize files for your department, you will copy files to the Income folder you created in Activity 2.3.

1. At the Windows desktop, open a Computer window.

   You can open a Computer window by either right-clicking the Start screen thumbnail and then clicking *File Explorer* or by clicking the File Explorer button on the Taskbar and then clicking *Computer* in the Navigation pane.

Tutorial 2.4
Selecting, Copying, and Moving Folders and Files

2. Double-click the icon representing the storage medium onto which you copied the WindowsS2 folder.

3. Double-click the *WindowsS2* folder in the Content pane.

4. Click the View tab and then click the *List* option in the Layout group.

5. Click the file named ***WEExcelRevenues.xlsx*** in the Content pane.

   Click once to select a file. Windows displays file properties for the selected file in the bottom left corner of the WindowsS2 window.

6. Hold down the Shift key, click the file named ***WETable02.docx***, and then release the Shift key.

   Clicking ***WETable02.docx*** while holding down the Shift key causes all files from ***WEExcelRevenues.xlsx*** through ***WETable02.docx*** to be selected.

7. Position the mouse pointer within the selected group of files, right-click, and then click *Copy* at the shortcut menu.

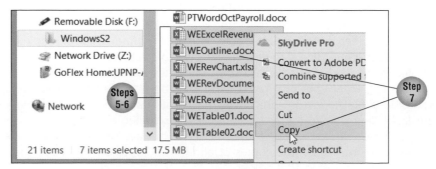

8 Click the Back button located left of the Address bar.

9 Double-click the *Income* folder.

10 Right-click in the Content pane and then click *Paste* at the shortcut menu.

When a large file or large group of files is copied, Windows displays a message box with a progress bar to indicate the approximate time required to copy the files, as shown in Figure 2.2. The message box closes when the copying process is complete.

In Brief

Copy Adjacent Files to New Folder
1. Display Computer window.
2. Navigate to desired drive and/or folder.
3. If necessary, change current view to *List*.
4. Click first file name.
5. Hold down Shift key and then click last file name.
6. Right-click in selected group of files and click *Copy*.
7. Navigate to desired destination drive and/or folder.
8. Right-click in blank area of Content pane and click *Paste*.

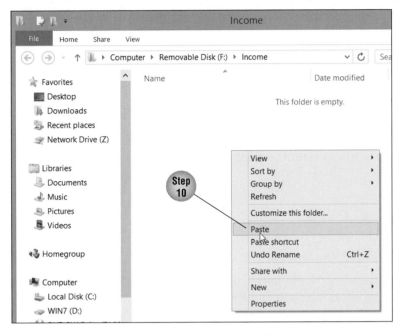

11 Click in a blank area of the Content pane to deselect the file names.

12 Close the Computer window.

FIGURE 2.2 Time to Complete Message Box

In Addition

Copying by Dragging

You can also copy a file or folder to another location using a drag-and-drop technique. To do this, open a Computer or Documents window and display the desired file or folder in the Content pane. Position the mouse pointer on the file or folder to be copied, hold down the left mouse button, drag to the destination drive or folder name in the *Favorites, Libraries,* or *Computer* list in the Navigation pane, and then release the mouse button. By default, if you drag a file from one disk drive to another, Windows copies the file. However, to copy a file from one folder to another on the same disk drive, you must hold down the Ctrl key as you drag. To make dragging and dropping easier, you can open two windows and arrange them side-by-side on the desktop. In one window, display the files you want to copy. In the other window, display the destination folder. Select the files to be copied and then hold down the Ctrl key while dragging them to the destination window.

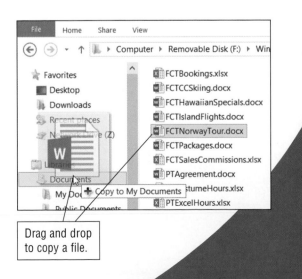

Drag and drop to copy a file.

Activity 2.5

Moving Folders and Files

Move files in a Computer or Documents window in a manner similar to copying files. Select the file(s) or folder(s) you want to move, position the mouse pointer over the selected file(s) or folder(s), right-click, and then click *Cut* at the shortcut menu. Navigate to the desired destination location, right-click a blank area in the Content pane, and then click *Paste* at the shortcut menu. You can also use the Copy, Cut, and Paste buttons in the Clipboard group on the Home tab.

Project

After further review of the files you copied into the Income folder, you decide to create another folder and move some of the files from the Income folder into the new folder.

Worldwide Enterprises

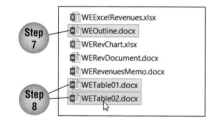
SNAP

Review Tutorial 2.4
Selecting, Copying, and Moving Folder and Files

1. At the Windows desktop, display a Computer window.

2. Double-click the icon representing the storage medium onto which you copied the WindowsS2 folder.

3. Click the New folder button on the Quick Access toolbar.

4. Type **Distribution** and then press Enter.

5. Double-click the *Income* folder.

6. Change the current view to *List*.

7. Click once on **WEOutline.docx**.

   Clicking once on the file selects the file name, thereby identifying the item you want to move; double-clicking the file would instruct Windows to open Word and then open the document.

8. Hold down the Ctrl key, click once on **WETable01.docx**, click once on **WETable02.docx**, and then release the Ctrl key.

   Using the Ctrl key, you can select nonadjacent files.

	WEExcelRevenues.xlsx
Step 7	WEOutline.docx
	WERevChart.xlsx
	WERevDocument.docx
	WERevenuesMemo.docx
	WETable01.docx
Step 8	WETable02.docx

9. Click the Home tab and then click the Cut button in the Clipboard group.

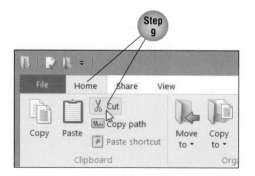

(10) Click the Back button at the left of the Address bar.

(11) Double-click the *Distribution* folder.

(12) Click the Home tab and then click the Paste button in the Clipboard group.

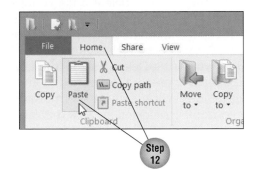

Step 12

In Brief

Move Nonadjacent Files to New Folder
1. Display Computer window.
2. Navigate to desired drive and/or folder.
3. If necessary, change current view to *List*.
4. Click first file name.
5. Hold down Ctrl key, click each additional file name, and then release Ctrl key.
6. Click Cut button in Clipboard group on Home tab.
7. Navigate to desired destination drive and/or folder.
8. Click Paste button in Clipboard group on Home tab.

(13) Click in a blank area of the Content pane to deselect the file names.

(14) Click the Back button at the left of the Address bar.

(15) Double-click the *Income* folder.

(16) Notice the three files ***WEOutline.docx***, ***WETable01.docx***, and ***WETable02.docx*** no longer reside in the Income folder.

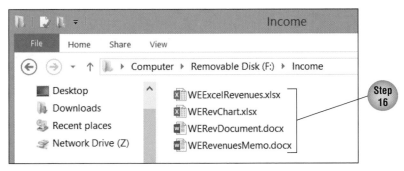

Step 16

(17) Close the Computer window.

In Addition

Displaying Disk or Drive Properties

Information such as the amount of used space and free space on a disk or drive and the disk or drive hardware is available at the Properties dialog box. To display the Local Disk (C:) Properties dialog box, similar to the one shown at the right, open a Computer window. At the Computer window, right-click *Local Disk (C:)* and then click *Properties* at the shortcut menu. With the General tab selected, information displays about used and free space on the drive. Click the Tools tab to display error-checking, backup, and defragmentation options. The Hardware tab displays the name and type of all disk drives as well as the device properties. The Sharing tab displays options for sharing folders, and change user permissions at the Security tab. To enable quota management wherein you can assign space limits for each user, click the Quota tab.

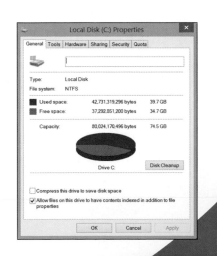

Activity 2.6

Deleting Folders and Files to the Recycle Bin

Deleting the wrong file can be a disaster, but Windows helps protect your work with the Recycle Bin. The Recycle Bin acts just like an office wastepaper basket: you can "throw away" (delete) unwanted files, but you also can "reach in" to the Recycle Bin and take out (restore) a file if you threw it away by accident. Files or folders deleted from a hard disk drive are automatically sent to the Recycle Bin. However, files or folders deleted from a removable disk such as your USB flash drive are deleted permanently.

To delete a file or folder, display a Computer or Documents window and then display in the Content pane the file(s) or folder(s) you want to delete. Select the file(s) or folder(s) and then press the Delete key on the keyboard or right-click the selected files or folders and click *Delete* at the shortcut menu. At the message asking you to confirm the deletion, click the Yes button.

Project

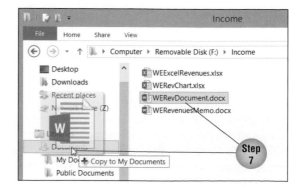

Tutorial 2.6
Using the Recycle Bin

As you continue to organize your files, you will copy a file and a folder from your storage medium to the My Documents folder on the hard drive and then delete a file and folder, moving them to the Recycle Bin.

1. At the Windows desktop, display a Computer window.

2. Double-click the icon representing the storage medium onto which you copied the WindowsS2 folder.

3. Click once to select the *Distribution* folder.

4. Position the mouse pointer over the selected folder name, hold down the left mouse button, drag to *Documents* in the *Libraries* section of the Navigation pane, and then release the mouse button.

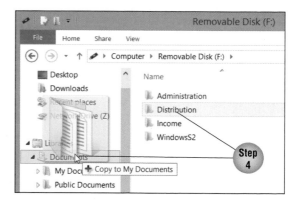

As you point to the Documents library in the Navigation pane, Windows displays the ScreenTip *Copy to My Documents*. If you drag a file or folder from a removable storage device to a location on the computer's hard drive, the file or folder is copied. However, if you drag a file or folder from a location on the hard drive to another location on the hard drive, the file or folder is moved rather than copied.

5. Double-click the *Income* folder.

6. Click once to select **WERevDocument.docx**.

7. Position the mouse pointer over the selected file name, hold down the left mouse button, drag to *Documents* in the *Libraries* section of the Navigation pane, and then release the mouse button.

8 Click *Documents* in the *Libraries* section of the Navigation pane to display the files and folders associated with the Documents library in the Content pane.

In Brief
Delete File/Folder
1. Display Computer window and navigate to desired drive and/or folder.
2. Click file/folder to select it.
3. Press Delete key.
4. At confirmation message, click Yes.

> The Documents library displays the contents of two folders by default: *My Documents* and *Public Documents*. My Documents is the default folder in which files and folders associated with the Documents library are stored. You can add and remove folders associated with a library. You will learn more about libraries in an assessment at the end of this section.

9 Click once to select the *Distribution* folder.

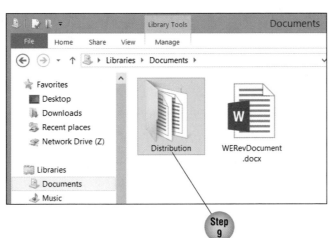

Step 8

Step 9

10 Press the Delete key on the keyboard.

11 Right-click **WERevDocument.docx** in the Content pane and then click *Delete* at the shortcut menu.

12 Close the Documents library window.

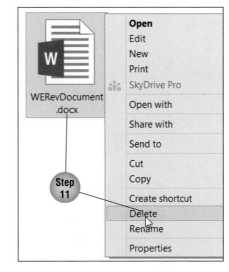

Step 11

In Addition

Dragging and Dropping Files and Folders

Another method for deleting a file or folder is to drag the file or folder to the Recycle Bin icon on the desktop. This moves the file into the Recycle Bin. You can also select multiple files or folders and then drag and drop the selected items into the Recycle Bin.

Restoring Folders and Files;
Emptying Files from the Recycle Bin

A file or folder deleted to the Recycle Bin can be restored. Restore a file or folder with options at the Recycle Bin window. Display this window by double-clicking the Recycle Bin icon on the Windows desktop. Once you restore a file or folder, it is removed from the Recycle Bin and returned to its original location. Just like a waste-paper basket can overflow, the Recycle Bin can contain too many files and folders. Emptying the Recycle Bin permanently deletes all files and folders. You can also delete a single file or folder from the Recycle Bin (rather than all files and folders).

Project You decide to experiment with the Recycle Bin by learning how to restore a file and how to empty the Recycle Bin.

Worldwide Enterprises

SNAP

Review Tutorial 2.4
Selecting, Copying, and Moving Folders and Files

1. At the Windows desktop, display the contents of the Recycle Bin by double-clicking the Recycle Bin icon.

   Step 1

   The Recycle Bin window displays, similar to the one shown in Figure 2.3.

2. At the Recycle Bin window, change the current view to *List*.

3. Click once to select **WERevDocument.docx**.

   Depending on the contents of the Recycle Bin, you may need to scroll down the list to display this document.

FIGURE 2.3 Recycle Bin Window

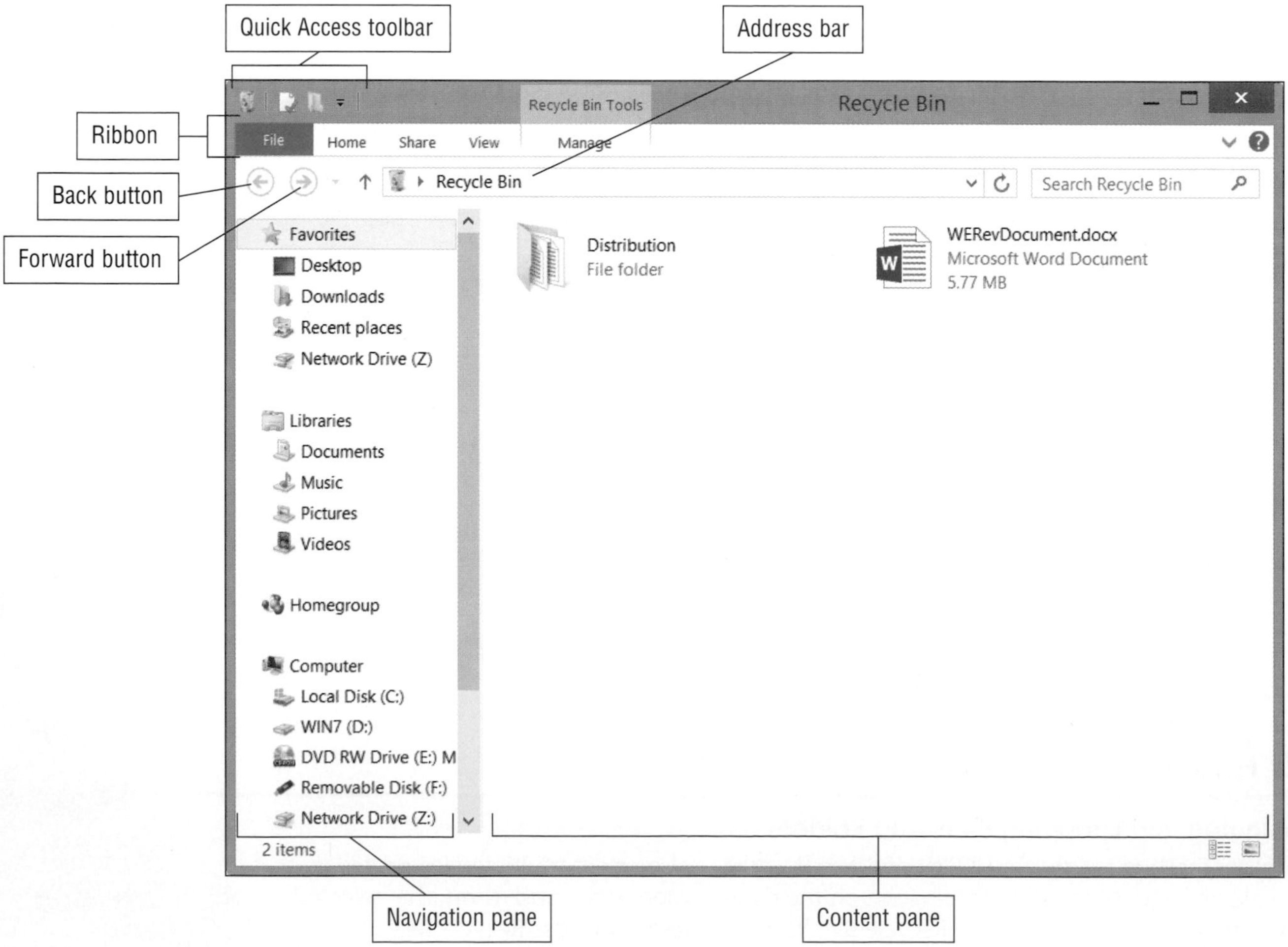

Quick Access toolbar · Address bar · Ribbon · Back button · Forward button · Navigation pane · Content pane

4 Click the Recycle Bin Tools Manage tab and then click the Restore the selected items button in the Restore group.

> The file is removed from the Recycle Bin and returned to the location from which it was deleted. Once a file or folder is moved into the Recycle Bin, you are limited to the following options: Restore, Cut, or Delete.

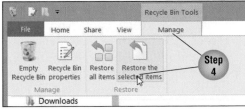

In Brief

Restore File/Folder from Recycle Bin
1. At Windows desktop, double-click Recycle Bin icon.
2. At Recycle Bin window, click file/folder to select it (or select multiple files/folders).
3. Click Restore the selected items button on Recycle Bin Tools Manage tab.

Delete File/Folder from Recycle Bin
1. At Windows desktop, double-click Recycle Bin icon.
2. At Recycle Bin window, click file/folder to select it (or select multiple files/folders).
3. Press Delete key.
4. At confirmation message, click Yes.

5 Click once to select the *Distribution* folder.

6 Click the Restore the selected items button in the Restore group.

7 Close the Recycle Bin window.

8 At the Windows desktop, open a Computer window.

9 Click *Documents* in the *Libraries* section of the Navigation pane.

> Notice that the file and folder have been restored from the Recycle Bin.

10 Delete the file and folder you restored. To do this, click once on the *Distribution* folder, hold down the Ctrl key, click once on the **WERevDocument.docx** file name, and then release the Ctrl key.

11 Press the Delete key.

12 Close the Documents window.

13 At the Windows desktop, double-click the Recycle Bin icon.

14 Click once on the *Distribution* folder, hold down the Ctrl key, click once on the **WERevDocument.docx** file name, and then release the Ctrl key.

15 Click the Home tab and then click the Delete button in the Organize group.

16 At the Delete Multiple Items message box asking if you are sure you want to permanently delete the two items, click Yes.

> To empty the entire contents of the Recycle Bin, click the Empty Recycle Bin button in the Manage group on the Recycle Bin Tools Manage tab.

17 Close the Recycle Bin window.

In Addition

Showing or Hiding the Recycle Bin on the Desktop

The Recycle Bin icon is displayed on the desktop by default. To remove it, right-click a blank area of the desktop and then click *Personalize* at the shortcut menu. At the Personalization window, click Change desktop icons in the left pane. At the Desktop Icon Settings dialog box, shown at the right, click the *Recycle Bin* check box to remove the check mark and then click OK. Note the other desktop icons you can choose to show or hide at this dialog box.

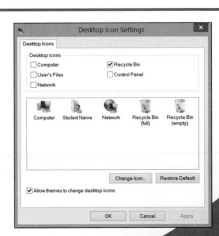

Activity 2.8

Exploring the Control Panel

The Control Panel offers a variety of categories, each containing icons you can use to customize the functionality of your computer. Display the Control Panel window by right-clicking the Start screen thumbnail and then clicking *Control Panel* at the pop-up list. At the Control Panel window, available categories display in the Content pane. (By default, the Control Panel window opens in Category view. If your window opens in Large icons view or Small icons view, click the down-pointing arrow next to *View by*, located near the top right of the Control Panel window, and then click *Category* at the drop-down list.) Click a category or hyperlinked option below a category and a list of tasks, a list of icons, or a separate window displays.

Project

You want to know how to customize your computer, so you decide to explore the Control Panel window.

Worldwide Enterprises

1. At the Windows desktop, right-click the Start screen thumbnail and then click *Control Panel* at the pop-up list.

   The Control Panel window displays, similar to the one shown in Figure 2.4.

SNAP

Tutorial 2.8
Exploring the Control Panel

2. At the Control Panel window, click the <u>Appearance and Personalization</u> hyperlink.

3. After viewing the tasks and icons available in the Appearance and Personalization category, click the Back button.

4. Click the <u>Hardware and Sound</u> hyperlink.

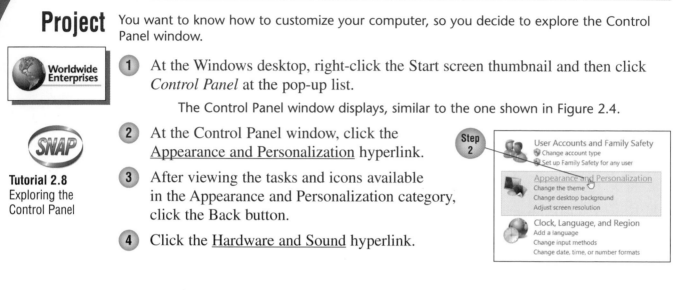

FIGURE 2.4 Control Panel Window

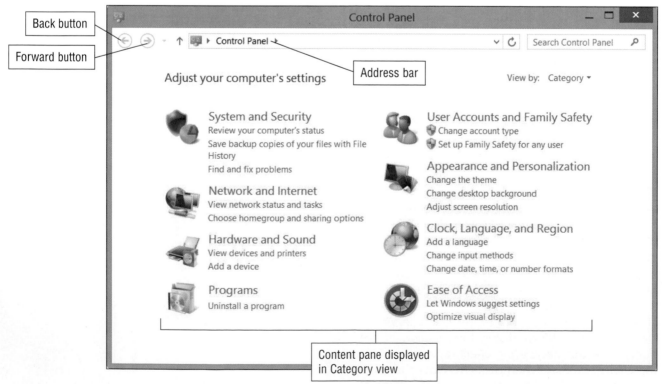

5 Click the <u>Mouse</u> hyperlink in the Devices and Printers category.

    This displays the Mouse Properties dialog box.

In Brief
Display Control Panel Window
1. Right-click Start screen thumbnail.
2. Click *Control Panel*.

6 At the Mouse Properties dialog box, click each tab and review the available options.

7 Click the Cancel button to close the Mouse Properties dialog box.

8 Click the Back button.

9 Click the <u>Programs</u> hyperlink in the Content pane.

10 At the Programs window, click the <u>Programs and Features</u> hyperlink.

    This is where you would uninstall a program on your computer.

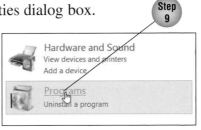

11 Click the Back button twice.

12 Click the <u>System and Security</u> hyperlink.

13 Click the <u>System</u> hyperlink.

14 Maximize the window.

15 Close the System window.

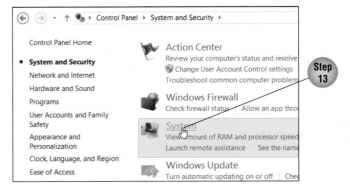

In Addition

Changing the Control Panel View

By default, the Control Panel window displays categories of tasks in what is called Category view. This view can be changed to *Large icons* or *Small icons*. In the Large icons view, shown at the right, options in the Control Panel window are shown alphabetically by icon name. To change from Category view to Large icons or Small icons, click the down-pointing arrow next to *View by* located near the top right of the Control Panel window and then click the desired option at the drop-down list.

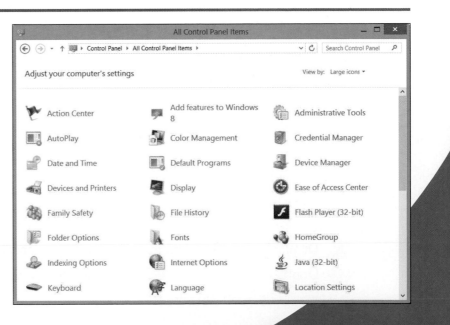

Activity 2.9

Windows includes a Search feature you can access through the Charm bar. You can quickly find an application, setting, or file by typing the first few letters of the application, setting, or file name. You can choose whether to search for an application, setting or file by selecting one of the three tiles located below the search text box—Apps, Settings, or Files. If your computer has many applications and files stored on the hard disk, using the search tool allows you to locate what you need in a few seconds and with minimal mouse clicks. At the right of the Address bar in a Computer or Documents window is a search text box. Type in this text box the first few letters of a file you need to locate. The Content pane is filtered instantly to display items that match your criterion.

Windows performs fast searching because the operating system maintains an index in the background in which all of the key words associated with the applications, settings, and files on your computer are referenced. This index is constantly updated as you work. When you type an entry in a search text box, Windows consults the index rather than conducting a search of the entire hard drive.

Project

You want to experiment with the search capabilities of Windows to see how you can quickly locate applications and files.

Tutorial 2.9
Using Windows
Search Tools

1 At the Windows desktop, display the Charm bar and then click the Search button.

2 With the insertion point positioned in the search text box located at the top of the Search panel, make sure the Apps tile is selected below the search text box, and then type **calc** in the search text box.

As soon as you begin typing an entry in the search text box, Windows begins to display relevant results. Notice that the Calculator program is shown below the heading *Apps* at the top of the list. Depending on the contents stored in the computer you are using, additional items may be displayed below *Calculator*.

3 Click the Calculator tile in the *Apps* list at the upper left side of the Start screen.

4 Close the Calculator window.

5 Display the Charm bar and then click the Search button.

6 Make sure the Apps tile is selected below the search text box and then type **note** in the search text box.

Windows lists all app elements stored on the computer you are using that are associated with the text *note*, including the Notepad application, which you can use to create, edit, and save simple, text-based documents.

7 Press the Esc key.

Pressing the Esc key clears the search results list and the search text box.

8 Display the desktop and then open a Computer window.

9 Double-click the icon representing the storage medium onto which you copied the WindowsS2 folder.

10 Double-click the *WindowsS2* folder and then change the view to Large Icons.

11 Click in the Search WindowsS2 text box located at the right of the Address bar.

12 Type **werev**.

As soon as you begin typing in the search WindowsS2 text box, Windows filters the list of files in the Content pane to those that begin with the letters you type. Notice that the Address bar displays *Search Results in WindowsS2* to indicate that the files displayed that match your criteria were limited to the current folder. If you want to search other locations or by other file properties, click one of the option buttons located on the Search Tools Search tab.

Step
12

WErev - Search Results in WindowsS2

| File | Home | Share | View | Search |

Search Results in WindowsS2   werev

Favorites
Desktop
Downloads
Recent places
Network Drive (Z:)

Libraries
Documents
Music
Pictures
Videos

Homegroup

Computer
Local Disk (C:)
WIN7 (D:)
DVD RW Drive (E:) M
Removable Disk (F:)

WERevDocument.docx   Date modified: 11/29/2009 12:14 ...   Size: 5.77 MB
F:\WindowsS2

WERevenuesMemo.docx   Date modified: 11/29/2009 12:14 ...   Size: 197 KB
F:\WindowsS2

WERevChart.xlsx   Date modified: 11/29/2009 12:13 ...   Size: 5.77 MB
F:\WindowsS2

search results for files that begin with *werev*

3 items

13 With the insertion point still positioned in the search text box, press the Backspace key to remove *werev* and then type **pte**.

The list of files in the Content pane is updated to display those files that begin with *pte*.

WindowsS2

pte

Step
13

14 Double-click the file named ***PTExcelOctPayroll.xlsx***.

The file opens in Microsoft Excel.

15 Close Microsoft Excel by clicking the Close button at the right side of the Title bar.

16 Close the Computer window.

In Brief

Search for Applications or Documents from Charm bar
1. Click Search button on Charm bar.
2. Click Apps, Settings, or Files tile.
3. Type search criteria in search text box.

Search for Document
1. Open Computer or Documents library window.
2. Type search criteria in search text box.

In Addition

Using a Wildcard Character in a Search

When conducting a search, you can type an asterisk (*) in place of any number of letters, numbers, or symbols within a file name to find files based on a pattern of characters. For example, typing ***hours*** would locate the files listed at the right in your WindowsS2 folder. Notice the pattern is that all files have *hours* in the middle of the file name but any number of other characters before and after *hours*.

PTWordHours.docx
PTExcelHours.xlsx
PTCostumeHours.xlsx

Activity 2.10

Customizing the Desktop

The Windows operating environment is customizable. You can change background patterns and colors; specify a screen saver that will display when the screen sits idle for a specific period of time; change the scheme for windows, title bars, and system fonts; and change screen resolution and text size. Make these types of changes at the Control Panel Personalization window. Many companies adopt a corporate standard for display properties on their computers.

Project

You decide to look at the customization options available for the desktop and set the screen resolution to the corporate standard for computers at Worldwide Enterprises.

Note: Before completing this activity, check with your instructor to determine if you can customize the desktop. If necessary, practice these steps on your home computer.

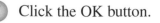

SNAP

Tutorial 2.10
Customizing the Desktop

1. At the Windows desktop, position the arrow pointer in a blank area of the desktop, right-click the mouse, and then click *Personalize* at the shortcut menu.

2. At the Personalization window, click the <u>Desktop Background</u> hyperlink located along the bottom of the window.

   Make a note of the current background.

3. Make sure *Windows Desktop Backgrounds* displays in the Picture location option box. If necessary, scroll up or down the available images, click an image that you like, and click the Save changes button.

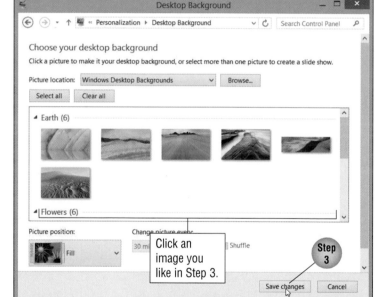

4. Click the <u>Screen Saver</u> hyperlink.

   Make a note of the current screen saver name.

5. At the Screen Saver Settings dialog box, click the option box arrow below *Screen saver* and then click *Ribbons* at the drop-down list.

   A preview of the screen saver displays in the screen located toward the top of the dialog box.

6. Click the up- or down-pointing arrow next to the *Wait* measurement box until *1* displays.

7. Click the OK button.

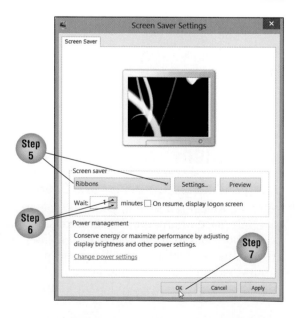

8 Click the Color hyperlink.

> Make a note of the color box that is currently selected.

9 Click the *Color 9* color box (second column in the bottom row) and then click the Save changes button. ***Note: Skip this step if your window does not display as shown below.***

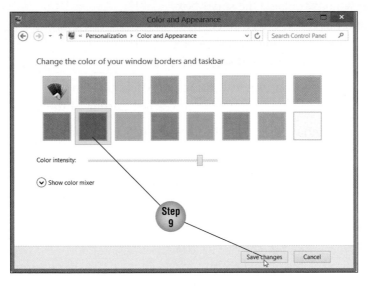

10 Close the Personalization window. Let the screen remain idle for one minute so that the screen saver displays.

11 Move the mouse to deactivate the screen saver and then double-click the Recycle Bin icon.

> Notice the Color 9 color scheme applied to the Taskbar and the window borders.

12 Close the Recycle Bin window.

13 Reinstate the original desktop settings by right-clicking a blank area of the desktop, clicking *Personalize* at the shortcut menu, and then returning the desktop background, screen saver, and window color to the original settings.

> In the next steps, you will set the screen resolution to *1600 × 900 pixels,* which is the corporate standard for all desktop computers at Worldwide Enterprises. Standardizing display properties is considered a best practice in large companies that support many computer users.

14 Right-click a blank area of the desktop and then click *Screen resolution* at the shortcut menu.

15 At the Screen Resolution window, look at the current setting displayed in the *Resolution* option box. For example, your screen may be currently set at *1920 × 1080*. If your screen is already set to *1600 × 900*, click OK to close the window and complete this activity.

> Screen resolution is set in pixels. ***Pixel*** is the abbreviation of *picture element* and refers to a single dot or point on the display monitor. Changing the screen resolution to a higher number of pixels means that more information can be seen on the screen as items are scaled to a smaller size.

continues

16 Click the *Resolution* option box and then drag the slider bar up or down as necessary until the screen resolution is set to *1600 × 900*. If necessary, check with your instructor for alternate instructions.

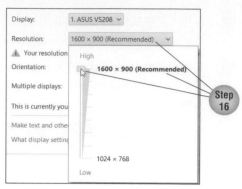

Step 16

17 Click in the window outside the slider box, click OK, and then click the Keep changes button at the Display Settings message box asking if you want to keep the display settings.

18 At the Screen resolution window, click the Make text and other items larger or smaller hyperlink located toward the lower left corner of the window.

19 At the display window, click the Medium – 125% option.

20 Click the Apply button.

21 At the message indicating that you must sign out of your computer, click the Sign out now button.

22 Log back into your account.

The screen captures in this textbook were taken using 1600 × 900 screen resolution and the display of text and items set to Medium - 125%. If the computer you are using has a different screen resolution, what you will see on your screen may not match the textbook illustrations. For additional information, refer to the In Addition section below.

In Addition

Windows Screen Resolution and the Microsoft Office Ribbon

Before you begin learning the applications in the Microsoft Office 2013 suite, take a moment to check the display settings on the computer you are using. The ribbon in the Microsoft Office suite adjusts to the screen resolution setting of your computer monitor. A computer monitor set at a high resolution will have the ability to show more buttons in the ribbon than will a monitor set to a low resolution. The screen captures in this textbook were taken at a resolution of 1600 x 900 pixels. Below, the Word ribbon is shown three ways: at a lower screen resolution (1366 x 768 pixels), at the screen resolution featured throughout this textbook, and at a higher screen resolution (1920 x 1080 pixels). Note the variances in the ribbon in all three examples. If possible, set your display to 1600 x 900 pixels to match the illustrations you will see in this textbook.

Appearance of Microsoft Word ribbon with computer monitor set at:

1366 x 768 screen resolution

1600 x 900 screen resolution (featured in this textbook)

1920 x 1080 screen resolution

Features Summary

Feature	Button/Icon	Action
Computer window		Right-click Start screen thumbnail, click *File Explorer*.
Control Panel window		Right-click Start screen thumbnail, click *Control Panel*.
copy selected files/folders		At Computer or Documents library window, select files/folders to be copied, right-click in selected group, click *Copy*, navigate to destination folder, right-click in Content pane, click *Paste*.
create new folder		At Computer or Documents library window, click New Folder button on Quick Access toolbar.
delete selected files/folders		At Computer or Documents library window, select files to be deleted, press Delete key, click Yes.
folder options		Click View tab, click Options button.
move selected files/folders		At Computer or Documents library window, select files/folders to be moved, right-click in selected group, click *Cut*, navigate to destination folder, right-click in Content pane, click *Paste*.
Recycle Bin		Double-click *Recycle Bin* icon.
rename file/folder		At Computer or Documents library window, right-click file or folder, click *Rename*, type new name, press Enter.
restore files/folders from Recycle Bin		At Recycle Bin, select desired files/folders, click Recycle Bin Tools Manage tab, click Restore the selected items button on tab.
search for programs or documents		Display Charm bar, click Search button, type search criterion in search text box; or open Computer or Documents library window, type search criterion in search text box.
select adjacent files/folders		Click first file/folder, hold down Shift key, click last file/folder.
select nonadjacent files/folders		Click first file/folder, hold down Ctrl key, click any other files/folders.

Knowledge Check SNAP

Completion: In the space provided at the right, indicate the correct term, command, or option.

1. Navigate to any other device or folder from the current device and folder using the Navigation pane or this bar in the Computer window. _____

2. Specify the option to open each folder in its own window at this dialog box. _____

3. Click this button on the Quick Access toolbar to create a new folder in the Computer window. _____

4. Change the display of files and folders in the Computer window to *List* or *Details* using this group on the View tab. _____

5. To select adjacent files, click the first file, hold down this key, and then click the last file. _____

6. To select nonadjacent files, click the first file, hold down this key, and then click any other desired files. _____

7. Click this button to display in the Content pane the files in the previous folder viewed. _____

8. Click this button in the Clipboard group on the Home tab to move selected files. _____

9. Files deleted from the hard drive are sent here. _____

10. Open this window to display a list of categories or icons in which you can customize the appearance and functionality of your computer. _____

11. Access search tools using this bar at the desktop. _____

12. Customize the desktop by changing the background, screen saver, and/or color option at this window. _____

Skills Review

Review 1 Browsing Devices and Changing the View

1. Open the Computer window.
2. Change to Large Icons view.
3. Change the folder option to open each folder in its own window.
4. Display the contents of your storage medium.
5. Display the contents of the WindowsS2 folder.
6. Change to Details view.
7. Close the WindowsS2 window.
8. Close the window for your storage medium.
9. Change the folder option to open each folder in the same window.
10. Change to Tiles view and then close the Computer window.

Review 2 Creating a Folder

1. Open the Computer window.
2. Display the contents of your storage medium.
3. Right-click a blank area in the Content pane, point to *New*, and then click *Folder*.
4. Type **Worksheets** and then press Enter.
5. Close the window.

Review 3 Selecting, Copying, Moving, and Deleting Files

1. Open the Computer window.
2. Display the contents of your storage medium.
3. Display the contents of the WindowsS2 folder.
4. Change the current view to List if the display is not already set to List.
5. Click once on *FCTBookings.xlsx* to select it, hold down the Shift key, and then click *FCTPackages.docx*.
6. Right-click within the selected group of files and then click *Copy* at the shortcut menu.
7. Click the Back button.
8. Double-click the *Worksheets* folder.
9. Right-click in the Content pane, click *Paste*, and then click in a blank area to deselect the files.
10. Click the Back button and then double-click *WindowsS2*.
11. Click *WEExcelRevenues.xlsx* in the Content pane, hold down the Ctrl key, and then click *WERevChart.xlsx*.
12. Click the Cut button in the Clipboard group on the Home tab.
13. Click the Back button and then double-click *Worksheets*.
14. Click the Paste button in the Clipboard group on the Home tab.
15. Click the right-pointing arrow next to your storage medium in the Address bar and then click *WindowsS2* at the drop-down list.
16. Click *FCTCCSkiing.docx* in the Content pane, hold down the Ctrl key, and then click *FCTNorwayTour.docx*.
17. Press the Delete key and then click Yes at the Delete Multiple Items confirmation message.
18. Close the Computer window.

Review 4 Renaming a File

1. Open the Computer window.
2. Display the contents of your storage medium.
3. Display the contents of the WindowsS2 folder.
4. Right-click *WETable01.docx* and then click *Rename*.
5. Type **WEPreviewDistribution** and then press Enter.
6. Right-click *WETable02.docx* and then click *Rename*.
7. Type **WEGeneralDistribution** and then press Enter.
8. Close the Computer window.

Review 5 Searching for Files

1. Open the Computer window.
2. Display the contents of the WindowsS2 folder on your storage medium.
3. Type ***rev*** in the search WindowsS2 text box.
4. Press the Esc key until the filter is cleared and all files are redisplayed.
5. Type ***excel*** in the search WindowsS2 text box.
6. Close the Computer window.
7. Click the Search button on the Charm bar.
8. Type ***word*** in the search text box. Notice the applications displayed in the Start screen.
9. Press the Esc key and then click in the Start screen area outside the Search panel to close the Search panel.

Skills Assessment

Assessment 1 Managing Folders and Files

1. Create a new folder on your storage medium named PerformanceThreads.
2. Display the contents of the WindowsS2 folder.
3. If necessary, change to List view.
4. Copy all files beginning with *PT* to the PerformanceThreads folder.
5. If necessary, display the contents of the PerformanceThreads folder and change to List view.
6. Create a new folder within PerformanceThreads named Payroll. (A folder created within a folder is referred to as a subfolder.)
7. Move **PTExcelOctPayroll.xlsx** and **PTWordOctPayroll.docx** from the PerformanceThreads folder into the Payroll subfolder.
8. Delete **PTMarqueeLetter.docx** from the PerformanceThreads folder.
9. Rename the file named **PTAgreement.docx** located in the PerformanceThreads folder to **CostumeAgreement.docx**.

Assessment 2 Managing Folders and Files

1. Display the contents of your storage medium.
2. Create a new folder named FirstChoiceTravel.
3. Display the contents of the WindowsS2 folder.
4. Copy all files beginning with *FCT* to the FirstChoiceTravel folder.
5. If necessary, display the contents of the FirstChoiceTravel folder and change to List view.
6. Create a new folder within FirstChoiceTravel and name it *Accounting*.
7. Create a new folder within the Accounting folder and name it *Commissions*.
8. Move **FCTBookings.xlsx** from the FirstChoiceTravel folder into the Accounting subfolder.
9. Move **FCTSalesCommissions.xlsx** from the FirstChoiceTravel folder into the Commissions subfolder.
10. Delete **FCTIslandFlights.docx** from the FirstChoiceTravel folder.
11. Rename the file named **FCTPackages.docx** located in the FirstChoiceTravel folder to **FCTOregonNevadaPkgs.docx**.

Assessment 3 Managing Folders and Files

1. Display the contents of your storage medium.
2. Create a new folder named WorldwideEnt.
3. Display the contents of the WindowsS2 folder.
4. Copy all files beginning with *WE* to the WorldwideEnt folder.
5. If necessary, display the contents of the WorldwideEnt folder and change to List view.
6. Delete **WEOutline.docx** from the WorldwideEnt folder.
7. Change the name of the WorldwideEnt folder to *WorldwideEnterprises*.

Assessment 4 Deleting Folders and Files

Note: Check with your Instructor before completing this assessment in case you need to show him or her that you completed the activities within this section before deleting the folders.

1. Display the contents of your storage medium.
2. Delete the folder named Administration.
3. Delete the folder named Distribution.
4. Delete the folder named Income.

Assessment 5 Copying Folders from the Student CD to Storage Medium

1. Display the contents of the Marquee student CD that accompanies this textbook in the Computer window.
2. Display the contents of the Word folder in the Content pane.
3. Select all of the subfolders in the Word folder and then copy them to your storage medium.
4. Display the contents of the Excel folder in the Content pane and then copy all of the subfolders in the Excel folder to your storage medium.
5. Display the contents of the Access folder in the Content pane and then copy all of the subfolders in the Access folder to your storage medium.
6. Display the contents of the PowerPoint folder in the Content pane and then copy all of the subfolders in the PowerPoint folder to your storage medium.
7. Copy the AudioandVideo folder to your storage medium.
8. Display the contents of the Integrating folder and then copy all of the subfolders to your storage medium.

Assessment 6 Searching for Information on User Accounts

1. You have been asked by your supervisor at First Choice Travel to learn about sharing your computer with other users. Your supervisor is considering adding an evening shift and wants to find out how existing computer equipment can be set up for other users. Using the Windows Help and Support feature, search for information on user accounts. *Hint: Type user accounts in the search text box and press Enter. Consider reading the topic* **Which user account is right for me** *as your first step.*

2. Locate topics with information about the three types of user accounts: *Standard, Administrator*, and *Guest*. Specifically, your supervisor is interested in which type of account would be best suited for day-to-day work and why this type of account is your recommendation.

3. Create a new folder on your storage medium named WindowsEOS.

4. Using WordPad or Word, compose a memo to your instructor that describes the differences among the three types of user accounts and then provide your recommendation for which type of account should be used for individuals on each shift.

5. Save the memo in the WindowsEOS folder and name it **WS2-UserAccounts**.

6. Print the memo and then close the application you used to compose the memo.

Assessment 7 Searching for Information on Windows Libraries

HELP

1. You have been asked by your supervisor at First Choice Travel to learn about a feature in Windows 8 called Libraries. Your supervisor is not sure about the difference between a library and a normal folder for managing folders and files. She wants you to find out how a library can be useful to her and how to create her own library and add folders to it. She also wonders if the default libraries Windows created can have other folders added to them. Using the Windows Help and Support feature, search for information on libraries. *Hint: Type libraries in the search text box and then press Enter. Consider reading the topic* **Library basics** *as your first step.*

2. Locate topics with information about libraries.

3. Using WordPad or Word, compose a memo to your instructor that provides her or him with answers to the following questions:
   a. What is the difference between a library and a folder?
   b. How can I create my own library?
   c. How can I add or remove folders in a library?
   d. What is the limit on the number of folders that can be added to a library?

4. Save the memo and name it **WS2-Libraries** in the WindowsEOS folder.

5. Print the memo and then close the application you used to compose the memo.

MICROSOFT®

INTERNET EXPLORER 10

Nita Rutkosky
Pierce College at Puyallup,
Puyallup, Washington

Denise Seguin
Fanshawe College,
London, Ontario

Audrey Roggenkamp
Pierce College at Puyallup,
Puyallup, Washington

Ian Rutkosky
Pierce College at Puyallup,
Puyallup, Washington

Paradigm PUBLISHING

St. Paul

Contents

Managing Editor	Christine Hurney
Director of Production	Timothy W. Larson
Production Editor	Sarah Kearin
Cover and Text Designer	Leslie Anderson
Copy Editor	Sid Korpi, Proof Positive Editing
Design and Production Specialists	Jack Ross and Sara Schmidt Boldon
Testers	Desiree Carvel; Ann E. Mills, Ivy Tech Community College of Indiana, Indianapolis, IN; Brienna McWade
Indexer	Terry Casey
VP & Director of Digital Projects	Chuck Bratton
Digital Project Manager	Tom Modl

Internet Explorer

Browsing the Internet Using Internet Explorer 10

Skills

- Visit sites by typing a web address
- Use hyperlinks to navigate to web pages
- Search for information using search tools
- Narrow a search using advanced search options
- Download content from a web page
- Evaluate content found on a web page

Projects Overview

Visit websites for two national parks. Search for websites pertaining to historical costume design. Use advanced search options to locate information on skydiving companies in the state of Oregon. Locate and save images of Banff National Park. Find information on Apollo lunar missions and evaluate the source and date of publication of the information.

Visit the home pages for the *New York Times* and *USA Today* and read a current article.

Search for and locate the web page for the Theatre Department at York University and the web page for the Department of Drama at New York University.

Locate a website for a snow skiing resort in Utah and then download an image from the web page.

1

Navigating the Internet Using Web Addresses

In today's world, the Internet is used for a variety of tasks, including locating information about any topic one can imagine, communicating with others through email or social networking sites, and buying and selling goods and services. In this section, you will use Microsoft's Internet Explorer web browser to locate information on the Internet. A **web browser** is software that allows you to view the text, images, and other content that has been stored on a web page on the Internet. **Uniform Resource Locators**, referred to as URLs, identify web servers that have content on the Internet. A URL is often referred to as a **web address**. Just as you need a specific mailing address to identify your location to the post office, a web server needs a unique web address to identify its location to the Internet.

Project

Dennis Chun, the location director for Marquee Productions, is gathering information for a new movie project. He has asked you to browse the websites for Yosemite National Park and Glacier National Park.

Note: Printing instructions are not included in the project steps in this section. Check with your instructor to find out if you need to print the web pages you visit.

SNAP

Tutorial 1.1
Navigating the Internet Using Web Addresses

1. Make sure you are connected to the Internet and that the Windows desktop displays.

   Check with your instructor to determine if you need to complete steps to access the Internet.

2. Open Microsoft Internet Explorer by clicking the Internet Explorer icon 🄴 on the Windows Taskbar.

   Figure 1.1 identifies the elements of the Internet Explorer window. The web page that displays in your Internet Explorer window may vary from what you see in Figure 1.1. Refer to Figure 1.2 on the next page for descriptions of the tools available in Internet Explorer.

3. At the Internet Explorer window, click in the Address bar (refer to Figure 1.1), type **www.nps.gov/yose**, and then press Enter.

Step 3

FIGURE 1.1 Internet Explorer Window

navigation buttons

Address bar

browser controls

tab

④ Scroll down the home page for Yosemite National Park by pressing the Down Arrow key on the keyboard, or by clicking the down-pointing arrow on the vertical scroll bar located at the right side of the Internet Explorer window.

In Brief

Display Specific Website
1. At Windows desktop, click *Internet Explorer* icon on Taskbar.
2. Click in Address bar, type web address, and then press Enter.

The first web page that appears for a website is called the site's *home page*.

⑤ Display the home page for Glacier National Park by clicking in the Address bar, typing **www.nps.gov/glac**, and then pressing Enter.

As you begin to type the first few characters in the Address bar, a drop-down list appears with the names of websites you have already visited that are spelled the same. Matched characters are displayed in blue for quick reference. If the web address you want displays in the drop-down list, you do not need to type the entire address—simply click the desired web address in the drop-down list.

Step 5

⑥ Click the <u>History & Culture</u> hyperlink in the navigation area at the left side of the page.

Most web pages contain hyperlinks that you click to connect to another page within the website or to another site on the Internet. Hyperlinks display in a web page in a variety of ways such as underlined text, text in a navigation bar, buttons, images, or icons. To use a hyperlink, position the mouse pointer on the hyperlink until the mouse pointer turns into a hand and then click the left mouse button.

⑦ Scroll down and view the content on the History & Culture web page.

⑧ Click the Back button located in the upper left corner of the screen (see Figure 1.2) to return to the Glacier National Park home page.

⑨ Click the Forward button located to the right of the Back button to return to the History & Culture page.

Step 8

Step 9

FIGURE 1.2 Browsing, Navigating, and Other Internet Explorer Tools

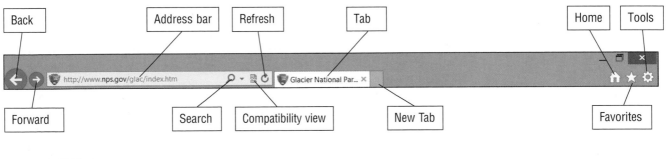

Back | Address bar | Refresh | Tab | Home | Tools

Forward | Search | Compatibility view | New Tab | Favorites

In Addition

Using Internet Explorer in the Modern UI

Windows 8 contains a new user interface, which has been optimized for touch devices. If you access Internet Explorer through the Windows 8 start screen, the Modern UI version of Internet Explorer displays. This version displays differently than the desktop version of Internet Explorer and is designed for use on touch devices. To open the Modern UI version of Internet Explorer, display the Windows 8 start screen and then click the Internet Explorer tile. The address bar and buttons appear at the bottom of the screen and are increased in size. All of the activities in this section use the desktop version of Internet Explorer. If the Internet Explorer button does not appear on the Taskbar, ask your instructor for help on how to access the desktop version of Internet Explorer.

Activity 1.2

Finding Information Using Search Tools

If you do not know the web address for a specific site or you want to find information on the Internet but do not know what site to visit, you can search the Internet using a search engine. A variety of search engines are available, and each offers the opportunity to search for specific information. One method for searching for information is to click in the Address bar, type a keyword or phrase related to your search, and then press Enter. Another method for completing a search is to go to the home page for a search engine and use options at the search engine's site.

Project

Tutorial 1.2
Finding Information
Using Search Tools

Allan Herron, research coordinator for Marquee Productions, has asked you to locate sites with historical costumes for a new movie project. Specifically, she has asked you to locate information on Elizabethan and Renaissance costumes.

1. With the Internet Explorer window active, click in the Address bar.

2. Type **Renaissance costumes** and then press Enter.

    When you press the Enter key, a Bing page with the search results displays. Bing is Microsoft's online search portal and is the default search engine used by Internet Explorer. Bing organizes search results by topic category and provides related search suggestions.

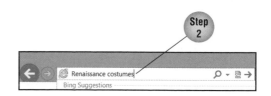

3. Scroll down the search results list and click a hyperlink that interests you by positioning the mouse pointer on the hyperlink text until the pointer turns into a hand and then clicking the left mouse button.

4. Browse the content at the page you selected.

5. Use the Yahoo! search engine to find sites on Renaissance costumes by clicking in the Address bar, typing **www.yahoo.com**, and then pressing Enter.

6. At the Yahoo! website, type **Renaissance costumes** in the search text box and then press Enter.

    As you begin to type, the Yahoo! search assist feature displays search suggestions in a list below the search text box. You can click a suggested phrase in the list instead of completing your typing. Characters in each suggested search phrase that match your typing are displayed in another font style for quick reference. Notice that Bing and Yahoo!'s suggested search phrases are different. Each search engine has its own way of cataloging and indexing search terms.

Web Images Video Local News More ▾		
Renaissance costumes	✕	**Search**

medieval renaissance costumes
cheap renaissance costumes
plus size renaissance costumes
renaissance costumes **patterns**
renaissance costumes **for kids**
authentic renaissance costumes
children's renaissance costumes
renaissance costumes **clothing**
italian renaissance costumes
renaissance costumes **for sale**

Step 6

Search Assist: On | Off

7 Click a hyperlink to a site that interests you.

8 Use the Google search engine to find sites on Elizabethan costumes by clicking in the Address bar, typing **www.google.com**, and then pressing Enter.

9 At the Google website, type **Elizabethan costumes** in the search text box and then press Enter.

Notice that Google also provides a drop-down list of suggested search phrases based on the characters you type.

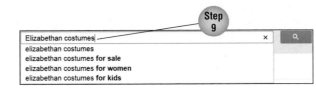

10 Click a hyperlink to a site that interests you.

11 Use the Dogpile search engine to find sites on Elizabethan costumes by clicking in the Address bar, typing **www.dogpile.com**, and then pressing Enter.

Dogpile is a metasearch search engine. A *metasearch search engine* sends your search phrase to other search engines and then compiles the results into one list, allowing you to type the search phrase once and access results from a variety of search engines that index web pages. Dogpile provides search results from Google, Yahoo!, and Yandex.

12 At the Dogpile website, type **Elizabethan costumes** in the search text box and then press Enter.

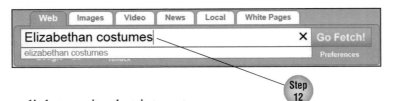

13 Click a hyperlink to a site that interests you.

In Addition

Customizing Internet Explorer

Internet Explorer 10 has been streamlined to provide users with more browsing space and reduced clutter. By default, Microsoft has turned off many features in Internet Explorer 10 such as the Menu bar, Command bar, and Status bar. You can turn these features on by right-clicking the empty space above the Address bar (see Figure 1.1 on page 2) and then clicking the desired option at the drop-down list that displays. For example, if you want to turn on the Menu bar (the bar that contains File, Edit, and so on), right-click the empty space above the Address bar and then click *Menu bar* at the drop-down list. (This inserts a check mark next to *Menu bar.*)

Adding Frequently Used Web Pages to Favorites

If you visit a web page on a regular basis, add the page to the Favorites Center or add a button to the web page on the Favorites bar. To display the Favorites bar, right-click the empty space above the

Address bar and then click *Favorites bar* at the drop-down list. To add the web page to the Favorites bar, display the web page and then click the Favorites button (which displays as a white star located in the upper right corner of the window). When the Favorites Center displays, click the down-pointing arrow on the Add to favorites button and then click *Add to Favorites bar* at the drop-down list. If you prefer, you can add the website to the Favorites Center list. To do this, click the Favorites button and then click the Add to favorites button at the Favorites Center. At the Add a Favorite dialog box that displays, make sure the information in the *Name* text box is the title by which you want to refer to the website (if not, type your own title for the page) and then click the Add button. The new website is added to the Favorites Center drop-down list. Jump quickly to the site by clicking the Favorites button and then clicking the site name at the drop-down list.

Activity 1.3

Refining Your Search Using Advanced Search Tools

The Internet contains an extraordinary amount of information. Depending on what you are searching for on the Internet and the search engine you use, some searches can result in several thousand "hits" (sites). Wading through a large number of sites can be very time-consuming. You can achieve a more targeted search results list if you hone your search technique using the advanced search options offered by a search engine. Look for an advanced search options link at your favorite search engine site the next time you need to locate information, and experiment with various methods to limit the search results. Effective searching is a skill you obtain through practice.

Project

SNAP

Tutorial 1.3
Researching Information Using Advanced Search Tools

James Vecchio, stunt coordinator at Marquee Productions, has asked you to locate information on skydiving companies in the state of Oregon.

1. With the Internet Explorer window active, click in the Address bar, type **www.yahoo.com**, and then press Enter.

2. At the Yahoo! home page, click the Search button [Search] next to the search text box.

3. Click the *More* option located above the Search text box and then click *Advanced Search* at the drop-down list.

4. At the Advanced Web Search page, click in the *the exact phrase* text box and then type **skydiving in Oregon**.

   This limits the search to websites with the exact phrase "skydiving in Oregon."

5. Click the *Only .com domains* option.

   Clicking this option tells Yahoo! to only display websites with a *.com* extension and to ignore any other extension.

6. Click the Yahoo! Search button.

Step 3

Local Shopping Apps News More
- Answers
- Directory
- Sports
- Finance
- Blog
- All Search Services
- Advanced Search
- Preferences
- Advertising Programs
- About This Page

new Yahoo! Axis.
SEARCH. WAY BETTER. Get

Step 6

Advanced Web Search

You can use the options on this page to create a very specific search. Just fill in the fields you need for your current search. Yahoo! Search

Show results with
- all of these words [ ] any part of the page ⌄
- the exact phrase [skydiving in Oregon ×] any part of the page ⌄
- any of these words [ ] any part of the page ⌄
- none of these words [ ] any part of the page ⌄

Tip: Use these options to look for an exact phrase or to exclude pages containing certain words. You can also limit your search to certain parts of pages.

Site/Domain
- ○ Any domain
- ⦿ Only .com domains ○ Only .edu domains
- ○ Only .gov domains ○ Only .org domains

Step 5

Step 4

7 When the list of websites displays, click a hyperlink that interests you.

8 Click the Back button until the Yahoo! Advanced Web Search page displays.

9 Select and then delete the text *skydiving in Oregon* located in the *the exact phrase* text box.

10 Click in the *all of these words* text box and then type **skydiving Oregon tandem static line**.

> You want to focus on websites that offer tandem and static line skydiving in Oregon. Enter specific text in the *all of these words* text box to limit the search only to those websites containing all of the words.

11 Click the *Any domain* option.

12 Click the Yahoo! Search button.

In Brief

Complete Advanced Search Using Yahoo!
1. At Internet Explorer window, click in Address bar, type *www.yahoo.com*, then press Enter.
2. Click Search button, click *More* option, click *Advanced Search*.
3. Click in desired search text box, type search criteria text.
4. Select search method and search options.
5. Click Yahoo! Search button.

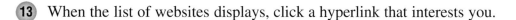

Step 10

Step 12

Step 11

Advanced Web Search

You can use the options on this page to create a very specific search. Just fill in the fields you need for your current search.

Yahoo! Search

Show results with	all of these words	skydiving Oregon tandem static line	any part of the page ∨
	the exact phrase		any part of the page ∨
	any of these words		any part of the page ∨
	none of these words		any part of the page ∨

Tip: Use these options to look for an exact phrase or to exclude pages containing certain words. You can also limit your search to certain parts of pages.

Site/Domain ● Any domain
○ Only **.com** domains ○ Only **.edu** domains
○ Only **.gov** domains ○ Only **.org** domains

13 When the list of websites displays, click a hyperlink that interests you.

In Addition

Displaying a List of Sites Visited

As you view various web pages, Internet Explorer keeps track of the websites you visit. Display the History pane by clicking the Favorites button and then clicking the History tab in the Favorites Center. Click a timeframe to expand the list and display the sites visited during that period. For example, click *Last Week* to expand the list and view the pages you visited within the past week. Click a hyperlink to revisit the page. At the top of the History pane, click the View option box (currently displays *View By Date*) to change the order in which the history list is displayed. You can display websites in the History pane to *View By Date*, *View By Site*, *View By Most Visited*, or *View By Order Visited Today*. Click *Search History* at the View button drop-down list to search the websites in the History pane by keyword or phrase.

Add to favorites

| Favorites | Feeds | History |

View By Date ∨
View By Date
View By Site
View By Most Visited
View By Order Visited Today
Search History

Activity 1.4

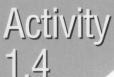

Downloading Content from a Web Page

Downloading content from a web page can involve saving to your hard disk or other storage medium images, text, video, audio, or an entire web page. Copyright laws protect much of the information on the Internet. Before using information or media files you have downloaded from the Internet, check the source site for restrictions. When in doubt, contact the website administrator or another contact person identified on the site and request permission to use the content. Finally, make sure to credit the source of any content you use that was obtained from a web page. Generally, you can use content from a website that is considered public domain, such as a government website, without obtaining permission.

Project

Tutorial 1.4
Downloading Content from a Web Page

Chris Greenbaum, the production manager of the new movie project at Marquee Productions, has asked you to locate on the Internet a picture of Banff National Park and an image that shows a map of the park. She wants you to save the images as separate files she can insert into her presentation for the next production meeting.

1. With the Internet Explorer window active, click in the Address bar, type **www.google.com**, and then press Enter.

2. At the Google home page, click the <u>Images</u> hyperlink at the top left of the home page.

3. At the Google images page, type **Banff National Park** in the search text box and then press Enter or click the Search button.

4. Browse the images that display in the search results.

5. Position the mouse pointer over an image you want to download, right-click the mouse, and then click *Save picture as* at the shortcut menu.

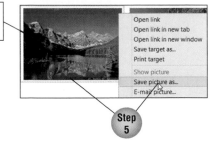

> The image you choose may vary from the one shown here.

6. At the Save Picture dialog box, click *Desktop* in the *Favorites* section of the Navigation pane, select the current text in the *File name* text box, type **BanffPicture1**, and then click Save or press Enter.

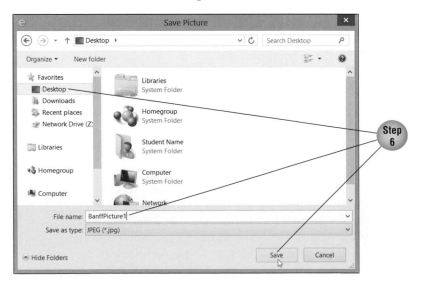

(7) Click in the Address bar, type **www.dogpile.com**, and then press Enter.

(8) Click the Images tab at the Dogpile home page.

(9) Click in the search text box, type **Banff National Park map**, and then press Enter or click the Go Fetch! button.

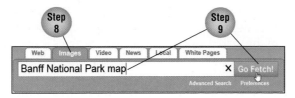

(10) Browse the map images that display in the search results, right-click the mouse over one of the maps you want to download, and then click *Save picture as* at the shortcut menu.

(11) At the Save Picture dialog box, with *Desktop* already selected in the Address bar and with the current file name already selected in the *File name* text box, type **BanffMap1** and then click Save or press Enter.

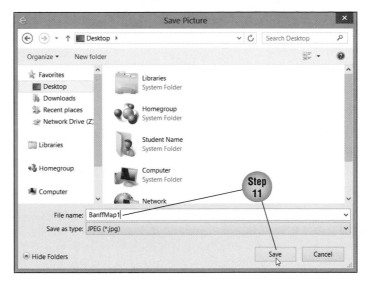

In Addition

Downloading an Application

Using Internet Explorer, you can download applications and programs to install onto your computer. When an application is downloaded, Internet Explorer displays the download bar toward the bottom of the screen (as shown below) asking if you want to run or save the application. If you want to install the application, click the Run button. Click the Save button if you want Internet Explorer to save the application in a temporary folder. If you want to save the application in a spe-

cific location on your computer, click the down-pointing arrow on the Save button and then click *Save As* at the drop-down list that displays. This displays the Save As dialog box where you can specify the drive or file in which you want to save the file. Applications downloaded from the Internet can potentially contain viruses, so make sure the website and file are from a trusted source.

Do you want to run or save **SnapSetup.exe** (3.24 MB) from **snap2010.emcp.com**? | Run | Save ▾ | Cancel | ✕

Activity 1.5

Evaluating Content on the Web

The Web is a vast repository of information that is easily accessible and constantly changing. Although a wealth of accurate and timely information is available at your fingertips, some information on the Internet may be outdated, inaccurate, or of poor quality, and therefore should not be relied upon. Since anyone with an Internet connection and the right software can publish information on the Web, knowing the clues to recognizing accurate and current content is a worthwhile skill. The following are some tips to help you develop this skill.

First, look for an author, publisher, or website owner name and consider if the source is credible. For example, is the author associated with a recognizable company, government, or news organization? Second, look for the date the information was published. Is the content outdated? If yes, consider the impact that more current information might have on the information you are evaluating. Third, look for indications that a bias may exist in the content. For example, is there a sponsor on the site that might indicate the information is one-sided? Can the information be validated by another source?

Project

Allan Herron, research coordinator at Marquee Productions, is working on research for a new documentary about the Apollo space missions. She has asked you to locate information on the Web that she can add to her research. You want to be careful that the information you provide for the project is credible.

1. With the Internet Explorer window active, click in the Address bar, type **www.google.com**, and then press Enter.

2. At the Google home page, type **Apollo lunar missions** in the search text box and then click the Search button or press Enter.

3. Click a hyperlink to a page that interests you.

4. At the web page, try to locate the author or publisher name, the date the article was published, and/or the date the page was last updated. If the web page contains any ads or sponsors, consider if this advertising has an impact on the content you are reading.

   Some pages put this information at the bottom of the page, while other pages place the author and date at the beginning of the article. If you cannot find an author or date, look for a Contact link on the website you are viewing to see if you can determine the name of the company that has published the information. Also, look over the web address to see if the address provides a clue to the authorship. For example, a web address with a *.edu* domain indicates the source is from a page connected with an educational institution.

5. Click the New Tab tab to open a new browsing window.

   > Your tab name may vary.
   >
   > Step 5
   >
   > Apollo Missions to t... ✕

6. Click in the Address bar, type **www.nasa.gov/mission_pages/apollo**, and then press Enter.

7. Scroll to the bottom of the page and read the information in the banner next to the NASA logo that provides information about the date the page was last updated, the page editor, and the NASA official.

   NASA

   Page Last Updated: July 20, 2012
   Page Editor: Yvette Smith
   NASA Official: Brian Dunbar

   NASA Information on the American Recovery and Reinvestment Act of 2009
   Budgets, Strategic Plans and Accountability Reports
   Equal Employment Opportunity Data Posted Pursuant to the No Fear Act
   Information-Dissemination Policies and Inventories

   Freedom of Information Act
   Privacy Policy & Important Notices
   NASA Advisory Council
   Aerospace Safety Advisory Panel
   Inspector General Hotline
   Office of the Inspector General
   NASA Communications Policy

   Contact NASA
   Site Map
   USA.gov
   Open Government at NASA
   Help and Preferences

   Step 7

8 Click the tab for the first web page you visited about Apollo lunar missions and click the Back button to return to the search results list.

9 Click another link that interests you and try to locate information about the date, author, and publisher similar to that which you viewed at NASA's website.

10 Compare the two pages shown side by side in Figure 1.3 below. Note that one page provides details about dates and authors while the other page does not have the same references.

> The page without the references may not necessarily have inaccurate data or be an otherwise poor-quality source of information about the Apollo missions; however, the absence of an author or date of revision means that you would have difficulty citing this source for a research paper or other academic assignment.

11 Close Internet Explorer. Click the Close all tabs button at the Internet Explorer dialog box.

FIGURE 1.3 Step 10

This page has source and date references.

This page has no author, publisher, or date reference.

Features Summary

Feature	Button	Keyboard Shortcut
go back to previous web page	←	Alt + Left Arrow OR Backspace
go forward to next web page	→	Alt + Right Arrow
go to home page	🏠	Alt + Home
display Favorites Center	★	Alt + C
display Tools drop-down list	⚙	Alt + X

Knowledge Check SNAP

Completion: In the space provided at the right, indicate the correct term, command, or option.

1. The letters *URL* stand for this. _____
2. Type a URL in this bar at the Internet Explorer window. _____
3. Click this button on the Internet Explorer toolbar to display the previous web page. _____
4. Bing is the default search engine in Internet Explorer. List two other search engines. _____
5. Reduce the number of search results by looking for these options at the search engine's website. _____
6. Download an image from a website to a file on your computer by right-clicking the image and then selecting this option at the shortcut menu. _____

Skills Review

Note: Check with your instructor before completing the Skills Review activities to find out if you have to print the pages you visit.

Review 1 Browsing the Internet and Navigating with Hyperlinks

1. Open Internet Explorer.
2. Click in the Address bar, type **www.si.edu**, and then press Enter. (This is the home page for the Smithsonian Institution.)
3. Click a hyperlink to a topic that interests you and then read the page.
4. Click another hyperlink and then read the page.
5. Click the Back button until the Smithsonian Institution home page displays.

Review 2 Searching for Specific Sites

1. At the Internet Explorer window, search for websites on mountain climbing.
2. In the search results, click a hyperlink to a site that interests you.
3. Display the Yahoo! website and then use advanced options to search for websites with the *.com* domain on mountain climbing in British Columbia, Canada.
4. Visit at least two sites in the search results that interest you.

Review 3 Downloading Content from a Web Page

1. Using your favorite search engine, search for websites on parasailing in Hawaii. Find a site that contains a parasailing image that you like.
2. Download the parasailing image to the desktop, saving it as **ParasailImage1**.
3. Search for maps of Hawaii.
4. Browse the map images and then select one to download to the desktop, saving it as **HawaiiMap1**.
5. Close Internet Explorer.

Skills Assessment

Note: Check with your instructor before completing the Skills Assessment activities to find out if you have to print the pages you visit.

Assessment 1 Visiting Web Pages for Current News Articles

1. Sam Vestering, a manager at Worldwide Enterprises, likes to keep up to date with current events by reading the daily headlines for various newspapers. He has asked you to scan the home pages for two online newspapers—the *New York Times* and *USA Today*—for articles of interest. To begin, open Internet Explorer.
2. Go to the website of the *New York Times* at www.nytimes.com. Scan the headlines for today's publication, click the hyperlink to an article that interests you, and then read the article.
3. Visit the website of *USA Today* at www.usatoday.com, click the hyperlink to an article that interests you, and then read the article.

Assessment 2 Navigating Websites for Theatre Programs

1. Cal Rubine, the chair of the Theatre Arts Division at Niagara Peninsula College, has asked you to visit the web pages for the theatre and/or drama departments at two universities to compare programs. Visit the home page for York University, Toronto, Canada, at www.yorku.ca.
2. Locate the web page for the Theatre Department and then read about the program.
3. Visit the home page for New York University at www.nyu.edu.
4. Using NYU's home-page search feature, locate the web page for the Department of Drama (undergraduate) and then read about the program. If necessary, click hyperlinks to more pages to find program details.

Assessment 3 Downloading Content on Ski Resorts

1. You work for First Choice Travel and are preparing a brochure on snow skiing vacations. You need some information and images for the brochure. Search for information on snow-skiing resorts in Utah.
2. Visit a website that interests you and that contains an image of a resort or mountains.
3. Download an image from the web page to the desktop, saving it as **UtahResortImage1**.
4. Close Internet Explorer.

Assessment 4 Deleting Downloaded Content on the Desktop

1. At the Windows 8 desktop, right-click the **UtahResortImage1** file and then click *Delete* at the shortcut menu. Click *Yes* at the Delete File dialog box to move the file to the Recycle Bin.
2. Delete all of the other downloaded files you saved to the desktop during this section.

Marquee Series

MICROSOFT®
EXCEL 2013

Nita Rutkosky
Pierce College at Puyallup,
Puyallup, Washington

Denise Seguin
Fanshawe College,
London, Ontario

Audrey Roggenkamp
Pierce College at Puyallup,
Puyallup, Washington

Ian Rutkosky
Pierce College at Puyallup,
Puyallup, Washington

Paradigm
PUBLISHING

St. Paul

Managing Editor	Christine Hurney
Director of Production	Timothy W. Larson
Production Editor	Sarah Kearin
Cover and Text Designer	Leslie Anderson
Copy Editor	Sid Korpi, Proof Positive Editing
Design and Production Specialists	Jack Ross and Sara Schmidt Boldon
Testers	Desiree Carvel; Ann E. Mills, Ivy Tech Community College of Indiana, Indianapolis, IN; Brienna McWade
Indexer	Terry Casey
VP & Director of Digital Projects	Chuck Bratton
Digital Projects Manager	Tom Modl

The authors, editors, and publisher thank the following instructors for their helpful suggestions during the planning and development of the Marquee Office 2013 series: Olugbemiga Adekunle, Blue Ridge Community College, Harrisonburg, VA; Letty Barnes, Lake WA Institute of Technology, Kirkland, WA; Erika Nadas, Wilbur Wright College, Chicago, IL; Carolyn Walker, Greenville Technical College, Greenville, SC; Carla Anderson, National College, Lynchburg, VA; Judy A. McLaney, Lurleen B. Wallace Community College, Opp, AL; Sue Canter, Guilford Technical Community College, Jamestown, NC; Reuel Sample, National College, Knoxville, TN; Regina Young, Wiregrass Georgia Technical College, Valdosta, GA; William Roxbury, National College, Stow, OH; Charles Adams, II, Danville Community College, Danville, VA; Karen Spray, Northeast Community College, Norfolk, NE; Deborah Miller, Augusta Technical College, Augusta, GA; Wanda Stuparits, Lanier Technical College, Cumming, GA; Gale Wilson, Brookhaven College, Farmers Branch, TX; Jocelyn S. Pinkard, Arlington Career Institute, Grand Prairie, TX; Ann Blackman, Parkland College, Champaign, IL; Fathia Williams, Fletcher Technical Community College, Houma, LA; Leslie Martin, Gaston College, Dallas, NC; Tom Rose, Kellogg Community College, Battle Creek, MI; Casey Thompson, Wiregrass Georgia Technical College, Douglas, GA; Larry Bush, University of Cincinnati, Clermont College, Amelia, OH; Tim Ellis, Schoolcraft College, Liconia, MI; Miles Cannon, Lanier Technical College, Oakwood, GA; Irvin LaFleur, Lanier Technical College, Cumming, GA; Patricia Partyka, Schoolcraft College, Prudenville, MI.

Care has been taken to verify the accuracy of information presented in this book. However, the authors, editors, and publisher cannot accept responsibility for Web, email, newsgroup, or chat room subject matter or content, or for consequences from application of the information in this book, and make no warranty, expressed or implied, with respect to its content.

Trademarks: Some of the product names and company names included in this book have been used for identification purposes only and may be trademarks or registered trade names of their respective manufacturers and sellers. Access, Excel, Internet Explorer, Microsoft, PowerPoint, and Windows are trademarks of Microsoft Corporation in the United States and/or other countries. The authors, editors, and publisher disclaim any affiliation, association, or connection with, or sponsorship or endorsement by, such owners.

We have made every effort to trace the ownership of all copyrighted material and to secure permission from copyright holders. In the event of any question arising as to the use of any material, we will be pleased to make the necessary corrections in future printings. Thanks are due to the aforementioned authors, publishers, and agents for permission to use the materials indicated.

Text: ISBN 978-0-76385-247-4
Text & CD: ISBN 978-0-76385-268-9

© 2014 by Paradigm Publishing, Inc.
875 Montreal Way
St. Paul, MN 55102
Email: educate@emcp.com
Website: www.emcp.com

Printed in the United States of America

22 21 20 19 18 17 16 15 14 13   1 2 3 4 5 6 7 8 9 10

Contents

EXCEL 2013

Microsoft Excel 2013 is a popular choice among individuals and companies to organize, analyze, and present data in columns and rows in a file called a *worksheet*. More than one worksheet can be created and saved in a file called a *workbook*. Entries are placed in a worksheet in a *cell*, which is the intersection of a column with a row. A cell is labeled with the column letter and row number, such as A1. Worksheets can be created to track, analyze, and chart any type of data that can be set up in a column and row format. Expenses, sales, assets, liabilities, grades, statistics, research study data, machine production records, weather records, and gas usage are just a few examples of the type of information that can be stored in an Excel workbook. While working in Excel, you will create and edit worksheets for the following six companies.

First Choice Travel is a travel center offering a full range of traveling services from booking flights, hotel reservations, and rental cars to offering travel seminars.

The Waterfront Bistro offers fine dining for lunch and dinner and also offers banquet facilities, a wine cellar, and catering services.

Worldwide Enterprises is a national and international distributor of products for a variety of companies and is the exclusive movie distribution agent for Marquee Productions.

Marquee Productions is involved in all aspects of creating movies from script writing and development to filming. The company produces documentaries, biographies, as well as historical and action movies.

Performance Threads maintains an inventory of rental costumes and also researches, designs, and sews special-order and custom-made costumes.

The mission of the Niagara Peninsula College Theatre Arts Division is to offer a curriculum designed to provide students with a thorough exposure to all aspects of the theater arts.

In Section 1 you will learn how to
Create Worksheets to Analyze Data

Begin your work in Excel by entering labels in columns or rows to create the worksheet layout. Next, add the values that correspond to the labels. Finally, create formulas to add, subtract, multiply, or divide to calculate the desired results. Once a worksheet has been created, the power and versatility of Excel is put to use by performing what-if analyses. What happens to net profit if sales increase by 4 percent? What happens to monthly cash flow if the wages of all employees are raised 3 percent? To answer these types of questions, you edit a value and then watch Excel automatically update all other values dependent on the number you changed.

Start a new worksheet by entering labels to create the worksheet layout.

	A	B	C	D	E	F	G	H	I	J	K	L
1						Payroll						
2					Week Ended: September 26, 2015							
3										Total	Pay	Gross
4			Sun	Mon	Tue	Wed	Thu	Fri	Sat	Hours	Rate	Pay
5	Lou	Cortez										
6	Jasmine	Hill										
7	Heather	Kiley										
8	Dayna	McGuire										
9	Carla	Modano										
10	Tyler	Santini										
11	Pat	Soulliere										
12	Moira	Su-Lin										
13	Toni	Williams										
14												
15	Total											
16												
17	Hours Proof											
18	Gross Pay Proof											

Next, add the values to record quantities, rates, or other numeric entries.

	A	B	C	D	E	F	G	H	I	J	K
1						Payroll					
2					Week Ended: September 26, 2015						
3										Total	Pay
4			Sun	Mon	Tue	Wed	Thu	Fri	Sat	Hours	Rate
5	Lou	Cortez	8	0	6	8	0	8	8		8.25
6	Jasmine	Hill	8	0	8	8	0	8	6		8.25
7	Heather	Kiley	0	8	6	8	5	5	8		8.25
8	Dayna	McGuire	6	5	8	8	7	0	6		8.25
9	Carla	Modano	0	0	8	8	7	7	8		8.25
10	Tyler	Santini	8	0	8	8	6	7	0		8.25
11	Pat	Soulliere	8	8	0	8	7	7	0		8.25
12	Moira	Su-Lin	0	8	0	8	7	7	8		8.25
13	Toni	Williams	8	0	0	8	8	7	4		8.25

Create the formulas to add, subtract, multiply, or divide.

	A	B	C	D	E	F	G	H	I	J	K	L
1						Payroll						
2					Week Ended: September 26, 2015							
3										Total	Pay	Gross
4			Sun	Mon	Tue	Wed	Thu	Fri	Sat	Hours	Rate	Pay
5	Lou	Cortez	8	0	6	8	0	8	8	=SUM(C5:I5)	8.25	=J5*K5
6	Jasmine	Hill	8	0	8	8	0	8	6	=SUM(C6:I6)	8.25	=J6*K6
7	Heather	Kiley	0	8	6	8	5	5	8	=SUM(C7:I7)	8.25	=J7*K7
8	Dayna	McGuire	6	5	8	8	7	0	6	=SUM(C8:I8)	8.25	=J8*K8
9	Carla	Modano	0	0	8	8	7	7	8	=SUM(C9:I9)	8.25	=J9*K9
10	Tyler	Santini	8	0	8	8	6	7	0	=SUM(C10:I10)	8.25	=J10*K10
11	Pat	Soulliere	8	8	0	8	7	7	0	=SUM(C11:I11)	8.25	=J11*K11
12	Moira	Su-Lin	0	8	0	8	7	7	8	=SUM(C12:I12)	8.25	=J12*K12
13	Toni	Williams	8	0	0	8	8	7	4	=SUM(C13:I13)	8.25	=J13*K13
14												
15	Total		=SUM(C5:C14)	=SUM(D5:D14)	=SUM(E5:E14)	=SUM(F5:F14)	=SUM(G5:G14)	=SUM(H5:H14)	=SUM(I5:I14)	=SUM(J5:J14)		=SUM(L5:L14)
16												
17	Hours Proof	=SUM(C5:I13)										
18	Gross Pay Proof	=B17*K5										

The desired results are shown in the finished worksheet.

	A	B	C	D	E	F	G	H	I	J	K	L
1						Payroll						
2					Week Ended: September 26, 2015							
3										Total	Pay	Gross
4			Sun	Mon	Tue	Wed	Thu	Fri	Sat	Hours	Rate	Pay
5	Lou	Cortez	8	0	6	8	0	8	8	38	8.25	$ 313.50
6	Jasmine	Hill	8	0	8	8	0	8	6	38	8.25	$ 313.50
7	Heather	Kiley	0	8	6	8	5	5	8	40	8.25	$ 330.00
8	Dayna	McGuire	6	5	8	8	7	0	6	40	8.25	$ 330.00
9	Carla	Modano	0	0	8	8	7	7	8	38	8.25	$ 313.50
10	Tyler	Santini	8	0	8	8	6	7	0	37	8.25	$ 305.25
11	Pat	Soulliere	8	8	0	8	7	7	0	38	8.25	$ 313.50
12	Moira	Su-Lin	0	8	0	8	7	7	8	38	8.25	$ 313.50
13	Toni	Williams	8	0	0	8	8	7	4	35	8.25	$ 288.75
14												
15	Total		46	29	44	72	47	56	48	342		$2,821.50
16												
17	Hours Proof		342									
18	Gross Pay Proof	$2,821.50										

Edit and Format Worksheets

Excel allows you to apply formatting attributes and add color to enhance the appearance of the worksheet and draw a reader's attention to important titles, totals, or other results. Excel provides the ability to apply a theme which coordinates colors, fonts, and effects to create a worksheet with a professional appearance in just a few mouse clicks. A variety of formats, grouped into categories, are available for numbers, dates, and times. Insert images such as clip art or a logo to enhance a worksheet or add a corporate identity.

The Waterfront Bistro

3104 Rivermist Drive
Buffalo, NY 14280
716 555 3166

Quotation

TO: Marquee Productions
955 South Alameda Street
Los Angeles, CA 90037

DATE: 5-Nov-15

ATT: Camille Matsui

RE: Remote Location Filming
July 11 to August 31

Note: All prices include tax.

Item	No. of Persons	Price per Person	No. of Days	Total
Buffet Lunch	56	8.34	52	$ 24,286.08
Soup and salad				
Vegetable tray with dip				
Seafood hors d'oeuvres				
Hot entrée				
Deli tray and rolls				
Dessert				
Beverages	56	3.91	52	11,385.92
Coffee and tea				
Assorted juice				
Mineral water				
Snacks	56	3.91	52	11,385.92
Muffins				
Donuts				
Fruit tray				
Vegetable tray with dip				
Transport		33.00	52	1,716.00
Total				$ 48,773.92

Terms: Due upon receipt of invoice payable in U.S. funds

Apply formatting enhancements including:

- adding borders
- adding fill color
- adjusting row height
- adjusting column width
- applying a cell style
- applying a theme
- changing text alignment within cells
- changing font, font size, font color
- changing font attributes to bold and/or italic
- indenting text within a cell
- formatting numbers

The Waterfront Bistro

2015 Special Event Bookings

Contact Name	Contact Phone	Event	Date	Room	Guests	Special Menu	Price Per Person
Cecily Hillmore	716 555 6598	Business Meeting	1/15/2015	Starlake	42	No	23.95
Frances Corriveau	716 555 3256	Birthday Party	1/18/2015	Westview	82	Yes	29.95
Orlando Fagan	716 555 3694	25th Wedding Anniversary	3/14/2015	Westview	95	Yes	29.95
Kim Pockovic	905 555 3698	Birthday Party	3/21/2015	Westview	65	Yes	36.95
Lane Gill	416 555 3264	Business Meeting	3/25/2015	Starlake	55	No	22.95
Percy Bresque	716 555 1248	50th Wedding Anniversary	4/12/2015	Westview	102	Yes	35.95
Max Santore	905 555 3264	Wedding	4/25/2015	Sunset	188	Yes	27.95
Omar Hamid	716 555 8796	Engagement Party	5/10/2015	Sunset	67	Yes	29.95
Jack Torrance	716 555 1469	Business Meeting	5/15/2015	Westview	34	No	24.95
Dana Russell	716 555 4965	Birthday Party	5/30/2015	Starlake	54	No	28.95
Walter Szucs	905 555 6998	Birthday Party	6/6/2015	Starlake	84	No	34.95
Nicole Griffin	905 555 4166	25th Wedding Anniversary	6/14/2015	Starlake	78	Yes	34.95
Zack Doucet	716 555 3488	Wedding	6/27/2015	Sunset	215	Yes	29.95
Jesse Golinsky	716 555 4218	Business Meeting	6/30/2015	Westview	60	No	25.95
Cora Jin Ping	716 555 7774	Baby Shower	7/11/2015	Sunset	75	Yes	22.95
Elizabeth McMaster	716 555 9442	Engagement Party	7/18/2015	Sunset	94	Yes	28.95
Reed Pavelich	716 555 2286	Wedding	7/25/2015	Starlake	145	Yes	34.95
Alfredo Juanitez	716 555 4668	Business Meeting	7/30/2015	Westview	37	No	24.95
Yanfang Guo	716 555 4856	50th Wedding Anniversary	8/2/2015	Starlake	62	No	34.95
Jelena Boskovic	716 555 3456	Business Meeting	8/7/2015	Westview	27	Yes	29.95
Priscilla Melo	716 555 3145	Business Meeting	8/21/2015	Westview	34	Yes	25.95
Tracie McIntyre	716 555 3496	Birthday Party	9/5/2015	Sunset	26	No	22.95
Krista Pressey	716 555 7469	50th Wedding Anniversary	9/13/2015	Sunset	95	No	28.95
Langford Hill	716 555 8798	Wedding	9/19/2015	Starlake	185	No	34.95
Naomi Sayers	905 555 3486	Wedding	10/10/2015	Starlake	245	Yes	24.95
Lesley Reedman	716 555 4123	Wedding	10/18/2015	Westview	110	Yes	34.95
Mitchell Langley	905 555 4637	Wedding	11/14/2015	Sunset	85	Yes	29.95
Sally Ramirez	716 555 9648	Engagement Party	12/5/2015	Starlake	34	No	25.95

Insert images and clip art, display gridlines, and apply shading to enhance the appearance of a worksheet.

In Section 3 you will learn how to
Use Function Formulas and Add Visual Elements

Excel's functions make the task of writing formulas easier. Functions are grouped into categories such as statistical, financial, date, and logical. Excel provides over 300 prebuilt formulas to perform calculations. The Insert Function dialog box is available to assist with locating and creating a function. Create charts from data to emphasize trends or compare data sets. Add emphasis to worksheets or charts by drawing arrows and adding text boxes.

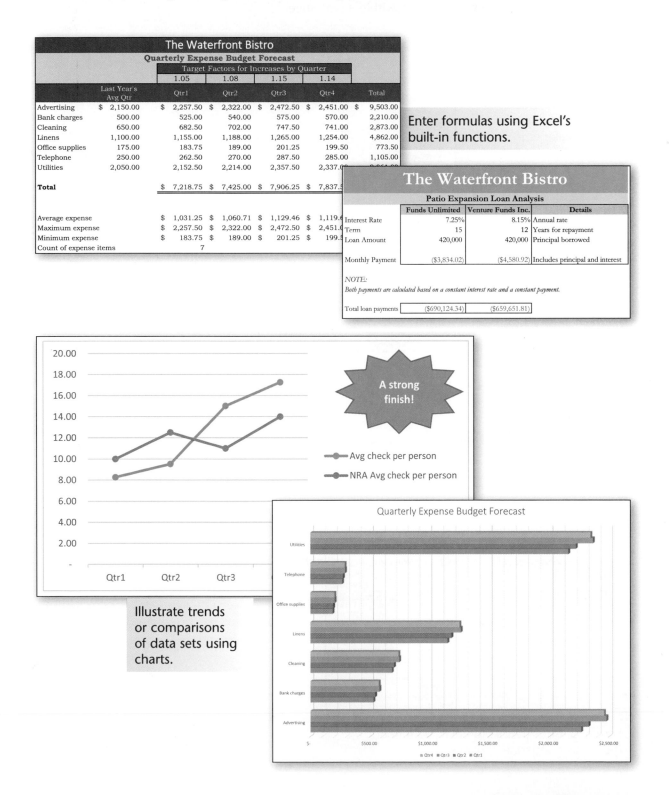

The Waterfront Bistro

Quarterly Expense Budget Forecast

		Target Factors for Increases by Quarter			
		1.05	1.08	1.15	1.14	
	Last Year's Avg Qtr	Qtr1	Qtr2	Qtr3	Qtr4	Total
Advertising	$ 2,150.00	$ 2,257.50	$ 2,322.00	$ 2,472.50	$ 2,451.00	$ 9,503.00
Bank charges	500.00	525.00	540.00	575.00	570.00	2,210.00
Cleaning	650.00	682.50	702.00	747.50	741.00	2,873.00
Linens	1,100.00	1,155.00	1,188.00	1,265.00	1,254.00	4,862.00
Office supplies	175.00	183.75	189.00	201.25	199.50	773.50
Telephone	250.00	262.50	270.00	287.50	285.00	1,105.00
Utilities	2,050.00	2,152.50	2,214.00	2,357.50	2,337.0	
Total		$ 7,218.75	$ 7,425.00	$ 7,906.25	$ 7,837.5	
Average expense		$ 1,031.25	$ 1,060.71	$ 1,129.46	$ 1,119.6	
Maximum expense		$ 2,257.50	$ 2,322.00	$ 2,472.50	$ 2,451.0	
Minimum expense		$ 183.75	$ 189.00	$ 201.25	$ 199.5	
Count of expense items		7				

Enter formulas using Excel's built-in functions.

The Waterfront Bistro

Patio Expansion Loan Analysis

	Funds Unlimited	Venture Funds Inc.	Details
Interest Rate	7.25%	8.15%	Annual rate
Term	15	12	Years for repayment
Loan Amount	420,000	420,000	Principal borrowed
Monthly Payment	($3,834.02)	($4,580.92)	Includes principal and interest

NOTE:
Both payments are calculated based on a constant interest rate and a constant payment.

| Total loan payments | ($690,124.34) | ($659,651.81) | |

A strong finish!

Avg check per person
NRA Avg check per person

Illustrate trends or comparisons of data sets using charts.

Quarterly Expense Budget Forecast

In Section 4 you will learn how to

Work with Multiple Worksheets and Tables

Excel allows you to easily manage large amounts of data by separating the data into different worksheets. Worksheets can be copied or moved to rearrange the order and logically organized by renaming and applying a tab color to the sheet tabs. Formulas can be created that reference cells in other worksheets or a cell can be linked to another worksheet to ensure the data flows from one worksheet to another. A list can be formatted as a table, which can be sorted, filtered, and formatted as a separate entity within a worksheet.

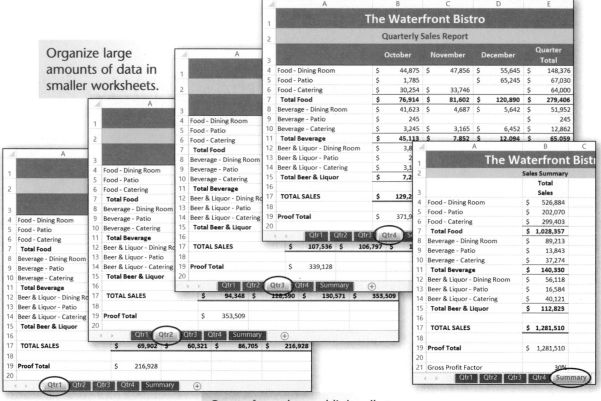

Organize large amounts of data in smaller worksheets.

Create formulas and link cells to summarize worksheets.

The Waterfront Bistro								
Catering Contracts								
First Name	Last Name	Contact Phone	Event	Date	Room	Guests	Special Menu	Price Per Person	Contract Total
Nicole	Griffin	905 555 4166	25th Wedding Anniversary	6/17/2015	Starlake	54	Yes	31.95	$ 1,725.30
Dana	Russell	716 555 4965	Birthday Party	5/30/2015	Starlake	36	No	26.95	$ 970.20
Walter	Szucs	905 555 6998	Birthday Party	6/10/2015	Starlake	42	No	28.95	$ 1,215.90
Sofia	Delgado	716 555 8465	Birthday Party	8/10/2015	Starlake	55	No	21.95	$ 1,207.25
Carlotta	Balducci	716 555 9665	Birthday Party	8/22/2015	Starlake	62	Yes	25.95	$ 1,608.90
Sonora	Yee	716 555 2668	Birthday Party	12/31/2015	Starlake	73	Yes	31.95	$ 2,332.35
Cecily	Hillmore	716 555 6598	Business Meeting	1/15/2015	Starlake	35	No	21.95	$ 768.25
Lane	Gill	416 555 3264	Business Meeting	3/29/2015	Starlake	71	No	21.95	$ 1,558.45
Mei-Yin	Zhang	716 555 2121	Business Meeting	12/1/2015	Starlake	28	Yes	31.95	$ 894.60
Cristian	Martinez	716 555 4331	Business Meeting	12/15/2015	Starlake	18	No	31.95	$ 575.10
Bianca	Vargas	716 555 3884	Engagement Party	10/15/2015	Starlake	40	Yes	31.95	$ 1,278.00
Reed	Pavelich	716 555 2286	Wedding	7/25/2015	Starlake	110	Yes	31.95	$ 3,514.50
Total						624		28.28	$ 17,648.80

Format a list as a table to filter and format the list as a separate entity.

Excel SECTION 1

Analyzing Data Using Excel

Skills

- Start Excel and identify features in the Excel window
- Save a workbook using Save and Save As
- Enter labels and values
- Use the fill handle to enter a series
- Enter formulas
- Create a formula using SUM
- Copy a formula
- Test a worksheet for accuracy
- Apply the Accounting format to values
- Right-align labels
- Sort a selection
- Use the Help feature
- Center a label across multiple columns
- Change the page orientation to landscape
- Preview and print a worksheet
- Display cell formulas in a worksheet
- Navigate a large worksheet using the mouse and the keyboard
- Jump to a specific cell using Go To

Student Resources

Before beginning the activities in Excel, copy to your storage medium the Excel folder on the Student Resources CD. This folder contains the data files you need to complete the projects in each Excel section.

Projects Overview

Edit a weekly sales report, create a payroll worksheet, create a condensed quarterly income statement, and sort a standard inventory list.

Create a projected distribution revenue schedule for a new movie release.

Complete an estimated travel costs worksheet.

Create an international student registration report and a target enrollment report.

Prepare a price quotation for costume alterations and rental.

1

Model Answers for Projects

These model answers for the projects you complete in Section 1 provide a preview of the finished projects before you begin working and also allow you to compare your own results with these models to ensure you have created the materials accurately.

ES1-WBWeeklySales.xlsx **is the project in Activity 1.1.**

Weekly Sales Report

For the week ended:	21-Sep							
	Sunday	**Monday**	**Tuesday**	**Wednesday**	**Thursday**	**Friday**	**Saturday**	**Total**
Food - Dining Room	2,585.00	1,006.00	1,255.00	1,345.00	1,488.00	1,596.00	2,137.00	11,412.00
Food - Patio	1,154.00	312.00	488.00	578.00	1,065.00	1,147.00	1,549.00	6,293.00
Food - Catering	2,477.00	-	-	1,865.00	1,855.00	4,266.00	3,157.00	13,620.00
Total Food	**6,216.00**	**1,318.00**	**1,743.00**	**3,788.00**	**4,408.00**	**7,009.00**	**6,843.00**	**31,325.00**
Beverage - Dining Room	341.00	88.00	195.00	229.00	214.00	198.00	235.00	1,500.00
Beverage - Patio	244.00	49.00	88.00	97.00	96.00	84.00	128.00	786.00
Beverage - Catering	652.00	-	-	314.00	247.00	394.00	214.00	1,821.00
Total Beverage	**1,237.00**	**137.00**	**283.00**	**640.00**	**557.00**	**676.00**	**577.00**	**4,107.00**
Beer & Liquor - Dining Room	1,577.00	175.00	269.00	492.00	323.00	224.00	485.00	3,545.00
Beer & Liquor - Patio	652.00	56.00	96.00	78.00	184.00	168.00	227.00	1,461.00
Beer & Liquor - Catering	984.00	-	-	344.00	411.00	884.00	774.00	3,397.00
Total Beer & Liquor	**3,213.00**	**231.00**	**365.00**	**914.00**	**918.00**	**1,276.00**	**1,486.00**	**8,403.00**
TOTAL SALES	**10,666.00**	**1,686.00**	**2,391.00**	**5,342.00**	**5,883.00**	**8,961.00**	**8,906.00**	**43,835.00**
Gross Profit Factor	**32%**							
Estimated Gross Profit	**3,413.12**	**539.52**	**765.12**	**1,709.44**	**1,882.56**	**2,867.52**	**2,849.92**	**14,027.20**

ES1-WBPayroll.xlsx **is the project in Activities 1.2 to 1.8.**

Payroll
Week Ended: September 26, 2015

		Sun	Mon	Tue	Wed	Thu	Fri	Sat	Total Hours	Pay Rate	Gross Pay
Lou	Cortez	8	0	6	8	0	8	8	38	8.25	$ 313.50
Jasmine	Hill	8	0	8	8	0	8	6	38	8.25	$ 313.50
Heather	Kiley	0	8	6	8	5	5	8	40	8.25	$ 330.00
Dayna	McGuire	6	5	8	8	7	0	6	40	8.25	$ 330.00
Carla	Modano	0	0	8	8	7	7	8	38	8.25	$ 313.50
Tyler	Santini	8	0	8	8	6	7	0	37	8.25	$ 305.25
Pat	Soulliere	8	8	0	8	7	7	0	38	8.25	$ 313.50
Moira	Su-Lin	0	8	0	8	7	7	8	38	8.25	$ 313.50
Toni	Williams	8	0	0	8	8	7	4	35	8.25	$ 288.75
Total		46	29	44	72	47	56	48	342		$ 2,821.50

Hours
Proof 342
Gross
Pay Proof $ 2,821.50

Student Name

ES1-WBPayroll.xlsx **is the project in Activity 1.9.**

Payroll
Week Ended: September 26, 2015

			Sun	Mon	Tue	Wed
Lou	Cortez	8	0	6	8	0
Jasmine	Hill	8	0	8	8	0
Heather	Kiley	0	8	6	8	5
Dayna	McGuire	6	5	8	8	7
Carla	Modano	0	0	8	8	7
Tyler	Santini	8	0	8	8	6
Pat	Soulliere	8	8	0	8	7
Moira	Su-Lin	0	8	0	8	7
Toni	Williams	8	0	0	8	8
Total		=SUM(C5:C14)	=SUM(D5:D14)	=SUM(E5:E14)	=SUM(F5:F14)	=SUM(G5:G14)

Hours
Proof =SUM(C5:I13)
Gross
Pay Proof =B17*K5

Student Name

Thu	Fri	Sat	Total Hours	Pay Rate	Gross Pay
8	8	=SUM(C5:I5)	8.25	=J5*K5	
8	6	=SUM(C6:I6)	8.25	=J6*K6	
5	8	=SUM(C7:I7)	8.25	=J7*K7	
0	6	=SUM(C8:I8)	8.25	=J8*K8	
7	8	=SUM(C9:I9)	8.25	=J9*K9	
7	0	=SUM(C10:I10)	8.25	=J10*K10	
7	0	=SUM(C11:I11)	8.25	=J11*K11	
7	8	=SUM(C12:I12)	8.25	=J12*K12	
7	4	=SUM(C13:I13)	8.25	=J13*K13	
=SUM(H5:H14)	=SUM(I5:I14)	=SUM(J5:J14)			=SUM(L5:L14)

Activity 1.1

Completing the Excel Worksheet Cycle

Information is created in Excel in a *worksheet* and is saved in a file called a *workbook*. A workbook can contain several worksheets. Imagine a worksheet as a page with horizontal and vertical lines drawn in a grid representing columns and rows. Data is entered into a *cell*, which is the intersection of a column with a row. Columns are lettered A to Z, AA to AZ, BA to BZ, and so on. The last column in the worksheet is labeled *XFD*. Rows are numbered 1, 2, 3, and so on. A column letter and a row number identify each cell. For example, A1 is the cell address for the intersection of column A with row 1. Each worksheet in Excel contains 16,384 columns and 1,048,576 rows. By default, an Excel workbook contains one worksheet labeled *Sheet1*. Additional sheets can be inserted as needed.

Project

You have been asked to update a weekly sales report for The Waterfront Bistro by adding data and viewing the impact of changing a cell used to calculate gross margin.

Tutorial 1.1
Opening, Saving, and Closing an Excel Workbook

1. At the Windows 8 Start screen, click the Excel 2013 tile.

   Depending on your system configuration, this step may vary.

2. At the Excel 2013 opening screen, click the Blank workbook template.

3. At the Excel screen, identify the various features by comparing your screen with the one shown in Figure 1.1. If necessary, maximize the Excel window. Depending on your screen resolution, your screen may vary slightly. Refer to Table 1.1 for a description of the screen features.

4. Click the FILE tab and then click the *Open* option at the backstage area.

   The backstage area organizes file management tasks into options such as *Open, Save, Save As,* and *Print.*

FIGURE 1.1 The Excel Screen

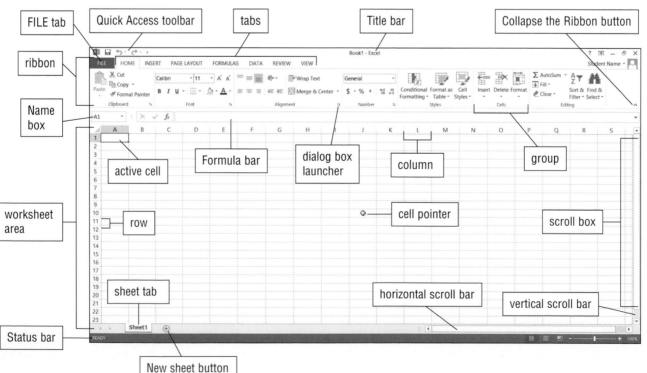

TABLE 1.1 Excel Screen Features

Feature	Description
active cell	location in the worksheet that will display typed data or that will be affected by a command
cell pointer	select cells when you see this icon by clicking or dragging the mouse
Collapse the Ribbon button	click to remove the ribbon; double-click a tab to redisplay the ribbon
dialog box or task pane launcher	click the downward-pointing diagonal arrow at the bottom right in a group to open a dialog box or task pane with more options for that group
FILE tab	displays the backstage area that contains options for working with and managing files
Formula bar	displays the contents stored in the active cell
Name box	displays the active cell address or name assigned to active cell
New sheet button	click the button to insert a new worksheet in the workbook
Quick Access toolbar	contains buttons for commonly used commands that can be executed with a single mouse click
ribbon	area containing the tabs with commands and buttons divided into groups
sheet tab	identifies the worksheet in the workbook
Status bar	displays current mode, action messages, view buttons, and Zoom slider bar
tabs	contains commands and buttons organized into groups
Title bar	displays workbook name followed by Microsoft Excel
vertical and horizontal scroll bars	used to view various parts of the worksheet beyond the current screen
worksheet area	contains cells used to create the worksheet

5 At the Open backstage area, click the desired location in the middle panel of the backstage area (the panel containing the four location options). For example, click the *SkyDrive* option preceded by your name if you are opening a workbook from your SkyDrive or click the *Computer* option if you are opening a workbook from your computer's hard drive or a USB flash drive.

6 Click the Browse button.

> Press Ctrl + F12 to display the Open dialog box without displaying the Open backstage area.

7 At the Open dialog box, double-click the *ExcelS1* folder.

> To change to a different drive, click the drive letter in the *Computer* section of the Open dialog box Navigation pane. (You may need to scroll down the Navigation pane to see the *Computer* section.) Change to a different folder by double-clicking the folder name in the Content pane.

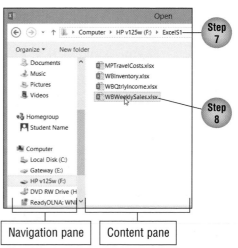

8 Double-click **WBWeeklySales.xlsx** in the Open dialog box Content pane.

> This workbook contains one worksheet with sales for The Waterfront Bistro for the week ended September 21, 2015. The formulas to sum the sales have already been created. Notice some of the cells in the column labeled *Saturday* are empty. You will enter these values in Steps 12 through 15.

continues

9 Click the FILE tab and then click the *Save As* option.

10 At the Save As backstage area, click the current folder (the end of the current folder path name should end in *ExcelS1*) that displays below the *Current Folder* heading.

> Use the *Save* option to save a file using the same name. If you want to keep the original workbook and save the workbook with the changes under a new name, use *Save As*.

11 At the Save As dialog box, with ExcelS1 the active folder on your storage medium, press the Home key, type **ES1-** at the beginning of the current file name in the *File name* text box, and then press Enter or click the Save button.

> Press the F12 function key to display the Save As dialog box without displaying the Save As backstage area. Excel files have the file extension *.xlsx* at the end of a workbook name. When naming a file, do not change or delete this file extension because the operating system recognizes files ending with *.xlsx* as Microsoft Excel workbooks. If you change or delete the extension, the operating system will not know which program is associated with the data.

12 Move the cell pointer over the intersection of column H with row 6 (cell H6) and then click to make cell H6 the active cell.

13 Type **3157** and then press Enter.

> Notice that the entry in cell H7 has changed. This is because the formula created in cell H7 was dependent on cell H6. As soon as you enter a value in cell H6, any other dependent cells are automatically updated. Can you identify other cells that changed as a result of the new value in cell H6?

Need Help?

Typing mistake? Make corrections as you type by pressing the Backspace key to delete characters to the left of the insertion point; or, if you notice the mistake after you have left the cell, make the cell active and double-click the cell to open the cell for editing.

14 Click cell H10 to make it the active cell and then type **214**.

15 Click cell H14 to make it the active cell, type **774**, and then press Enter.

16 Look at the entry in cell B19. This percentage is used to calculate the Estimated Gross Profit in row 20 (Total Sales times the Gross Profit Factor). Click cell B19 to make the cell active, type **32**, and then press Enter.

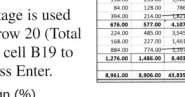

Step 13

Step 14

Step 15

> Excel automatically inserts the percent sign (%) when you type 32. Notice the new estimated gross profit values in cells B20 through I20.

Step 16

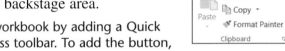

17	TOTAL SALES	10,666.00	1,686.00	2,391.00	5,342.00	5,883.00	8,961.00	8,906.00	43,835.00
18									
19	Gross Profit Factor	32%							
20	Estimated Gross Profit	3,413.12	539.52	765.12	1,709.44	1,882.56	2,867.52	2,849.92	14,027.20

17 Click the Save button 🖫 on the Quick Access toolbar.

18 Click the FILE tab, click the *Print* option, and then click the Print button at the Print backstage area.

Step 17

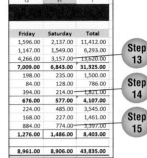

> You can save steps to print a workbook by adding a Quick Print button to the Quick Access toolbar. To add the button, click the Customize Quick Access Toolbar button that displays at the right side of the toolbar and then click *Quick Print* at the drop-down list. The worksheet's page layout options have been set to print the worksheet in landscape orientation and centered horizontally between the left and right margins. You will learn how to set these options in a later activity.

Step 18

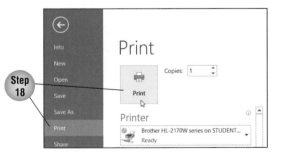

19 Click the FILE tab and then click the *Close* option to close the workbook. Click the FILE tab and click the Close option to close the blank workbook.

> When no workbooks are currently open, Excel displays a blank gray screen.

In Addition

Using AutoComplete

The AutoComplete feature in Excel will complete text entries for you as you start to type a new entry in a cell. If the first few letters that you type match another entry in the column, Excel automatically fills in the remaining text. Press Tab, Enter, or one of the arrow keys to accept the text Excel suggests, or continue typing the correct text. You can turn off AutoComplete by clicking the FILE tab and then clicking *Options*. Click *Advanced* in the left pane of the Excel Options dialog box, click the *Enable AutoComplete for cell values* check box to clear the box, and then click OK.

Activity 1.1   7

In Brief

Open Workbook
1. Click FILE tab.
2. Click *Open* option.
3. At Open backstage area, click desired location.
4. Click Browse button.
5. At Open dialog box, navigate to desired folder.
6. Double-click workbook name.

Save Workbook
1. Click Save button on Quick Access toolbar.
2. At Save As backstage area, click desired location.
3. Click Browse button.
4. At Save As dialog box, navigate to the desired folder.
5. Type document name.
6. Click Save or press Enter.

Save Workbook with New Name
1. Click FILE tab.
2. Click *Save As* option.
3. At Save As backstage area, click desired location.
4. Click Browse button.
5. At Save As dialog box, navigate to the desired folder.
6. Type document name.
7. Click Save or press Enter.

Activity 1.2

Entering Labels and Values; Using Fill Options

A *label* is an entry in a cell that helps the reader relate to the values in the corresponding column or row. Labels are generally entered first when creating a new worksheet since they define the layout of the data in the columns and rows. By default, Excel aligns labels at the left edge of the column. A *value* is a number, formula, or function that can be used to perform calculations in the worksheet. By default, Excel aligns values at the right edge of the column. Take a few moments to plan or sketch out the layout of a new worksheet before entering labels and values. Decide the calculations you will need to execute and how to display the data so that it will be easily understood and interpreted.

Project

Tutorial 1.2
Entering Data in Cells and Saving a Workbook with a New Name

You need to calculate gross pay in a new payroll worksheet for the hourly paid staff at The Waterfront Bistro. Begin by entering labels and values.

1. At the blank Excel screen, click the FILE tab, click the *New* option, and then click the Blank workbook template at the New backstage area.

    You can also open a new blank workbook with the keyboard shortcut, Ctrl + N. To execute this command, hold down the Ctrl key on your keyboard, press the N key, and then release the Ctrl key. You can also insert a New button on the Quick Access toolbar. To insert the button, click the Customize Quick Access Toolbar button that displays at the right side of the toolbar and then click *New* at the drop-down list.

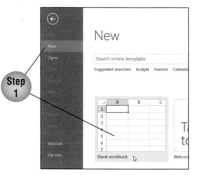

2. With cell A1 the active cell, type **Payroll** as the title for the new worksheet.

    When you type a new entry in a cell, the entry appears in the Formula bar as well as within the active cell in the worksheet area. To end a cell entry, press Enter, move to another cell in the worksheet, or click the Enter button on the Formula bar.

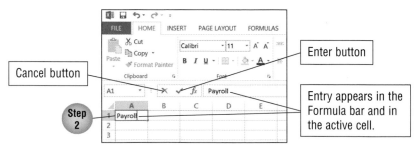

3. Press Enter.

4. With cell A2 the active cell, type **Week Ended: September 26, 2015**, and then press Enter.

    Notice the entry in cell A2 is overflowing into columns B, C, and D. You can allow a label to spill over into adjacent columns as long as you do not plan to enter other data in the overflow cells. In a later section, you will learn how to adjust column widths.

5 Enter the remaining labels as shown below by making the appropriate cell the active cell, typing the label, and then pressing Enter or clicking another cell. (Do not complete the labels for the days of the week beyond *Sun*, as this will be completed in Steps 6 through 8.)

Step 4

	A	B	C	D	E	F	G	H	I	J	K	L
1	Payroll											
2	Week Ended: September 26, 2015											
3										Total	Pay	Gross
4			Sun							Hours	Rate	Pay
5	Dayna	McGuire										
6	Heather	Kiley										
7	Pat	Soulliere										
8	Jasmine	Hill										
9	Moira	Su-Lin										
10	Carla	Modano										
11	Toni	Williams										
12	Tyler	Santini										
13	Lou	Cortez										
14												
15	Total											

Step 5

6 Click in cell C4 to make it the active cell.

> A thick green border surrounds the active cell. A small green square displays at the bottom right corner of the active cell. This green square is called the **fill handle**. The fill handle is used to fill adjacent cells with the same data or consecutive data. The entries that are automatically inserted in the adjacent cells are dependent on the contents of the active cell. You will use the fill handle in cell C4 to automatically enter the remaining days of the week in cells D4 through I4.

7 Point at the fill handle in cell C4. The cell pointer changes from the large white cross ✛ to a thin black cross ✚.

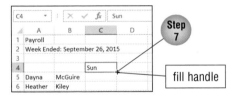

Step 7

fill handle

8 Hold down the left mouse button, drag the pointer to cell I4, and then release the mouse.

> The entries *Mon* through *Sat* appear in cells D4 to I4. As you drag the pointer to the right, a green border surrounds the selected cells and a ScreenTip appears below the pointer indicating the label or value that will be inserted. When you release the left mouse button, the cells remain selected and the Auto Fill Options button 🔡 appears. Clicking the Auto Fill Options button causes a drop-down list to display with various alternative actions for filling text or data in the cells.

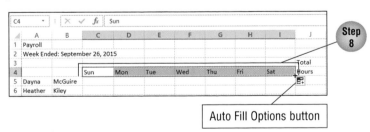

Step 8

Auto Fill Options button

Need Help?

The entries *Mon* through *Sat* do not appear? You probably dragged the mouse using the cell pointer instead of the fill handle. This action selects cells instead of filling them. Go back to Step 6 and try again, making sure you drag when you see the thin black cross.

continues

9 Click in cell C5 to make it the active cell.

10 Type **6** and then press the Right Arrow key.

11 Type **5** in cell D5 and then press the Right Arrow key.

12 Type the following values in the cells indicated:

E5: **8**

F5: **8**

G5: **7**

H5: **0**

I5: **6**

13 Make cell F5 the active cell.

14 Point at the fill handle in cell F5 and then drag the pointer down to cell F13.

> This time the active cell contained a value. The value 8 is copied to the adjacent cells.

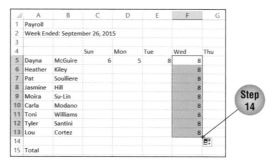

Step 14

15 Enter the remaining values for employee hours as shown below. Use the fill handle where duplicate values appear in adjacent cells to enter the data as efficiently as possible.

	A	B	C	D	E	F	G	H	I	J
1	Payroll									
2	Week Ended: September 26, 2015									
3										Total
4			Sun	Mon	Tue	Wed	Thu	Fri	Sat	Hours
5	Dayna	McGuire	6	5	8	8	7	0	6	
6	Heather	Kiley	0	8	6	8	5	5	8	
7	Pat	Soulliere	8	8	0	8	7	7	0	
8	Jasmine	Hill	8	0	8	8	0	8	6	
9	Moira	Su-Lin	0	8	0	8	7	7	8	
10	Carla	Modano	0	0	8	8	7	7	8	
11	Toni	Williams	8	0	0	8	8	7	4	
12	Tyler	Santini	8	0	8	8	6	7	0	
13	Lou	Cortez	8	0	6	8	0	8	8	
14										

Step 15

16 Make cell K5 the active cell, type **8.25**, and then press Enter.

17 Position the cell pointer over cell K5, hold down the left mouse button, drag down to cell K13, and then release the mouse.

> A group of adjacent cells is referred to as a *range*. A range is two or more cells. Select a range of cells when you want to perform an action on a group of cells.

In Brief

Using Fill Handle
1. Enter data in cell.
2. Drag fill handle to desired cell.

18 With HOME the active tab, click the Fill button 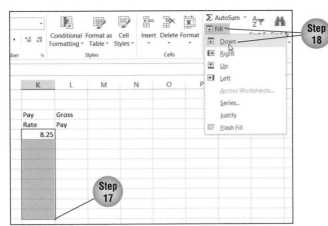 in the Editing group and then click *Down* at the drop-down list.

19 Click in any cell in the worksheet to deselect the range of cells in column K.

20 Click the Save button on the Quick Access toolbar.

21 At the Save As backstage area, click the recent folder that displays below the *Recent Folders* heading. (Before clicking the folder, make sure it is the ExcelS1 folder at the location where you want to save the workbook.)

22 At the Save As dialog box, type **ES1-WBPayroll** in the *File name* text box and then press Enter.

In Addition

Using the Fill Handle

The fill handle is versatile and can be used to enter a series of values, dates, times, or other labels as a pattern. The pattern is established based on the cells you select before dragging the fill handle. In the worksheet shown below, the cells in columns C through J were all populated using the fill handle. In each row, the first two cells in columns A and B were selected and then the fill handle dragged right to column J. Notice the variety of patterns used to extend a series.

Use the Auto Fill Options button drop-down list to control how the series is entered. After dragging the fill handle, the Auto Fill Options button displays at the end of the series. Pointing at the button causes the button to expand and display a down-pointing arrow. Click the down-pointing arrow and then select the desired fill action from the options in the drop-down list. By default, *Fill Series* is selected.

	A	B	C	D	E	F	G	H	I	J	K	L	M
1	Examples using the fill handle to continue a series in adjacent cells												
2	In each row below, the first two cells were selected and then the fill handle dragged right.												
3	1	2	3	4	5	6	7	8	9	10			
4	10	20	30	40	50	60	70	80	90	100			
5	9:00	10:00	11:00	12:00	13:00	14:00	15:00	16:00	17:00	18:00			
6	2015	2016	2017	2018	2019	2020	2021	2022	2023	2024			
7	Quarter 1	Quarter 2	Quarter 3	Quarter 4	Quarter 1	Quarter 2	Quarter 3	Quarter 4	Quarter 1	Quarter 2			
8	Period 1	Period 2	Period 3	Period 4	Period 5	Period 6	Period 7	Period 8	Period 9	Period 10			
9	Year 1	Year 2	Year 3	Year 4	Year 5	Year 6	Year 7	Year 8	Year 9	Year 10			
10													
11											○ Copy Cells		
12											⊙ Fill Series		
13											○ Fill Formatting Only		
14											○ Fill Without Formatting		
15													

Activity 1.3

Performing Calculations Using Formulas

A *formula* is entered into a cell to perform mathematical calculations in a worksheet. All formulas in Excel begin with the equals sign (=) as the first character. After the equals sign, the cell addresses that contain the values you want to calculate are entered between mathematical operators. The mathematical operators are + (addition), - (subtraction), * (multiplication), / (division), and ^ (exponentiation). An example of a valid formula is =A3*B3. In this formula, the value in cell A3 is multiplied by the value in cell B3 and the result is placed in the formula cell. By including the cell address in the formula rather than typing the actual value, you can utilize the powerful recalculation feature in Excel. If you change a cell's content, the worksheet is automatically recalculated so that all values are current.

Project

You will use two methods to enter formulas to calculate total hours and gross pay for the first two employees listed in the payroll worksheet for The Waterfront Bistro.

The Waterfront B·I·S·T·R·O

SNAP

Tutorial 1.3
Performing Calculations Using Formulas

1 With **ES1-WBPayroll.xlsx** open, make cell J5 the active cell.

Begin a formula by activating the cell in which you want the result placed.

2 Type **=C5+D5+E5+F5+G5+H5+I5** and then press Enter.

The values in cells C5 through I5 are added and the result, *40*, is displayed in cell J5. You can type cell column letters in a formula in uppercase or lowercase letters. If you type lowercase column letters in a formula, Excel will convert the letters to uppercase when you press Enter.

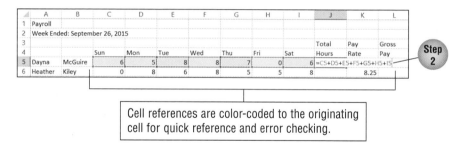

Cell references are color-coded to the originating cell for quick reference and error checking.

3 Press the Up Arrow key to make cell J5 the active cell.

Notice that the result of the formula displays in the worksheet area and the formula used to calculate the result displays in the Formula bar.

4 Make cell J6 the active cell, type the formula **=C6+D6+E6+F6+G6+H6+I6**, and then press Enter.

Seem like too much typing? A more efficient way to add a series of cells is available. This method will be introduced in the next activity after you learn the pointing method for entering formulas.

5 Make cell L5 the active cell.

To calculate gross pay, you need to multiply the total hours times the pay rate. In Steps 6 through 10, you will enter this formula using the pointing method.

6 Type the equals sign (=).

7 Click in cell J5.

A moving dashed border (called a *marquee*) displays around cell J5, indicating it is the cell included in the formula, and the cell address is added to the formula cell (J5) with a blinking insertion point after the reference. Notice also that the word *POINT* displays at the left side of the Status bar.

In Brief

Enter Formula
1. Make formula cell active.
2. Type =.
3. Type first cell address.
4. Type operator symbol.
5. Type second cell address.
6. Continue Steps 3–5 until finished.
7. Press Enter or click Enter button.

Enter a Formula Using the Pointing Method
1. Make formula cell active.
2. Type =.
3. Click first cell.
4. Type operator symbol.
5. Click second cell.
6. Repeat Steps 3–5 until finished.
7. Press Enter or click Enter button.

8 Type an asterisk (*), which is the multiplication operator.

> The marquee surrounding cell J5 disappears and cell J5 is color-coded with the cell reference *J5* within the formula cell.

9 Click in cell K5.

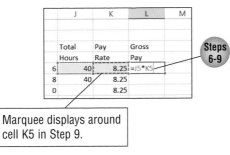

Steps 6-9

Marquee displays around cell K5 in Step 9.

10 Click the Enter button ✓ on the Formula bar.

> The result *330* is displayed in cell L5. In Activity 1.6, you will learn how to display two decimal places for cells containing dollar values.

Step 10

11 Type the formula **=J6*K6** in cell L6 (calculates the gross pay for Heather Kiley) and then press Enter.

12 Click the Save button on the Quick Access toolbar.

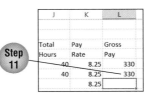

Step 11

In Addition

Order of Operations

If you include several operators in a formula, Excel calculates the result using the order of operations as follows: negations (e.g., -1) first, then percents (%), then exponentiations (^), then multiplication and division (* and /), and finally addition and subtraction (+ and -). If a formula contains more than one operator at the same level of precedence—for example, both an addition and a subtraction operation—Excel calculates the equation from left to right. To change the order of operations, use parentheses around the part of the formula you want calculated first.

Formula	Calculation
=B5*C5/D5	Both operators are at the same level of precedence—Excel would multiply the value in B5 times the value in C5 and then divide the result by the value in D5.
=B5+B6+B7*C10	Multiplication takes precedence over addition, so Excel would first multiply the value in B7 times the value in C10. Excel would then take the value in B5, add to it the value in B6, and then add the result of the multiplication.
=(B5+B6+B7)*C10	Because of the parentheses, Excel would first add the values in B5 through B7, then multiply this sum times the value in C10.

Activity 1.4

Using the SUM Function

The formulas to calculate the hours worked by the first two employees were lengthy. A more efficient way to calculate the total hours for Dayna McGuire in cell J5 would be to enter the formula =SUM(C5:I5). This formula includes one of Excel's built-in functions called SUM. A *function* is a pre-programmed formula. The structure of a formula utilizing a function begins with the equals sign (=), followed by the name of the function, and then the *argument*. Argument is the term given to the values identified within parentheses. In the example provided, the argument C5:I5 contains the starting cell and the ending cell separated by a colon (:). The colon is used to indicate a range is to be summed; a *range* is a rectangular-shaped block of cells. Since the SUM function is used frequently, an AutoSum button is available on the HOME tab.

Project

You decide to use a more efficient method of payroll calculation, so you will use the SUM function to complete the hours worked for the payroll worksheet.

Tutorial 1.4
Performing
Calculations Using
the AutoSum Button

1. With **ES1-WBPayroll.xlsx** open, make cell J5 the active cell and then press the Delete key.

   This deletes the cell contents. There was nothing wrong with the formula already entered in cell J5. You are deleting it so that the formulas in the completed worksheet will be consistent.

2. Click the AutoSum button Σ in the Editing group on the HOME tab. (Do not click the down-pointing arrow to the right of the AutoSum button.)

   A moving marquee surrounds cells C5 through I5 and a ScreenTip appears below the formula cell indicating the correct format for the SUM function. Excel enters the formula =*SUM(C5:I5)* in cell J5. The suggested range C5:I5 is selected within the formula so that you can highlight a different range with the mouse if the suggested range is not correct.

Excel enters formula with suggested range.

Step 2

ScreenTip displays correct format for SUM function.

3. Press Enter.

   Since the range Excel suggests is the correct range, you can finish the formula by pressing Enter or by clicking the Enter button on the Formula bar.

4. With cell J6 the active cell, press the Delete key to delete the existing formula in the cell.

5. Click the AutoSum button. When Excel displays the formula =*SUM(C6:I6)*, click the Enter button in the Formula bar.

6. Make cell J7 the active cell and then click the AutoSum button.

   Notice this time the range of cells Excel is suggesting to add (*J5:J6*) is the wrong range. When you click the AutoSum button, Excel looks for multiple values in the cells immediately above the active cell. In this case, there are multiple values above cell J7 so Excel inserts J5:J6 as the range in the SUM formula. You need to correct the range of cells that you want to add.

7 Position the cell pointer over cell C7, hold down the left mouse button, drag the pointer to the right to cell I7, and then release the mouse button.

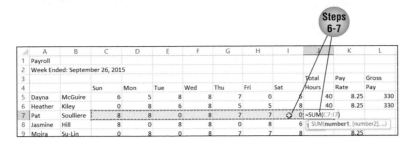

8 Press Enter.

Now that you have seen how the AutoSum button operates, you already know that the suggested range for the next employee's total hours will be incorrect. In Step 9, you will select the range of cells *first* to avoid the incorrect suggestion.

9 Position the cell pointer over cell C8, hold down the left mouse button, drag the pointer right to cell J8, and then release the mouse button.

Notice you are including cell J8, the cell that will display the result, in the range of cells.

10 Click the AutoSum button.

The result, *38*, appears in cell J8.

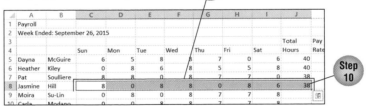

11 Click cell J8 and look in the Formula bar at the formula the SUM function created: *=SUM(C8:I8)*.

Since Excel created the correct SUM formula from a range of selected cells, you decide to try calculating total hours for more than one employee in one step using the method employed in Steps 9 and 10 but with an expanded range.

12 Position the cell pointer over cell C9, hold down the left mouse button, drag the pointer down and right to cell J13, and then release the mouse button.

13 Click the AutoSum button.

14 Click in cells J9, J10, J11, J12, and J13 to confirm that the correct formulas appear in the Formula bar.

15 Click the Save button on the Quick Access toolbar.

Activity 1.5

Copying Formulas

Many times you may create a worksheet in which several formulas are basically the same. For example, in the payroll worksheet, the formula to total the hours for Dayna McGuire is =SUM(C5:I5), for Heather Kiley =SUM(C6:I6), and so on. The only difference between the two formulas is the row number. Whenever formulas are this similar, you can use the Copy and Paste feature to copy the formula from one cell to another. The cell containing the original formula is called the *source*, and the cell(s) to which the formula is copied is called the *destination*. When the formula is pasted, Excel automatically changes column letters or row numbers to reflect the destination location. By default, Excel assumes *relative addressing*—cell addresses update relative to the destination.

Project

Tutorial 1.5
Copying and Testing
Formulas

To simplify your completion of the Payroll worksheet, you will copy formulas using two methods: Copy and Paste and the fill handle.

1 With **ES1-WBPayroll.xlsx** open, make cell L6 the active cell.

> This cell contains the formula =*J6*K6* to calculate the gross pay for Heather Kiley. You will copy this formula to the remaining cells in column L to finish the *Gross Pay* column.

2 Click the Copy button in the Clipboard group on the HOME tab. (Do not click the down-pointing arrow to the right of the Copy button.)

> A moving marquee surrounds the active cell indicating the source contents are copied to the *Clipboard*, which is a temporary storage location. The source being copied is the formula =*J6*K6*, not the value *330*.

3 Select the range L7:L13. To do this, position the cell pointer over cell L7, hold down the left mouse button, drag the pointer down to cell L13, and then release the mouse button.

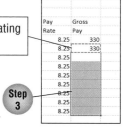

marquee indicating source range

4 Click the Paste button in the Clipboard group. (Do not click the down-pointing arrow on the button.)

> Excel copies the formula to the selected cells, displays the results, and the Paste Options button appears. Clicking the Paste Options button will display a drop-down list with various alternatives for pasting the data. The moving marquee remains around the source cell and the destination cells remain highlighted. The moving marquee disappears as soon as you start another activity or press the Esc key.

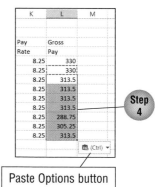

Paste Options button

5 Press the Esc key to remove the marquee and the Paste Options button, click in cell L7, and then look at the entry in the Formula bar: =*J7*K7*.

> The row number in the source formula was increased by one to reflect the destination. The actions you completed in Steps 1 through 4 are called *relative copying*.

6 Use the Down Arrow key to check the remaining formulas in column L.

7 Make cell C15 the active cell.

In Brief
Copy Formula
1. Make source cell active.
2. Click Copy button.
3. Select destination cell(s).
4. Click Paste button.

8 Click the AutoSum button and then click the Enter button in the Formula bar.

> The SUM function inserts the formula =SUM(C5:C14). Next, you will copy the formula using the fill handle.

9 Drag the fill handle in cell C15 right to cell L15.

> When the active cell contains a formula, dragging the fill handle causes Excel to copy the formula and change cell references relative to each destination location.

	A	B	C	D	E	F	G	H	I	J	K	L
1	Payroll											
2	Week Ended: September 26, 2015											
3										Total	Pay	Gross
4			Sun	Mon	Tue	Wed	Thu	Fri	Sat	Hours	Rate	Pay
5	Dayna	McGuire	6	5	8	8	7	0	6	40	8.25	330
6	Heather	Kiley	0	8	6	8	5	5	8	40	8.25	330
7	Pat	Soulliere	8	8	0	8	7	7	0	38	8.25	313.5
8	Jasmine	Hill	8	0	8	8	0	8	6	38	8.25	313.5
9	Moira	Su-Lin	0	8	0	8	7	7	8	38	8.25	313.5
10	Carla	Modano	0	0	8	8	7	7	8	38	8.25	313.5
11	Toni	Williams	8	0	0	8	8	7	4	35	8.25	288.75
12	Tyler	Santini	8	0	8	8	6	7	0	37	8.25	305.25
13	Lou	Cortez	8	0	6	8	0	8	8	38	8.25	313.5
14												
15	Total		46	29	44	72	47	56	48	342	74.25	2821.5
16												

Step 9

Need Help?
If the results do not appear in cells D15 through L15, you probably dragged the cell pointer instead of the fill handle. Click cell C15 and try again, making sure you drag using the thin black cross.

10 Make cell K15 the active cell and then press the Delete key.

> The sum of the *Pay Rate* column is not useful information.

11 Make cell D15 the active cell and look at the entry in the Formula bar: =SUM(D5:D14).

> The column letter in the source formula was changed to reflect the destination.

12 Use the Right Arrow key to check the formulas in the remaining columns.

13 Click the Save button on the Quick Access toolbar.

In Addition

Understanding Copy and Paste versus Fill

What is the difference between Copy and Paste and the fill handle? When you use Copy, the contents of the source cell(s) are placed in the Clipboard. The data will remain in the Clipboard and can be pasted several times in the current worksheet, into any other worksheet that is open, or into an open file in another program. Use Copy and Paste when the formula is to be inserted more than once or into nonadjacent cells. Use the fill handle when the formula is only being copied to adjacent cells.

Testing the Worksheet;
Improving the Worksheet Appearance; Sorting

When you have finished building the worksheet, verifying that the formulas you entered are accurate is a good idea. The worksheet could contain formulas that are correct in structure but not mathematically correct for the situation. For example, the wrong range may be included in a SUM formula, or parentheses missing from a multioperator formula may cause an incorrect result. Various methods can be employed to verify a worksheet's accuracy. One method is to create a proof formula in a cell beside or below the worksheet that will verify the totals. For example, in the payroll worksheet the *Total Hours* column can be verified by creating a formula that adds all of the hours for all of the employees.

Data in Excel can be rearranged by sorting rows in either ascending order or descending order. You can select a single column or define a custom sort to specify multiple columns that determine the sort order.

Project

To confirm the accuracy of your calculations in the payroll worksheet, you will enter proof formulas to test the worksheet and then use two formatting options to improve the worksheet's appearance.

SNAP

Tutorial 1.6
Sorting Data

1. With **ES1-WBPayroll.xlsx** open, make cell A17 the active cell.

2. Type **Hours**, press Alt + Enter, type **Proof**, and then press Enter.

   Alt + Enter is the command to insert a line break in a cell. This command is used when you want multiple lines within the same cell. The height of the row is automatically expanded to accommodate the multiple lines.

3. Make cell B17 the active cell.

4. Click in the Formula bar, type **=SUM(C5:I13)**, and then click the Enter button or press Enter. (Alternatively, you could click the AutoSum button and then drag the pointer across the range of cells C5 through I13.)

   Excel displays the result, *342*, which verifies that your total hours in cell J15 is correct. Can you think of another formula that would have accomplished the same objective? ***Hint: Think of the direction you added to arrive at the total hours in cell J15.***

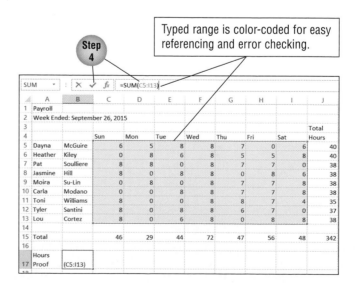

5 Make cell A18 the active cell.

6 Type **Gross**, press Alt + Enter, type **Pay Proof**, and then press Enter.

7 Make cell B18 the active cell.

> Since all of the employees are paid the same rate of pay, you can verify the *Gross Pay* column by multiplying the total hours times the pay rate.

8 Type **=B17*K5** and then press the Right Arrow key.

> The result, *2,821.5,* confirms that the value in cell L15 is correct. The importance of testing a worksheet cannot be emphasized enough. Worksheets often contain important financial or statistical data that can form the basis for strategic business decisions.

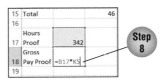

Step 8

9 Look at the completed worksheet shown below. Notice that some of the values in column L show no decimals, while others show 1 or 2 decimal places. Also notice the labels do not align directly over the values below them.

Labels do not align directly over values.

	A	B	C	D	E	F	G	H	I	J	K	L
1	Payroll											
2	Week Ended: September 26, 2015											
3										Total	Pay	Gross
4			Sun	Mon	Tue	Wed	Thu	Fri	Sat	Hours	Rate	Pay
5	Dayna	McGuire	6	5	8	8	7	0	6	40	8.25	330
6	Heather	Kiley	0	8	6	8	5	5	8	40	8.25	330
7	Pat	Soulliere	8	8	0	8	7	7	0	38	8.25	313.5
8	Jasmine	Hill	8	0	8	8	0	8	6	38	8.25	313.5
9	Moira	Su-Lin	0	8	0	8	7	7	8	38	8.25	313.5
10	Carla	Modano	0	0	8	8	7	7	8	38	8.25	313.5
11	Toni	Williams	8	0	0	8	8	7	4	35	8.25	288.75
12	Tyler	Santini	8	0	8	8	6	7	0	37	8.25	305.25
13	Lou	Cortez	8	0	6	8	0	8	8	38	8.25	313.5
14												
15	Total		46	29	44	72	47	56	48	342		2821.5
16												
17	Hours Proof	342										
18	Gross Pay Proof	2821.5										

Decimal places are not consistent.

continues

10 Select the range of cells L5:L15.

These final steps in building a worksheet are meant to improve the appearance of cells. In column L, Excel uses up to 15 decimal places for precision when calculating values. Since the *Gross Pay* column represents a sum of money, you will format these cells to display a dollar sign and show two decimal places.

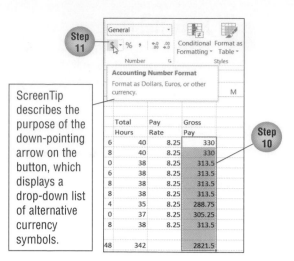

Step 11

ScreenTip describes the purpose of the down-pointing arrow on the button, which displays a drop-down list of alternative currency symbols.

Step 10

11 Click the Accounting Number Format button $ in the Number group on the HOME tab. (Do not click the down-pointing arrow to the right of the button.)

The Accounting format adds a dollar sign, a comma in the thousands place, and two decimal places to each value in the selection.

12 Make cell B18 the active cell and then click the Accounting Number Format button.

13 Select the range of cells C3:L4.

As previously mentioned, labels are aligned at the left edge of a column while values are aligned at the right edge. In the next step, you will align the labels at the right edge of the column so they appear directly over the values they represent.

14 Click the Align Right button ≡ in the Alignment group on the HOME tab.

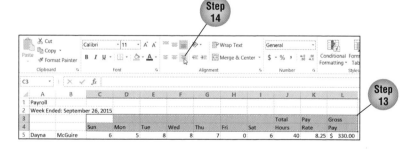

Step 14

Step 13

15 Click in any cell to deselect the range.

In the next steps, you will rearrange the names in the payroll worksheet so that they are in alphabetical order by last name. Since the last name is not the first column in the worksheet, you will need to define a custom sort.

16 Select the range of cells A5:L13.

You are selecting the range before executing the sort command since you do not want to include the cells above and below the list of names in the sort action.

17 Click the Sort & Filter button in the Editing group on the HOME tab.

18 Click *Custom Sort* at the drop-down list.

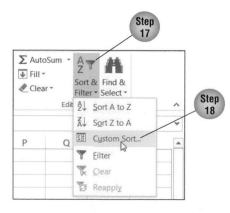

Step 17

Step 18

19 At the Sort dialog box, click the down-pointing arrow at the right of *Sort by* in the *Column* section and then click *Column B* at the drop-down list.

> The default entries of *Values* for *Sort On* and *A to Z* for *Order* are correct since you want the cells sorted by the text entries in column B in ascending order.

20 Click OK.

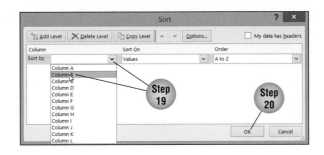

21 Click in any cell to deselect the range. Compare your sorted worksheet to the one shown below.

	A	B	C	D	E	F	G	H	I	J	K	L
1	Payroll											
2	Week Ended: September 26, 2015											
3										Total	Pay	Gross
4			Sun	Mon	Tue	Wed	Thu	Fri	Sat	Hours	Rate	Pay
5	Lou	Cortez	8	0	6	8	0	8	8	38	8.25	$ 313.50
6	Jasmine	Hill	8	0	8	8	0	8	6	38	8.25	$ 313.50
7	Heather	Kiley	0	8	6	8	5	5	8	40	8.25	$ 330.00
8	Dayna	McGuire	6	5	8	8	7	0	6	40	8.25	$ 330.00
9	Carla	Modano	0	0	8	8	7	7	8	38	8.25	$ 313.50
10	Tyler	Santini	8	0	8	8	6	7	0	37	8.25	$ 305.25
11	Pat	Soulliere	8	8	0	8	7	7	0	38	8.25	$ 313.50
12	Moira	Su-Lin	0	8	0	8	7	7	8	38	8.25	$ 313.50
13	Toni	Williams	8	0	0	8	8	7	4	35	8.25	$ 288.75
14												
15	Total		46	29	44	72	47	56	48	342		$2,821.50
16												
17	Hours Proof	342										
18	Gross Pay Proof	$2,821.50										

22 Click the Save button on the Quick Access toolbar.

In Addition

Rotating Text in Cells

The Alignment group on the HOME tab contains an Orientation button, which you can use to rotate text within cells. Text can be rotated counterclockwise, clockwise, changed to a vertical alignment, rotated up vertically, or rotated down vertically. Often, text set in narrow columns is angled to improve the label appearance. In the screen shown at the right, the cells containing the days of the week in the payroll worksheet are angled counterclockwise.

Activity 1.7

An extensive online Help resource is available that contains information on Excel features and commands. Click the Microsoft Excel Help button located near the upper right corner of the screen to open the Excel Help window. By default, the Help feature searches for an Internet connection. If you are not connected to the Internet, an offline message displays in the Excel Help window. Make sure you are connected to the Internet to complete the steps in this activity. Another method to use Help resources is to point to a button on a tab and then press the F1 function key.

Project

After reviewing the payroll worksheet, you think the first two title rows would look better if the text was centered over the columns in the worksheet. You will use the Help feature to look up the steps to do this.

SNAP

Tutorial 1.7
Getting Help at the Excel Help Window

① With **ES1-WBPayroll.xlsx** open, make cell A1 the active cell.

To center the title rows above the columns in the worksheet, you decide to browse the buttons in the Alignment group on the HOME tab. The Merge & Center button in the Alignment group seems appropriate, but you are not sure of the steps to work with this feature.

② Point to the Merge & Center button in the Alignment group on the HOME tab and read the information that displays in the ScreenTip.

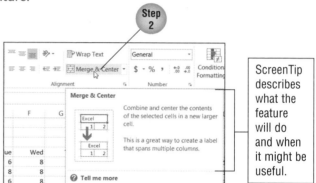

③ With the pointer still resting on the Merge & Center button, press the F1 function key and then read the information on merging cells that displays in the Excel Help window. Make sure you scroll down the window and read all of the information provided by Excel Help.

④ Close the Excel Help window by clicking the Close button located in the upper right corner of the window.

⑤ Select the range of cells A1:L1 and then click the Merge & Center button in the Alignment group on the HOME tab.

Cell A1 is merged across columns A through L and the text *Payroll* is automatically centered within the merged cell.

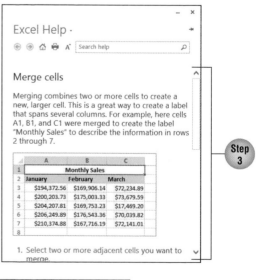

6 Select the range of cells A2:L2 and then click the Merge & Center button.

The two titles in the payroll worksheet are now centered over the cells below them.

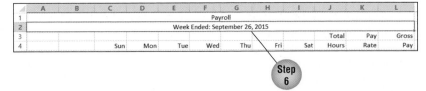

In Brief

Use Help
1. Click Microsoft Excel Help button.
2. Click desired option in Excel Help window.

Step 6

7 Click the Microsoft Excel Help button **?** located near the upper right corner of the screen.

You can also access Help resources by typing a search phrase and browsing related topics in the Help window.

8 Click in the search text box, type **preview worksheet**, and then click the Search online help button or press Enter.

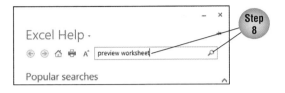

Step 8

9 Click the <u>Preview worksheet pages before you print</u> hyperlink and then read the information that displays in the window.

10 Close the Excel Help window.

11 Click the Save button on the Quick Access toolbar.

Step 9

Since Microsoft Office Online is updated frequently, your search results list may vary for this hyperlink, including its title or position in the list.

In Addition

Using Excel Help Window Buttons

The Excel Help window contains five buttons that display to the left of the search box. Use the Back and Forward buttons to navigate in the window. Click the Home button to return to the Excel Help window opening screen. If you want to print information on a topic or feature, click the Print button and then click the Print button at the Print dialog box. You can make the text in the Excel Help window larger by clicking the Use Large Text button. In addition to these five buttons, the Excel Help window contains a Keep Help on Top button located near the upper right corner of the window. Click this button and the Excel Help window remains on the screen even when you work in a worksheet. Click the button again to remove (unpin) the window from the screen.

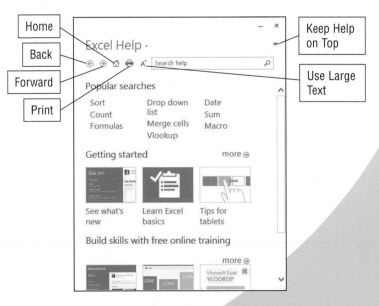

Previewing; Changing Page Orientation; Printing a Worksheet

Many times, a worksheet is printed to have a paper copy, or **hard copy**, to file or to attach to a report. Large, complex worksheets are often easier to proofread and check from a paper copy. Display the Print backstage area to preview the worksheet and modify print options. For example, to change the page orientation while previewing how the worksheet will print, click the FILE tab and then click the *Print* option. At the Print backstage area, a preview of how the worksheet will look when printed displays at the right side. The center of the Print backstage area is divided into three categories: *Print, Printer,* and *Settings.* Use the galleries available in each category to modify print options. Use the Print backstage area to preview the worksheet before printing to avoid wasted paper by checking in advance whether the entire worksheet will fit on one page, or to preview and/or change other print options.

Project The Payroll worksheet is finished. You want to preview the worksheet and then print a copy for the office manager.

1 With **ES1-WBPayroll.xlsx** open, make cell A20 the active cell and then type the student information your instructor has directed for printouts. For example, type your first and last names and then press Enter.

Make sure you have checked if other identifying information such as your program or class number should be included.

Tutorial 1.8
Printing a Worksheet

2 Click the FILE tab and then click the *Print* option to display the worksheet in the Print backstage area as shown in Figure 1.2.

FIGURE 1.2 Print Backstage Area

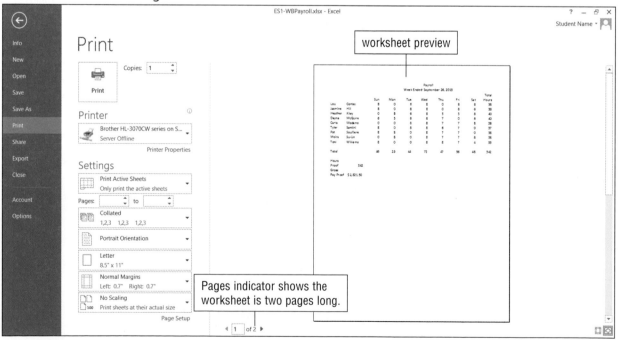

3 The right side of the backstage area displays the first page of the worksheet as it will print with the current print options. Notice the pages indicator at the bottom left of the preview shows that you are viewing page *1 of 2* pages. Click the Next Page button located at the right of the current page number to display page 2.

4 The second page of the printout appears showing the columns that could not fit on page 1.

5 Click the orientation gallery (currently displays *Portrait Orientation*) in the *Settings* category in the Print backstage area.

> One method to reduce the printout to one page is to change the orientation of the paper from portrait to landscape. In **portrait** orientation, the page is printed on paper taller than it is wide. In **landscape** orientation, the data is rotated to print on paper that is wider than it is tall.

6 Click *Landscape Orientation* at the drop-down list.

> The preview updates to show the worksheet in landscape orientation. Notice that all of the columns now fit on one page.

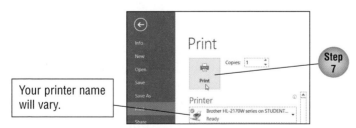

7 Click the Print button.

> The Print backstage area closes and the worksheet prints on the default printer. The default settings in the Print backstage area are to print one copy of all pages in the active worksheet. You will learn how to adjust page layout and print settings in a later section.

Your printer name will vary.

8 At the worksheet, scroll right if necessary until you see the vertical dashed line between columns located to the right of the *Gross Pay* column.

> The dashed vertical line is a page break. Page breaks appear after you have previewed or printed a worksheet. A worksheet that spans many rows will display a horizontal dashed line below the last row that can fit on the page. The dashed lines do not print.

9 Click the Save button on the Quick Access toolbar.

In Brief

Preview Worksheet
1. Click FILE tab.
2. Click *Print* option.

Change to Landscape Orientation
1. Click FILE tab.
2. Click *Print* option.
3. Click orientation gallery.
4. Click *Landscape Orientation*.

Activity 1.9

Displaying Formulas; Navigating a Worksheet

Sometimes you may want to print a worksheet with the cell formulas displayed rather than the formula results. Printing a second copy of a worksheet with the cell formulas is a good idea when complicated formulas that would take you a long time to redo exist in the worksheet. To display cell formulas, click the FORMULAS tab and then click the Show Formulas button in the Formula Auditing group. You can also display formulas with the keyboard shortcut Ctrl + `.

Once a worksheet becomes larger, you will need to scroll to the right or scroll down to locate cells with which you need to work. The horizontal and vertical scroll bars are used to scroll with the mouse. Scrolling using the scroll bars does not move the position of the active cell. You can also scroll using the arrow keys or with keyboard commands. Scrolling using the keyboard moves the active cell.

Project

You will print a second copy of the payroll worksheet with the cell formulas displayed and practice navigating the worksheet using the scroll bars and keyboard shortcuts.

1 With **ES1-WBPayroll.xlsx** open, click the FORMULAS tab.

2 Click the Show Formulas button in the Formula Auditing group.

The cells in the worksheet are automatically expanded and cells that contain formulas now display the formula in the worksheet area.

Tutorial 1.9A
Displaying Formulas in a Worksheet

Tutorial 1.9B
Navigating and Scrolling in a Worksheet

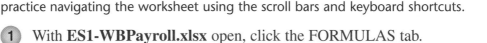

3 Click the FILE tab and then click the *Print* option.

4 At the Print backstage area, click the Print button.

The worksheet will print on two pages in the expanded cell formulas view. In a later section, you will learn how to adjust column widths and scale a worksheet to reduce the number of pages for a wide printout.

5 Position the mouse pointer on the right scroll arrow at the right edge of the horizontal scroll bar and then click the left mouse button a few times to scroll to the right edge of the worksheet.

6 Position the mouse pointer on the horizontal scroll box, hold down the left mouse button, drag the scroll box to the left edge of the horizontal scroll bar, and then release the mouse button.

The width or height of the scroll box indicates the proportional number of the used cells in the worksheet that are visible in the current window. The position of the scroll box within the scroll bar indicates the relative location of the visible cells within the remainder of the worksheet.

7 Press Ctrl + Home.

> Ctrl + Home makes cell A1 the active cell.

8 Press the Page Down key once.

> Each time you press the Page Down key, you move the active cell down one screen.

9 Press the Page Up key once.

> Each time you press the Page Up key, you move the active cell up one screen.

10 Click the Find & Select button 🔍 in the Editing group on the HOME tab and then click *Go To* at the drop-down list.

Step 10

11 At the Go To dialog box, type **L15** in the *Reference* text box and then click OK or press Enter.

> Notice that using Go To moved the position of the active cell. Cell L15 is now the active cell.

12 Use the Up, Down, Left, and Right Arrow keys to practice moving around the worksheet.

> Holding down a directional arrow key causes the screen to scroll very quickly. Table 1.2 below illustrates more keyboard scrolling techniques.

Step 11

13 Press Ctrl + ` to turn off the display of formulas.

> The ` symbol is the grave symbol. On the keyboard, it is usually located on the key immediately to the left of the number 1 key.

14 Click the Save button on the Quick Access toolbar.

15 Click the FILE tab and then click the *Close* option in the backstage area.

In Brief

Display Formulas
1. Click FORMULAS tab.
2. Click Show Formulas button.
OR
Press Ctrl + `.

Go to a Specific Cell
1. Click Find & Select button.
2. Click *Go To*.
3. Type cell address.
4. Click OK.

TABLE 1.2 Keyboard Movement Commands

Press	To move to
Arrow keys	one cell up, down, left, or right
Ctrl + Home	A1
Ctrl + End	last cell in worksheet
Home	beginning of row
Page Down	down one screen
Page Up	up one screen
Alt + Page Down	one screen to the right
Alt + Page Up	one screen to the left

In Addition

Displaying Formulas at the Excel Options Dialog Box

In addition to the Show Formulas button on the FORMULAS tab and the keyboard shortcut, you can also display formulas at the Excel Options dialog box. Display this dialog box by clicking the FILE tab and then clicking *Options*. At the Excel Options dialog box, click *Advanced* in the left pane, click the *Show formulas in cells instead of their calculated results* check box in the *Display options for this worksheet* section to insert a check mark, and then click OK.

Features Summary

Feature	Ribbon Tab, Group	Button	FILE Tab Option	Keyboard Shortcut
Accounting format	HOME, Number	$		
align right	HOME, Alignment	≡		
cell formulas	FORMULAS, Formula Auditing		*Options*	Ctrl + `
close a workbook			*Close*	Ctrl + F4
copy	HOME, Clipboard			Ctrl + C
fill down	HOME, Editing	, *Down*		Ctrl + D
fill left	HOME, Editing	, *Left*		
fill right	HOME, Editing	, *Right*		Ctrl + R
fill up	HOME, Editing	, *Up*		
Go To	HOME, Editing	, *Go To*		Ctrl + G
Help		?		F1
insert line break				Alt + Enter
merge and center	HOME, Alignment			
new workbook			*New*	Ctrl + N
Open backstage area			*Open*	Ctrl + O
Open dialog box				Ctrl + F12
paste	HOME, Clipboard			Ctrl + V
Print backstage area			*Print*	Ctrl + P or Ctrl + F2
save			*Save*	Ctrl + S
save with a new name			*Save As*	F12
sort	HOME, Editing	A/Z▼		
SUM function	HOME, Editing	Σ		Alt + =

Knowledge Check   SNAP

Completion: In the space provided at the right, indicate the correct term, command, or option.

1. This area contains commands and buttons for performing actions divided into tabs and groups.   _____

2. This area displays the formula stored within the cell (not the result).   _____

3. The cell pointer changes to this when pointing at the small green square in the bottom right corner of the active cell.   _____

4. This would be the formula entry to divide the contents of cell C6 by the contents in cell C12.   _____

5. This is the term for the method used to create a formula by typing the equals sign and operator symbols while clicking reference cells between the typed symbols.   _____

6. This term is used to refer to the values identified within parentheses in the SUM function.   _____

7. The AutoSum button is located in this group on the HOME tab.   _____

8. Do this action if Excel suggests the wrong range after you click the AutoSum button.   _____

9. This button appears after copied cells are pasted into the destination range.   _____

10. This is the term for the formulas entered beside or below a worksheet that are designed to verify the worksheet's accuracy.   _____

11. This format adds a dollar sign, a comma in the thousands place, and two decimal places to each value in the selected range.   _____

12. Click the Sort & Filter button in the Editing group on the HOME tab and then click this option at the drop-down list to display the Sort dialog box.   _____

13. This keyboard shortcut will open the Excel Help window when pointing to a button.   _____

14. Display this backstage area to change the page orientation.   _____

15. This keyboard command displays formulas in a worksheet.   _____

16. Open this dialog box to type a cell reference to which you want to move the active cell.   _____

Skills Review

Note: If you submit your work in hard copy, check with your instructor before completing these reviews to find out if you need to print two copies of each worksheet with one of the copies showing the cell formulas instead of the calculated results.

Review 1 Creating Labels, Values, and Formulas

1. Create a new folder on your storage medium and name it **ExcelEOS**.
2. Open **WBQtrlyIncome.xlsx**. Save the workbook in the ExcelEOS folder you created and name the workbook **ES1-R-WBQtrlyIncome**.
3. Type **Jul** in cell E5.
4. Use the fill handle in cell E5 to enter sequential monthly labels in cells F5 and G5.
5. Type **1,300** in cell E12.
6. Use the fill handle in cell E12 to copy the same value to cells F12 and G12.
7. Click in cell E13 and then use the AutoSum button to enter a formula that adds cells E10:E12.
8. Copy the formula in cell E13 to cells F13 and G13.
9. Click in cell E15 and then enter a formula that subtracts Total Expenses from Gross Margin by typing **=E8-E13**.
10. Copy the formula in cell E15 to cells F15 and G15.
11. Click in cell E16 and then enter a formula that multiplies Net Income by Taxes of 22% by typing **=E15*.22**.
12. Copy the formula in cell E16 to cells F16 and G16.
13. Click in cell E17 and then enter a formula that subtracts Taxes from Net Income Before Taxes by typing **=E15-E16**.
14. Copy the formula in cell E17 to cells F17 and G17.
15. Save **ES1-R-WBQtrlyIncome.xlsx**.

Review 2 Improving the Appearance of the Worksheet; Previewing and Printing

1. With **ES1-R-WBQtrlyIncome.xlsx** open, merge and center the title in row 1 across columns A through G.
2. Merge and center the text in row 2 across columns A through G.
3. Change the alignment of the range E5:G5 to right alignment.
4. Apply accounting formatting to cells E6:G17.
5. Display the worksheet in the Print backstage area to preview how the worksheet will look when printed.
6. Print the worksheet.
7. Display the worksheet with cell formulas displayed and then print another copy of the worksheet.
8. Turn off the display of formulas in the worksheet.
9. Save and then close **ES1-R-WBQtrlyIncome.xlsx**.

Skills Assessment

Note: If you submit your work in hard copy, check with your instructor before completing these assessments to find out if you need to print two copies of each worksheet with one of the copies showing the cell formulas instead of the calculated results.

Assessment 1 Adding Values and Formulas to a Worksheet

1. Open **MPTravelCosts.xlsx** and then save the workbook in the ExcelEOS folder and name it **ES1-A1-MPTravelCosts**.
2. This worksheet was started to calculate the travel costs for a remote location film shoot for July 11 to August 31, 2015. Melissa Gehring of First Choice Travel has just confirmed the following costs that you were waiting for to finish the worksheet. All costs are tax included.
   - Airfare to the location and back to Los Angeles airport is $588.15 per person.
   - The hotel is booked for two people per room and will cost $76.20 per room per night.
   - Each person traveling to the location will receive a daily expense allowance of $27.00.
3. Enter the appropriate values provided above in the *Unit Cost* column in the worksheet.
4. Enter the following formulas in the worksheet:
   - Enter a formula in cell G6 that multiplies the quantity by the unit cost (price of airfare).
   - Enter a formula in G7 that multiplies the quantity by the unit cost (room price) and then multiplies by extended cost. (You will need to use parentheses in this formula.)
   - Enter a formula in G8 that multiplies the quantity by the unit cost (daily allowance) and then multiplies by extended cost. (You will need to use parentheses in this formula.)
   - Enter a formula in G10 that sums the three extended cost amounts.
5. Apply alignment and formatting options you learned in this section to any cells that you consider would improve the appearance of the worksheet.
6. Save, print, and then close **ES1-A1-MPTravelCosts.xlsx**.

Assessment 2 Creating a New Workbook

1. You work with Bobbie Sinclair, business manager at Performance Threads. You are preparing a contract quotation for costume rental and alteration fees for costumes needed by Marquee Productions for its remote location film shoot July 11 to August 31, 2015. Create a new workbook that will calculate the contract price using the following information:
   - Seventeen Renaissance period costumes will be provided at a rental cost of $88.50 per day, tax included, for a total of 50 days.
   - A fee of $110.00 per costume, tax included, is charged for alterations provided on-site.
2. Make sure the total contract price is summed below the rental and alteration fee calculations.
3. Apply alignment and formatting options you learned in this section to any cells that you consider would improve the appearance of the worksheet.
4. Save the workbook in the ExcelEOS folder and name it **ES1-A2-PTCostumeCont**.
5. Print and then close **ES1-A2-PTCostumeCont.xlsx**.

Assessment 3 Creating a New Workbook

1. You work with Sam Vestering, manager of North American Distribution for Worldwide Enterprises. You are preparing a projected distribution revenue schedule for Marquee Productions' latest film *Going Global*, to be released September 2, 2015. Create a new workbook that will estimate Worldwide's projected revenue using the following information (see Table 1.3 below):
   • Group the preview cities and the general-release cities separately.
   • Preview cities receive the film a day before the general release and pay Worldwide Enterprises 15% of projected box office revenues.
   • General-release cities pay Worldwide Enterprises 10% of projected box office revenues.
   • Create a column for the estimated revenue for Worldwide Enterprises and write a formula that determines the estimated revenue for Worldwide Enterprises by multiplying the projected box office sales by 1000 and then multiplying by the revenue percentage (convert the percentage to the decimal number *0.1* for 10% and *0.15* for 15%). You will need to use parentheses when writing the formulas.
2. Apply alignment and formatting options you learned in this section to any cells that you consider would improve the appearance of the worksheet.
3. Use the Sort feature to rearrange the order of the preview cities in ascending order and then rearrange the order of the general-release cities in ascending order.
4. Save the workbook in the ExcelEOS folder and name it **ES1-A3-WEGGProjRev**.
5. Print and then close **ES1-A3-WEGGProjRev.xlsx**.

TABLE 1.3 Assessment 3

City	Release Category	Projected Box Office Sales in Thousands
New York	Preview	41.9
Tucson	General	15.3
Los Angeles	Preview	47.1
Denver	Preview	19.6
Orlando	General	29.6
Des Moines	General	10.4
Wichita	Preview	11.2
Boston	General	26.9
Philadelphia	General	21.4
Dallas	General	18.7
Milwaukee	General	12.6
Atlanta	Preview	33.1
Vancouver	General	31.7
Calgary	General	15.8
Toronto	Preview	29.2
Montreal	Preview	17.3

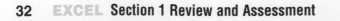

Assessment 4 Finding Information on Sorting

1. In Activity 1.6, you learned how to sort the employee names in the payroll worksheet using the Sort dialog box. Other methods are available for sorting data in a worksheet. Use Excel Help to find out more ways you can sort data in Excel.
2. Open **WBInventory.xlsx** and then save the workbook with Save As in the ExcelEOS folder and name it **ES1-A4-WBInventory**.
3. Sort the worksheet in ascending order by the *Item* column.
4. Print the worksheet.
5. Sort the worksheet in ascending order by the *Supplier Name* column.
6. Print the worksheet.
7. Save and then close **ES1-A4-WBInventory.xlsx**.

Assessment 5 Individual Challenge
Creating a School Budget

1. Create a worksheet to calculate the estimated total cost of completing your diploma or certificate. You determine the items that need to be included in the worksheet, such as tuition, fees, textbooks, supplies, accommodation costs, transportation, telephone, food, and entertainment. If necessary, use the Internet to find reasonable cost estimates if you want to include an item such as cell phone charges and want to research competitive rates for your area. Arrange the labels and values by quarter, semester, or academic year according to your preference. Make sure to include a total that shows the total cost of your education.
2. Save the worksheet in the ExcelEOS folder and name it **ES1-A5-SchoolBudget**.
3. Apply alignment and formatting options you learned in this section to any cells that you consider would improve the appearance of the worksheet.
4. If necessary, change the page orientation to landscape and then print the worksheet.
5. Save and then close **ES1-A5-SchoolBudget.xlsx**.

HELP

Marquee Challenge

Challenge 1 Preparing an International Student Registration Report

1. You work at Niagara Peninsula College in the Registrar's Office. The Registrar has asked you to create the annual report for international student registrations. Create the worksheet shown in Figure 1.3 below.
2. Calculate the tuition fees in column I by multiplying the credit hours times the fee per hour and then use the SUM function to calculate the total international student fees.
3. Apply format options as shown and format the amounts in columns H and I to the Accounting format.
4. Add the current date and your name in rows 4 and 19, respectively.
5. Change the page orientation to landscape.
6. Save the workbook in the ExcelEOS folder and name it **ES1-C1-NPCIntlRegRpt**.
7. Print and then close **ES1-C1-NPCIntlRegRpt.xlsx**.

FIGURE 1.3 Challenge 1

	A	B	C	D	E	F	G	H	I	J
1				Niagara Peninsula College						
2				International Student Registrations						
3				for the 2015/2016 Academic Year						
4				Report Date: Current Date						
5		Last	First	Home			Credit	Fee per	Tuition	
6	ID #	Name	Name	Country	Program	Semester	Hours	Hour	Fee	
7	241588	Cano	Sergio	Spain	BIS11	1	45	432		
8	241578	Flannigan	Maren	Ireland	BIS11	1	60	432		
9	241856	Chou	Terry	China	BMK12	1	45	432		
10	286953	Zhang	Joseph	China	BIN32	2	45	432		
11	274586	Alivero	Maria	Mexico	CMP12	2	45	432		
12	268451	Torres	Phillip	Ecuador	CTN14	2	60	432		
13	234851	Davis	Caitlyn	Australia	OAM24	3	60	432		
14	299635	Muir	Christa	Australia	GRD13	4	30	432		
15	247523	North	Marlo	Bahamas	HTC24	2	30	432		
16	277458	Cervinka	Mary	Croatia	TTM14	4	30	432		
17										
18					TOTAL INTERNATIONAL STUDENT FEES:					
19	Prepared by: Student Name									
20										

Challenge 2 Preparing a Theatre Arts Target Enrollment Report

1. You work with Cal Rubine, chair of the Theatre Arts division at Niagara Peninsula College. Cal needs the target student enrollment report to assist with the revenue projections for the upcoming budget. Cal has asked you to create the worksheet shown in Figure 1.4 below.
2. Cal uses the actual enrollments from the prior year (2014/2015) to calculate the target for the next year. In some programs, Cal expects that enrollment will be higher than the previous year due to new registrants, transfers from other programs, and students returning to pick up missed credits. In other programs, Cal expects that enrollment will decline from the previous year due to students dropping the program, transfers to other colleges, and students failing to meet the minimum GPA for progression. Cal has provided the percentages in Table 1.4 at the bottom of this page for you to use to create the formulas in the *Target* column.
3. Use the SUM function to calculate the total target estimated enrollments.
4. Apply alignment options as shown and add the current date and your name in rows 8 and 9, respectively.
5. If necessary, format the values in the *Target* column to zero decimal places and then change the page orientation to landscape.
6. Save the workbook in the ExcelEOS folder and name it **ES1-C2-NPCTargetEnrolRpt**.
7. Print and then close **ES1-C2-NPCTargetEnrolRpt.xlsx**.

FIGURE 1.4 Challenge 2

	A	B	C	D	E	F	G	H	I	J	K
1					Niagara Peninsula College						
2					Target Student Enrollments						
3					for the 2015/2016 Academic Year						
4					Theatre Arts Division						
5											
6	Academic chair: Cal Rubine										
7											
8	Report date: Current Date										
9	Prepared by: Student Name							Actual			
10					Program	Semester		Enrollment		Target	
11	Program Name				Code	Offering		2014/2015			
12	Theatre Arts: Acting				TAA12	1 2 3 4		210			
13	Theatre Arts: Stage Management				TAM23	1 2		55			
14	Theatre Arts: Lighting & Effects				TAL42	1 2		67			
15	Theatre Arts: Production				TAP32	1 2 3 4		221			
16	Theatre Arts: Sound				TAS14	1 2		38			
17	Theatre Arts: Businsess Management				TAB25	1 2 3 4		64			
18											
19					ESTIMATED ENROLLMENTS FOR 2015/2016:						
20											

TABLE 1.4 Challenge 2

Program Name	Target Percent
Theatre Arts: Acting	95%
Theatre Arts: Stage Management	106%
Theatre Arts: Lighting & Effects	112%
Theatre Arts: Production	85%
Theatre Arts: Sound	103%
Theatre Arts: Business Management	75%

Excel SECTION 2

Editing and Formatting Worksheets

Skills

- Edit the content of cells
- Clear cells and cell formats
- Use proofing tools
- Insert and delete columns and rows
- Move and copy cells
- Use Paste Options to link cells
- Adjust column width and row height
- Change the font, size, style, and color of cells
- Apply numeric formats and adjust the number of decimal places
- Use Undo and Redo
- Change cell alignment and indentation
- Use Repeat
- Add borders and shading
- Copy formats using Format Painter
- Apply cell styles
- Apply a theme
- Find and replace cell entries and formats
- Freeze and unfreeze panes
- Change the zoom percentage
- Insert, move, and resize clip art and pictures

Projects Overview

Edit and format a quotation and invoice for catering services. View and edit a special events booking worksheet.

Complete and format a costume cost report and an invoice for costume production.

Edit and format a revenue summary report for movie distribution.

Create a direct wages budget for a remote film shoot.

Create a room timetable.

Model Answers for Projects

These model answers for the projects you complete in Section 2 provide a preview of the finished projects before you begin working and also allow you to compare your own results with these models to ensure you have created the materials accurately.

ES2-WBQuoteToMP.xlsx is the project in Activities 2.1 to 2.9.

The Waterfront Bistro

3104 Rivermist Drive
Buffalo, NY 14280
716 555 3166

Quotation

TO: Marquee Productions
955 South Alameda Street
Los Angeles, CA 90037

DATE: 5-Nov-15

ATT: Camille Matsui

RE: Remote Location Filming
July 11 to August 31

Note: All prices include tax.

Item	No. of Persons	Price per Person	No. of Days	Total
Buffet Lunch	56	8.34	52	$ 24,286.08
Soup and salad				
Vegetable tray with dip				
Seafood hors d'oeuvres				
Hot entrée				
Deli tray and rolls				
Dessert				
Beverages	56	3.91	52	11,385.92
Coffee and tea				
Assorted juice				
Mineral water				
Snacks	56	3.91	52	11,385.92
Muffins				
Donuts				
Fruit tray				
Vegetable tray with dip				
Transport		33.00	52	1,716.00
Total				*$ 48,773.92*

Terms: Due upon receipt of invoice payable in U.S. funds

ES2-WBSpecEvents.xlsx is the project in Activities 2.10 to 2.12.

The Waterfront Bistro

2015 Special Event Bookings

Contact Name	Contact Phone	Event	Date	Room	Guests	Special Menu	Price Per Person
Cecily Hillmore	716 555 6598	Business Meeting	1/15/2015	Starlake	42	No	23.95
Frances Corriveau	716 555 3256	Birthday Party	1/18/2015	Westview	82	Yes	29.95
Orlando Fagan	716 555 3694	25th Wedding Anniversary	3/14/2015	Westview	95	Yes	29.95
Kim Pockovic	905 555 3698	Birthday Party	3/21/2015	Westview	65	Yes	36.95
Lane Gill	416 555 3264	Business Meeting	3/25/2015	Starlake	55	No	22.95
Percy Bresque	716 555 1248	50th Wedding Anniversary	4/12/2015	Westview	102	Yes	35.95
Max Santore	905 555 3264	Wedding	4/25/2015	Sunset	188	Yes	27.95
Omar Hamid	716 555 8796	Engagement Party	5/10/2015	Sunset	67	Yes	29.95
Jack Torrance	716 555 1469	Business Meeting	5/15/2015	Westview	34	No	24.95
Dana Russell	716 555 4965	Birthday Party	5/30/2015	Starlake	54	No	28.95
Walter Szucs	905 555 6998	Birthday Party	6/6/2015	Starlake	84	No	34.95
Nicole Griffin	905 555 4166	25th Wedding Anniversary	6/14/2015	Starlake	78	Yes	34.95
Zack Doucet	716 555 3488	Wedding	6/27/2015	Sunset	215	Yes	29.95
Jesse Golinsky	716 555 4218	Business Meeting	6/30/2015	Westview	60	No	25.95
Cora Jin Ping	716 555 7774	Baby Shower	7/11/2015	Sunset	75	Yes	22.95
Elizabeth McMaster	716 555 9442	Engagement Party	7/18/2015	Sunset	94	Yes	28.95
Reed Pavelich	716 555 2286	Wedding	7/25/2015	Starlake	145	Yes	34.95
Alfredo Juanitez	716 555 4668	Business Meeting	7/30/2015	Westview	37	No	24.95
Yanfang Guo	716 555 4856	50th Wedding Anniversary	8/2/2015	Starlake	62	No	34.95
Jelena Boskovic	716 555 3456	Business Meeting	8/7/2015	Westview	27	Yes	29.95
Priscilla Melo	716 555 3145	Business Meeting	8/21/2015	Westview	34	Yes	25.95
Tracie McIntyre	716 555 3496	Birthday Party	9/5/2015	Sunset	26	No	22.95
Krista Pressey	716 555 7469	50th Wedding Anniversary	9/13/2015	Sunset	95	No	28.95
Langford Hill	716 555 8798	Wedding	9/19/2015	Starlake	185	No	34.95
Naomi Sayers	905 555 3486	Wedding	10/10/2015	Starlake	245	Yes	24.95
Lesley Reedman	716 555 4123	Wedding	10/18/2015	Westview	110	Yes	34.95
Mitchell Langley	905 555 4637	Wedding	11/14/2015	Sunset	85	Yes	29.95
Sally Ramirez	716 555 9648	Engagement Party	12/5/2015	Starlake	34	No	25.95

Paulina Ordonez	905 555 1435	25th Wedding Anniversary	12/12/2015	Westview	45	No	22.95
Arietta Teneqja	905 555 1345	Business Meeting	12/16/2015	Sunset	67	Yes	28.95
Subrein El-Keri	416 555 9765	Engagement Party	12/19/2015	Westview	47	Yes	34.95
Edwina Blakely	716 555 3477	Birthday Party	12/20/2015	Westview	65	No	24.95
Laura Fernandez	416 555 1345	Shareholders Meeting	12/30/2015	Westview	194	No	39.95

Activity 2.1

Editing and Clearing Cells; Using Proofing Tools

The contents of a cell can be edited directly within the cell or in the Formula bar. Clearing a cell can involve removing the cell contents, format, or both. The Spelling feature is a useful tool to assist with correcting typing errors within a worksheet. After completing a spelling check, you will still need to proofread the worksheet since the spelling checker will not highlight all errors and cannot check the accuracy of values. Other proofing tools available include a Research feature to search for external information, a Thesaurus to find a word with similar meaning, and a Translate tool to translate a selected word into a different language.

Project

Dana Hirsch, manager of The Waterfront Bistro, has begun a catering services quotation for Marquee Productions. Dana has asked you to finish the quotation by correcting spelling, following up on costs, and improving the appearance of the document. You will be working on this quotation through most of this section.

The Waterfront B·I·S·T·R·O

SNAP

Tutorial 2.1
Editing Cells and Using Proofing Tools

1. Open **WBQuoteToMP.xlsx**. *Note: This worksheet contains intentional spelling errors that will be corrected in this activity.*

2. Save the workbook with Save As in the ExcelS2 folder and name it **ES2-WBQuoteToMP**.

3. Double-click in cell D18.

   Double-clicking a cell inserts a blinking insertion point in the cell and *Edit* appears in the Status bar. The insertion point position varies depending on the location of the cell pointer when the Edit mode is activated.

4. Press the Right or Left Arrow key as needed to move the insertion point between the decimal point and *7* and then press the Delete key.

5. Type **3** and then press Enter.

6. Make cell D30 the active cell.

7. Move the pointer after *7* in the Formula bar and then click the left mouse button.

   The cell pointer changes to an I-beam pointer I when positioned in the Formula bar.

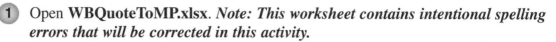

Step 5

8. Press Backspace to delete *7*, type **4**, and then click the Enter button on the Formula bar.

9. Make cell A7 the active cell and then press Delete.

   Delete or Backspace clears only the contents of the cell; formats applied to the cell remain in effect.

10. Make cell A1 the active cell and then press Delete.

    Notice the text is deleted from the cell but the color in the background of the cell remains.

11. Select the range A1:C1. Click the Clear button 🧹 in the Editing group on the HOME tab and then click *Clear All* at the drop-down list.

    Clear All removes everything from a cell, including formats or comments.

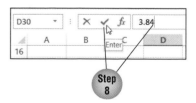

Step 8

Step 11

12 Click in cell A1, click the REVIEW tab, and then click the Spelling button 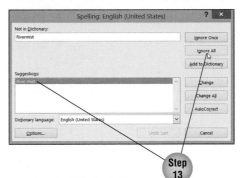 in the Proofing group.

> Spell check begins at the active cell. Words within the worksheet that are not found in the dictionary are highlighted as potential errors. Use buttons in the Spelling dialog box to skip the word (Ignore Once or Ignore All), replace the word with the highlighted word in the *Suggestions* list box (Change or Change All), or add the word to the dictionary (Add to Dictionary) if spelled correctly.

13 Click the Ignore All button in the Spelling dialog box to skip all occurrences of *Rivermist* in the worksheet since the street name is spelled correctly.

14 Click the Change button in the Spelling dialog box to replace *Remoat* with *Remote*.

15 Click the Change button in the Spelling dialog box to replace *Persns* with *Persons*.

16 Complete the spell check, changing words as required. Click OK at the message that the spelling check is complete for the entire sheet.

> Double-click the correct spelling in the *Suggestions* list box if the correct word is not initially selected. Click in the *Not in Dictionary* text box if the correct spelling is not in the list, edit as required, and then click Change. You can drag the Spelling dialog box out of the way if you need to see the selected word within the worksheet.

17 Make cell A36 the active cell.

18 Click the Thesaurus button  in the Proofing group on the REVIEW tab.

> Use the Thesaurus task pane to replace a word in the worksheet with another word of similar meaning. When you click the Thesaurus button, the Thesaurus task pane displays at the right side of the screen.

19 Point to the word *Transport* in the Thesaurus task pane word list, click the down-pointing arrow that appears, and then click *Insert* at the drop-down list.

> The word *Delivery* is replaced with *Transport* in cell A36.

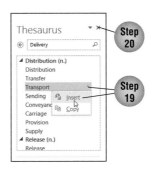

20 Click the Close button in the upper right corner of the Thesaurus task pane.

21 Save **ES2-WBQuoteToMP.xlsx**.

In Addition

Research Task Pane

Use the Research task pane to search for information online without leaving the worksheet. For example, you can conduct an Internet search and look up information in online encyclopedias or business reference sites. Display the Research task pane by clicking the Research button in the Proofing group on the REVIEW tab. Choose the online source by clicking the down-pointing arrow at the right of the *Resources* list box (located below the *Search for* text box).

Activity 2.2

Inserting and Deleting Columns and Rows

Insert rows or columns using options from the Insert button in the Cells group on the HOME tab or from the context-sensitive shortcut menu that displays when you right-click a selected area. Inserted rows are placed above the active cell or selected rows and existing rows are shifted down. Columns are inserted left of the active cell or selected columns and existing columns are shifted right. When rows or columns are deleted, data automatically is shifted up or left to fill space and relative references in formulas are updated.

Project

You will add items to and delete items from the quotation by inserting and deleting rows and columns.

SNAP

Tutorial 2.2
Inserting and Deleting Columns and Rows

(1) With **ES2-WBQuoteToMP.xlsx** open, position the cell pointer (displays as a right-pointing black arrow ➡) over row indicator *21*, hold down the left mouse button, drag the mouse down over row indicator *22*, and then release the mouse.

> This selects rows 21 and 22. Inserted rows are placed *above* the selected rows and columns are inserted to the *left*.

(2) Click the HOME tab, click the Insert button arrow ⊞ in the Cells group, and then click *Insert Sheet Rows* at the drop-down list.

> Two blank rows are inserted. All rows below the inserted rows are shifted down.

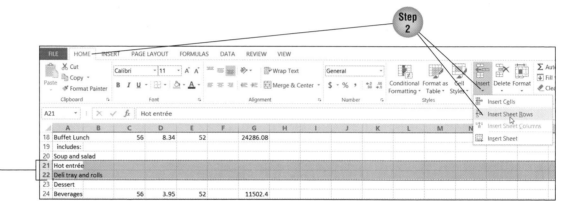

(3) Click in cell A21, type **Vegetable tray with dip**, and then press Enter.

(4) Type **Seafood hors d'oeuvres** and then press Enter.

(5) Make active any cell in row 29.

(6) Click the Delete button arrow ⊞ in the Cells group and then click *Delete Sheet Rows* at the drop-down list.

> The data in row *29* is removed from the worksheet. All rows below the deleted row shift up to fill in the space.

(7) Right-click the row 19 indicator to display the shortcut menu and Mini toolbar and then click *Delete*.

Mini toolbar

8 Right-click the row 26 indicator to display the shortcut menu and Mini toolbar and then click *Delete*.

9 Delete row 30 from the worksheet.

10 Position the cell pointer over column indicator letter *F* (displays as a down-pointing black arrow **↓**), right-click the mouse, and then click *Delete* at the shortcut menu.

Data in columns to the right of the deleted column are shifted left to fill in the space.

In Brief

Insert Rows or Columns
1. Select required number of rows or columns.
2. Click Insert button arrow.
3. Click *Insert Sheet Rows* or *Insert Sheet Columns*.

Delete Rows or Columns
1. Select rows or columns to be deleted.
2. Click Delete button arrow.
3. Click *Delete Sheet Rows* or *Delete Sheet Columns*.

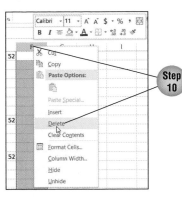

11 Click in any cell to deselect the column.

12 Make cell F8 the active cell, type **November 5, 2015**, and then press Enter.

By default, Excel displays dates in the format *d-mmm-yy* (5-Nov-15).

13 Save **ES2-WBQuoteToMP.xlsx**.

In Addition

Inserting and Deleting Cells

In this activity, you selected entire rows and columns before inserting or deleting. This practice is the more common method when you need to add to or delete data from a worksheet. Another method used less frequently is to insert new blank cells or delete a range of cells within the worksheet area. To insert new blank cells, select the range of cells you need to add and then click the Insert button in the Cells group on the HOME tab, or click the Insert button arrow and then click *Insert Cells* at the drop-down list to display the dialog box shown here. Using the dialog box, you can choose to shift existing cells right or down. Click the Delete button in the Cells group to delete a selected range of cells and shift up the cells below the deleted range. Click the Delete button arrow and then click *Delete Cells* to open the Delete dialog box with options similar to those for Insert.

Activity 2.3

Moving and Copying Cells

You learned how to use copy and paste to copy formulas in the payroll worksheet for The Waterfront Bistro. You can also use cut and paste to move the contents of a cell or range of cells to another location in the worksheet. The selected cells being cut or copied are called the *source*. The cell or range of cells that is receiving the source data is called the *destination*. If data already exists in the destination cells, Excel replaces the contents. Cells cut or copied to the Clipboard can be pasted more than once in the active workbook, in another workbook, or in another Office application.

Project

Tutorial 2.3
Moving and Copying Cells

Continue to work on the catering quotation by moving text in the quotation, duplicating a price, linking cells containing prices, and by copying a food item description.

1. With **ES2-WBQuoteToMP.xlsx** open, make cell A38 the active cell.

2. Click the Cut button in the Clipboard group on the HOME tab.

   A moving marquee surrounds the source after you use Cut or Copy, indicating the cell contents have been placed in the Clipboard.

3. Make cell E15 the active cell and then click the Paste button in the Clipboard group. (Do not click the down-pointing arrow on the Paste button because this displays a drop-down list of Paste options.)

   The text *Note: All prices include tax.* is removed from cell A38 and placed in cell E15. In the next step, you will move a range of cells using a method called *drag and drop*.

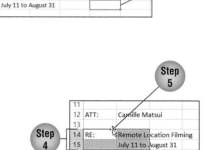

4. Select the range of cells A14:B15.

   You are only selecting to column B since the entries *Remote Location Filming* and *July 11 to August 31* are stored in cells B14 and B15, respectively.

5. Point at any one of the four borders surrounding the selected range.

   When you point at a border, the pointer changes from the thick white cross to a white arrow with the move icon attached to it (four-headed arrow).

6. Hold down the left mouse button, drag the top left corner of the range to cell E12, and then release the mouse button.

   A green border will appear as you drag, indicating the placement of the range when you release the mouse. The destination range displays in a ScreenTip below the green border.

7 Make cell D25 the active cell.

8 Click the Copy button 🗐 in the Clipboard group.

9 Make cell D29 the active cell, click the Paste button arrow in the Clipboard group, and then click the Paste Link button in the *Other Paste Options* section of the Paste Options gallery.

> The existing data in cell D29 is replaced with the value copied from cell D25, and the source and destination cells are now linked. Linking the cells means that any change made to the source cell (D25) will automatically be applied to the destination cell (D29). A Paste Options button appears next to the destination cell (D29). Click the button to return to the Paste Options gallery if you want to choose another paste option. See the In Addition section at the bottom of this page for more information on paste options.

10 Press Esc to remove the moving marquee from cell D25 and the Paste Options button near cell D29.

11 Make cell D25 the active cell and then edit the value to *3.91*.

> Notice the value in cell D29 is also changed automatically to 3.91.

Cell D29 changes automatically since the two cells are linked.

12 Make cell A20 the active cell. Point at any one of the four borders surrounding cell A20 until the pointer displays as a white arrow with the move icon attached to it, hold down the Ctrl key, and then drag the mouse to cell A33.

13 Release the mouse button first and then release the Ctrl key.

> A plus sign attached to the pointer indicates the source contents are being *copied* when you drag and drop using the Ctrl key.

14 Save **ES2-WBQuoteToMP.xlsx**.

In Brief

Move or Copy Cells
1. Select source cells.
2. Click Cut button or Copy button.
3. Select starting destination cell.
4. Click Paste button.

Copy and Link Cells
1. Select source cells.
2. Click Copy button.
3. Select destination cell.
4. Click Paste button arrow.
5. Click Paste Link button.

In Addition

Paste Options Gallery

The Paste Options gallery (shown at the right) appears in three places: click the Paste button arrow in the Clipboard group, click the Paste Options button that appears after an entry has been pasted into a cell, or the right-click shortcut menu. The gallery is divided into three sections: *Paste*, *Paste Values*, and *Other Paste Options*. Within each section, buttons are included for various paste options. Hover the mouse over a button in the gallery to view a ScreenTip that describes the button's purpose as well as to see a preview of the paste option applied to the cell in the worksheet. The Paste Options gallery is context sensitive, meaning the buttons that appear are dependent on the type of content that has been copied and the location in which the content is being pasted.

Activity 2.4

Adjusting Column Width and Row Height; Using AutoFit

By default, columns are all the same width and rows are all the same height with columns set by default to a width of 8.11 characters (80 pixels) and rows to a height of 14.40 points (24 pixels). In some cases, you do not have to increase the width when the text is too wide for the column, since labels "spill over" into the next cell if it is empty. Some column headings in the quotation are shortened because an entry exists in the column immediately to the right. Excel automatically adjusts the height of rows to accommodate the size of the text within the cells. Manually increasing the row height adds more space between rows, which can be used to improve readability or as a design technique to draw attention to a series of cells.

Project

You will widen the columns in which labels are shortened to make sure each entry is entirely visible to readers and increase the height of the row containing the column headings to make them stand out from the text below.

SNAP

Tutorial 2.4
Adjusting Column Width and Row Height

1. With **ES2-WBQuoteToMP.xlsx** open, make any cell active in column A.

2. Click the Format button ⊞ in the Cells group on the HOME tab and then click *Column Width* at the drop-down list.

    Step 2

3. At the Column Width dialog box, type **14** and then click OK or press Enter.

    In the next step, you will adjust the width of column D using the mouse.

    Step 3

4. Position the mouse pointer on the boundary line in the column indicator row between columns D and E until the pointer changes to a vertical line with a left-and-right-pointing arrow ↔.

5. Hold down the left mouse button, drag the boundary line to the right until *Width: 15.00 (142 pixels)* displays in the ScreenTip, and then release the mouse button.

    Step 5

    As you drag the boundary line to the right or left, a dotted line appears in the column in the worksheet area, indicating the new width. If, after decreasing a column's width, cells that previously had values in them now display as a series of pound symbols (######), the column is now too narrow. Widen the column to redisplay the values.

6. Position the mouse pointer on the boundary line in the column indicator row between columns C and D until the pointer changes to a vertical line with a left- and right-pointing arrow and then double-click the left mouse button.

    Double-clicking the boundary line sets the width to fit the length of the longest entry within the column, referred to as *AutoFit*.

7. Make cell E17 the active cell, click the Format button in the Cells group, and then click *AutoFit Column Width* at the drop-down list.

    AutoFit Column Width adjusts the width of the column to accommodate the amount of text in the active cell. After reviewing the worksheet, you decide all of the columns with numeric values should be the same width. In the next steps, you will learn how to set the width of multiple columns in one operation.

    Step 7

8 Position the mouse pointer on column indicator letter *C*, hold down the left mouse button, and then drag the mouse right to column F.

> This selects columns C through F.

9 Position the mouse pointer on the right boundary line for column E within the selected range of columns until the pointer changes to a vertical line with a left- and right-pointing arrow.

> Any changes made to the width of one column boundary will affect all of the selected columns.

10 Drag the boundary line right until *Width: 15.00 (142 pixels)* displays in the ScreenTip and then release the mouse button.

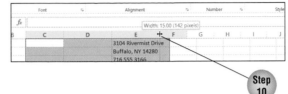

Step 10

11 Click in any cell to deselect the columns.

> Do not be concerned that the columns are now too wide after this step—you have many formatting tasks to complete that will improve the layout as you work through the next few activities.

12 Move E12:F13 to A14:B15 and then click in any cell to deselect the range. Refer to Activity 2.3 if you need assistance with this step.

> In the next steps, you will adjust row height using the mouse.

13 Position the mouse pointer on the boundary line below row 17 until the pointer changes to a horizontal line with an up- and down-pointing arrow ✛ .

14 Drag the boundary line down until *Height: 21.00 (35 pixels)* displays in the ScreenTip and then release the mouse button.

Step 14

15 Save **ES2-WBQuoteToMP.xlsx**.

In Brief

Increase or Decrease Column Width
1. Select column(s).
2. Click Format button in Cells group.
3. Click *Column Width*.
4. Type desired width.
5. Click OK.

Increase or Decrease Row Height
1. Select row(s).
2. Click Format button in Cells group.
3. Click *Row Height*.
4. Type desired height.
5. Click OK.

Adjust Width or Height Using Mouse
Drag boundary to right of column or below row, or double-click boundary to AutoFit.

In Addition

Row Height Dialog Box

A sequence of steps similar to the one used for adjusting column width using the Column Width dialog box can be used to increase or decrease the height of a row with the Row Height dialog box, shown at the right. Click any cell within the row, click the Format button in the Cells group  on the HOME tab, and then click *Row Height* at the drop-down list. Type the desired height and then press Enter or click OK.

Activity 2.5

Changing the Font, Size, Style, and Color of Cells

The *font* is the typeface used to display and print data. The default font in Excel is Calibri, but many other fonts are available. The size of the font is measured in units called *points*. A point is approximately 1/72 of an inch measured vertically. The default font size used by Excel is 11 points.

The larger the point size, the larger the type. Each font's style can be enhanced to **bold**, *italic*, or ***bold italic***. Cell entries display in black with a white background. Changing the color of the font and/or the color of the background (called *fill*) adds interest or emphasis to the cell entry.

Project
To add to the visual appeal of the quotation, you will change the font and font size and apply attributes such as font and fill color to the title *Quotation*.

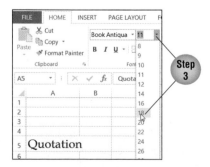

Tutorial 2.5
Applying Font
Formatting

1 With **ES2-WBQuoteToMP.xlsx** open, make cell A5 the active cell.

2 Click the Font button arrow in the Font group on the HOME tab, scroll down the list of fonts, and then point to *Book Antiqua* at the drop-down gallery. Notice that Excel applies the font you are pointing at to the active cell so that you can preview the result. This feature is called ***live preview***. Click *Book Antiqua* at the drop-down gallery.

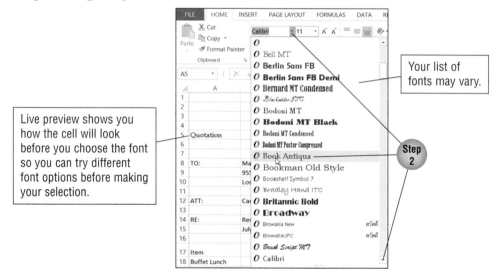

Live preview shows you how the cell will look before you choose the font so you can try different font options before making your selection.

Your list of fonts may vary.

Step 2

3 Click the Font Size button arrow in the Font group and then click *18* at the drop-down list.

The row height is automatically increased to accommodate the larger type size.

Step 3

4 With cell A5 still active, click the Font Color button arrow ![A] in the Font group and then click the *Blue* color option (eighth option) in the *Standard Colors* section of the color gallery.

5 Select the range of cells A5:F5 and then click the Merge & Center button ![icon] in the Alignment group.

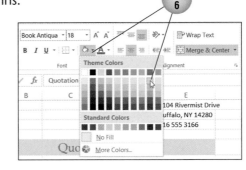

The cells in the range A5:F5 have now been merged into one large cell that spans across the six columns. The text within cell A5, *Quotation*, is now centered within this large cell. As you learned in Section 1, Merge & Center centers titles over multiple columns.

6 With merged cell A5 still selected, click the Fill Color button arrow ![icon] in the Font group and then click the *Blue, Accent 5, Lighter 80%* option (ninth column, second row) in the *Theme Colors* section of the color gallery.

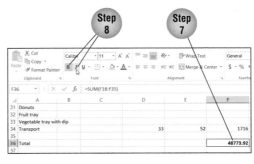

Fill is the color of the background in the cell. Changing the fill color is sometimes referred to as *shading* a cell.

7 Make cell F36 the active cell.

8 Click the Bold button ![B] and then click the Italic button ![I] in the Font group.

9 Save **ES2-WBQuoteToMP.xlsx**.

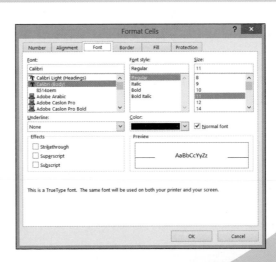

In Brief

Change Font
1. Select cells.
2. Click Font button arrow.
3. Click desired font.
4. Deselect cells.

Change Font Size
1. Select cells.
2. Click Font Size button arrow.
3. Click desired size.
4. Deselect cells.

Change Font Attributes
1. Select cells.
2. Click desired attribute button.
3. Deselect cells.

In Addition

Format Cells Dialog Box

You can use the Format Cells dialog box with the Font tab selected (shown at the right) to change the font, font size, font style, and color of text. Additional Underline style options such as *Single, Double, Single Accounting*, and *Double Accounting* are available, as well as special effects options *Strikethrough, Superscript*, and *Subscript*. Select the cells you want to change and then click the Font group dialog box launcher button ![icon] to open the Format Cells dialog box with the Font tab active.

Activity 2.6

Formatting Numeric Cells; Adjusting Decimal Places; Using Undo and Redo

In the payroll worksheet for The Waterfront Bistro, you learned how to format numeric cells by applying the Accounting format, which adds a dollar symbol ($), a comma in the thousands place, two decimal places, and displays negative values in brackets. Other numeric formats include Comma, Percent, and Currency. By default, cells are initially set to the General format, which has no specific numeric style. The number of decimal places in a selected range of cells can be increased or decreased using the Increase Decimal and Decrease Decimal buttons in the Number group on the HOME tab.

Use the Undo button on the Quick Access toolbar to reverse the last action. Excel stores up to 100 actions that can be undone or redone, and you can repeat actions as many times as you need. Some actions (such as Save) cannot be reversed with Undo.

Project

To display a consistent number of characters for the numeric values, you will apply the Accounting and Comma formats to selected ranges within the quotation.

SNAP

Tutorial 2.6
Applying Number Formatting

1. With **ES2-WBQuoteToMP.xlsx** open, make cell F18 the active cell.

2. Hold down the Ctrl key and click in cell F36.

3. Click the Accounting Number Format button $ in the Number group on the HOME tab.

4. Click in any cell to deselect the cells.

5. Select the range of cells F25:F34.

6. Click the Comma Style button , in the Number group.

   The Comma Style button formats cells the same as the Accounting Number Format button with the exception of the dollar or alternative currency symbol.

7. Click in any cell to deselect the range and review the numeric values in the worksheet. Notice that column D could be improved by applying a format option to the cell that is not showing the same number of decimal places as other values in the column.

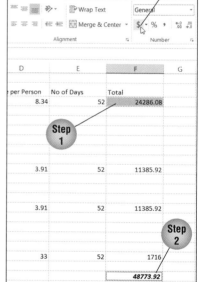

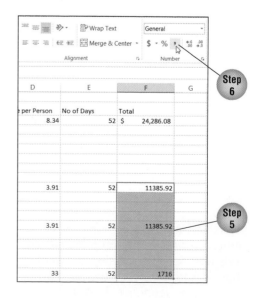

8 Make cell D34 the active cell.

9 Click the Increase Decimal button 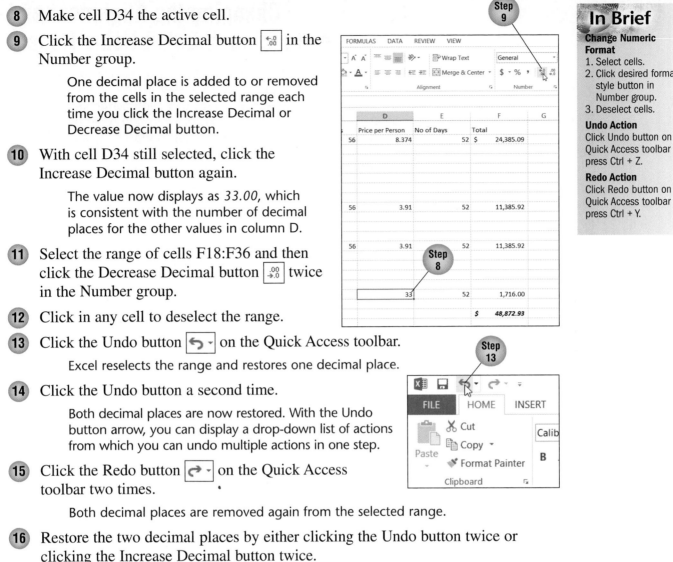 in the Number group.

> One decimal place is added to or removed from the cells in the selected range each time you click the Increase Decimal or Decrease Decimal button.

10 With cell D34 still selected, click the Increase Decimal button again.

> The value now displays as *33.00*, which is consistent with the number of decimal places for the other values in column D.

11 Select the range of cells F18:F36 and then click the Decrease Decimal button twice in the Number group.

12 Click in any cell to deselect the range.

13 Click the Undo button on the Quick Access toolbar.

> Excel reselects the range and restores one decimal place.

14 Click the Undo button a second time.

> Both decimal places are now restored. With the Undo button arrow, you can display a drop-down list of actions from which you can undo multiple actions in one step.

15 Click the Redo button on the Quick Access toolbar two times.

> Both decimal places are removed again from the selected range.

16 Restore the two decimal places by either clicking the Undo button twice or clicking the Increase Decimal button twice.

17 Click in any cell to deselect the range.

18 Save **ES2-WBQuoteToMP.xlsx**.

In Addition

Additional Number Format Options

Click the Number Format button arrow in the Number group on the HOME tab to display a drop-down list (shown at the right) with additional numeric format options including date, time, fraction, and scientific options. Click the *More Number Formats* option at the bottom of the list to open the Format Cells dialog box with the Number tab selected. Using this dialog box, you can access further customization options for a format, such as displaying negative values in red or creating your own custom format code.

Activity 2.7

Changing the Alignment and Indentation of Cells; Using Repeat

Data in a cell can be left-aligned, right-aligned, or centered within the column. Cells that have had Merge & Center applied can be formatted to align the text in the merged cell at the left or right. Use the Increase Indent and Decrease Indent buttons to indent text from the left edge of the cell approximately one character width each time the button is clicked. Using buttons along the top row in the Alignment group on the HOME tab, you can change vertical alignment, rotate text, or wrap text. Use the keyboard shortcut Ctrl + Y or F4 to repeat the last action on another cell. This is useful if you need to perform the same action several times in a row.

Project To improve the appearance of the quotation, you will change the alignment of column headings and values and indent labels from the left edge of column A.

The Waterfront
B·I·S·T·R·O

SNAP

Tutorial 2.7
Applying Alignment
Formatting

1. With **ES2-WBQuotetoMP.xlsx** open, edit the column headings in cells C17 and E17 to include a period (.) after the abbreviation for number. For example, the edited column heading in cell C17 will be *No. of Persons.*

2. Select the range of cells C17:F17.

3. Click the Center button ☰ in the Alignment group on the HOME tab.

4. Select the range of cells C18:C29 and then change the alignment to center.

5. Center the entries in the range of cells E18:E34.

6. Select the range of cells A19:A24.

7. Click the Increase Indent button ☰ in the Alignment group.

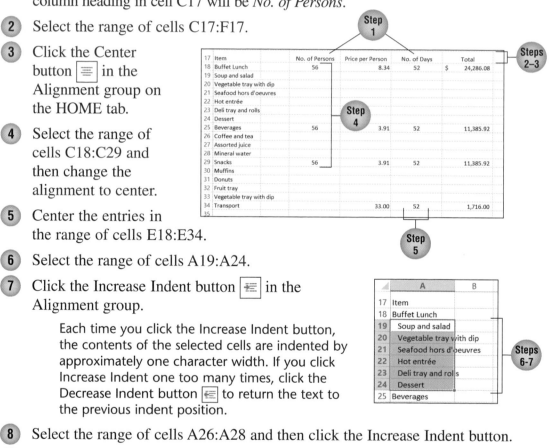

   Each time you click the Increase Indent button, the contents of the selected cells are indented by approximately one character width. If you click Increase Indent one too many times, click the Decrease Indent button ☰ to return the text to the previous indent position.

8. Select the range of cells A26:A28 and then click the Increase Indent button.

9. Select the range of cells A30:A33 and then click the Increase Indent button.

10. Select the range of cells A17:F17 and then bold the cells.

11. Make cell F8 the active cell and then click the Align Left button ☰ in the Alignment group.

    By default, Excel aligns date entries at the right edge of a column since dates are converted to a serial number and treated in a similar manner to values. You will learn more about using dates in Excel in Section 3.

12 Select the range of cells A17:F17.

> In Activity 2.4, you increased the height of row 17 to 21.00 points. The Alignment group contains buttons that also allow you to control the alignment of the text between the top and bottom of the cell boundaries. In the next step, you will center the text vertically within the cells.

13 Click the Middle Align button ≡ in the Alignment group.

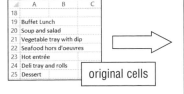

14 Deselect the range.

15 Select the range of cells E1:F1 and then click the Merge & Center button in the Alignment group.

16 Select the range of cells E2:F2 and then press Ctrl + Y (the Repeat command).

> You can also press the F4 function key to repeat an action or you can add a Repeat button to the Quick Access toolbar. To do this, click the Customize Quick Access Toolbar button ▾ that displays at the right side of the toolbar and then click *More Commands* at the drop-down list. At the Excel Options dialog box with *Quick Access Toolbar* selected in the left pane, scroll down the left list box, click *Repeat*, click the Add button, and then click OK.

17 Select the range of cells E3:F3 and then press Ctrl + Y.

> You can merge and center in only one row at a time in this situation because data already exists in all three rows.

18 Select the range of cells E1:E3 and then click the Align Right button ≡ in the Alignment group.

19 Deselect the range.

20 Save **ES2-WBQuoteToMP.xlsx**.

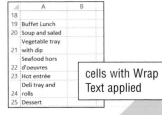

In Addition

Wrapping Text within a Cell

A Wrap Text button ⯐ is available in the Alignment group on the HOME tab. Use the Wrap Text button to wrap text within a cell if you do not want to widen the column width. Text too wide for the column is displayed on multiple lines and the height of the row is automatically increased. In the example shown at the right, the original cells are shown on the left and the wrapped cells in column A (which has also been made wider) are displayed on the right.

Activity 2.8

Adding Borders and Shading; Copying Formats with Format Painter

Borders in various styles and colors can be applied to display and print in selected cells within the worksheet. Borders can be added to the top, left, bottom, or right edge of a cell. Use borders to underscore headings or totals or to emphasize other cells. Shading adds color and/or a pattern to the background of a cell. Format Painter copies formats from a selected cell to another cell. Use this feature to apply multiple format options from one cell to another cell.

Project As you near completion of the quotation, you will spend time improving the presentation of the worksheet by adding borders and shading.

Tutorial 2.8
Using Format Painter and the Repeat Command

1 With **ES2-WBQuoteToMP.xlsx** open, select the range of cells A17:F17.

In the next steps, you will add a border to the top and bottom of the column headings using the Bottom Border button in the Font group on the HOME tab.

2 Click the Bottom Border button arrow in the Font group on the HOME tab.

A drop-down list of border style options displays. The *More Borders* option at the bottom of the list opens the Format Cells dialog box with the Border tab selected in which you can create a custom border.

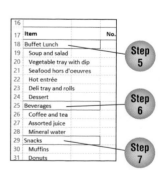

3 Click *Top and Bottom Border* at the drop-down list.

4 Click in any cell to deselect the range and view the border.

5 Select the range of cells A18:B18, click the Top and Bottom Border button arrow, and then click *Outside Borders* at the drop-down list.

6 Select the range of cells A25:B25 and then click the Outside Borders button. (Do not click the arrow.)

Since the Borders button updates to the most recently selected border style, you can apply the *Outside Borders* option to the active cell without displaying the drop-down list.

7 Select the range of cells A29:B29 and then click the Outside Borders button.

8 Deselect the range.

9 Make cell F36 the active cell, click the Outside Borders button arrow, and then click *Top and Double Bottom Border* at the drop-down list.

10 Make cell A8 the active cell, apply bold, and right-align the cell.

In the next steps, you will copy the formats from cell A8 to two other cells.

11 With cell A8 still the active cell, double-click the Format Painter button 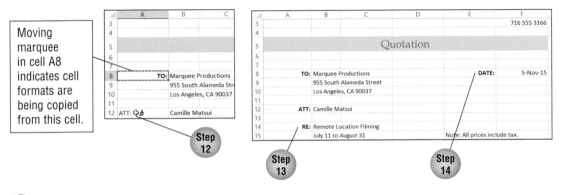 in the Clipboard group.

> A moving marquee surrounds the source cell and a paintbrush displays attached to the cell pointer. This icon means that the formats are copied from the source cell and can be pasted to multiple cells or ranges. Single-clicking the Format Painter button allows you to copy formats to the next cell or range that you click. Double-click the Format Painter button to toggle the feature on until you turn it off by clicking Format Painter again.

12 Click cell A12.

13 Click cell A14.

14 Click cell E8 and then click the Format Painter button to turn off the feature.

Moving marquee in cell A8 indicates cell formats are being copied from this cell.

Step 12

Step 13

Step 14

15 Save **ES2-WBQuoteToMP.xlsx.**

In Addition

Creating a Custom Border

If none of the borders available in the drop-down list suits your needs, you can create a custom border. Click the *More Borders* option at the bottom of the Borders button arrow drop-down list to open the Format Cells dialog box with the Border tab selected shown below. At this dialog box, you can change to a different line style by clicking another line option in the *Style* list box, and/or change the line color by clicking the down-pointing arrow at the right side of the *Color* option box and then choosing the desired color at the drop-down gallery. Next, specify the outside and/or inside border you want by clicking one of the buttons in the *Presets* section, clicking one or more of the Border buttons along the perimeter of the preview box, or by clicking inside the preview box at the edge of the cell along which you want the border to appear. When you are finished creating the border, click OK.

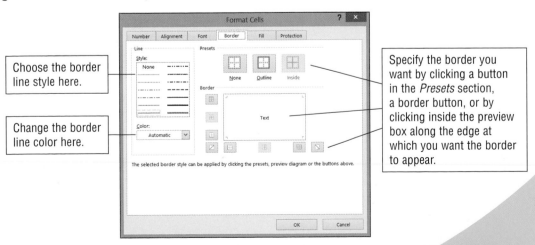

Choose the border line style here.

Change the border line color here.

Specify the border you want by clicking a button in the *Presets* section, a border button, or by clicking inside the preview box along the edge at which you want the border to appear.

Activity 2.9

Using Cell Styles and Themes

Cell styles contain a group of pre-defined formatting options stored in a name. *Styles* are an efficient method to consistently apply formats, creating a professional, consistent worksheet appearance. Excel includes several predefined styles that you can apply or modify; you also can choose to create your own cell style. A *theme* is a set of formatting choices that include a set of colors, a set of heading and body text fonts, and a set of lines and fill effects. Excel provides a variety of themes you can use to format text and cells in a worksheet.

Project

Your final steps in improving the presentation of the worksheet will involve applying cell styles and a theme.

The Waterfront B·I·S·T·R·O

SNAP

Tutorial 2.9
Applying Cell Styles and Themes

1 With **ES2-WBQuoteToMP.xlsx** open, make cell A5 the active cell.

You decide to change the formatting of the *Quotation* title to one of the predefined cell styles that Excel provides.

2 Click the Cell Styles button in the Styles group on the HOME tab.

A drop-down gallery appears with the predefined cell styles grouped into five sections: *Good, Bad and Neutral*; *Data and Model*; *Titles and Headings*; *Themed Cell Styles*; and *Number Format*.

3 Move the mouse over several of the cell style designs in the drop-down gallery and watch live preview show you the style applied to the title in cell A5.

4 Click the *Title* style in the *Titles and Headings* section of the gallery.

Step 2

Live preview shows how the cell will look when the Title style is applied to cell A5.

Step 4

5 Select the range of cells A17:F17, click the Cell Styles button in the Styles group, and then click the *Accent2* style in the *Themed Cell Styles* section.

6 Select the range of cells A18:B18, hold down the Ctrl key, select the range of cells A25:B25 and A29:B29, and then release the Ctrl key.

7 Click the Cell Styles button and then click the *Accent1* style in the *Themed Cell Styles* section at the drop-down gallery.

In the next steps, you will apply a theme to the quotation. Changing the theme will cause the fonts, colors, and effects to change for the cells. As with styles, you will be able to view a live preview of the changes before you choose a theme.

8 Deselect the cells.

continues

9 Click the PAGE LAYOUT tab.

10 Click the Themes button  in the Themes group.

11 Move the mouse over several of the themes in the drop-down gallery and watch live preview show you the changes that will take place in the worksheet.

12 Click *Retrospect* at the drop-down gallery.

> Notice that a theme affects the entire worksheet. You did not select a cell or range of cells before you applied a theme.

Colors and fonts associated with the Retrospect theme are shown in live preview.

13 Click the Colors button 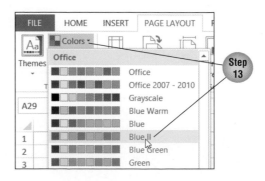 in the Themes group and then click *Blue II* at the drop-down gallery.

14 Click the Fonts button 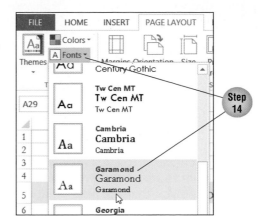 in the Themes group, scroll down the drop-down gallery, and then click *Garamond*.

15 Make cell A1 the active cell, type **The Waterfront Bistro**, and then press Enter.

16 Select the range of cells A1:D3 and then click the HOME tab.

17 Click the Merge & Center button in the Alignment group and then click the Middle Align button.

18 With cell A1 still the active cell, click the Cell Styles button and then click *Accent2* in the *Themed Cell Styles* section of the drop-down gallery.

19 With cell A1 still the active cell, change the font size to 28 points.

20 Select the range of cells E1:E3 and then apply the Accent2 cell style.

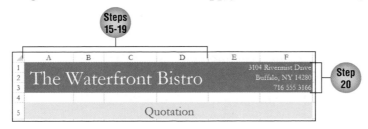

21 Click in any cell to deselect the range.

22 Click the FILE tab, click the *Print* option, and then click the Print button to print the finished quotation.

23 Save and then close **ES2-WBQuoteToMP.xlsx**.

In Brief

Apply Cell Styles
1. Select cells.
2. Click Cell Styles button.
3. Click desired style in drop-down gallery.

Apply Theme
1. Click PAGE LAYOUT tab.
2. Click Themes button.
3. Click desired theme in drop-down gallery.

In Addition

Creating a New Style

You can create your own style using the *New Cell Style* option at the bottom of the Cell Styles drop-down gallery. First, select a cell in the current worksheet and apply all of the formatting to the cell that you want saved in the style. Second, with the cell active to which you have applied the desired formats, click the Cell Styles button and then click *New Cell Style* at the drop-down gallery. At the Style dialog box shown at the right, type a name for the style in the *Style name* text box and then click OK. The new style will appear at the top of the Cell Styles gallery in a new section titled *Custom*. Custom styles are saved in the workbook in which they are created. You will not see the new style when you open a new workbook; however, you can copy styles from one workbook to another.

Activity 2.10

Using Find and Replace

Use the Find feature to search for specific labels or values that you want to verify or edit. The Find feature will move to each cell containing the text you specify. The Replace feature will search for a label, value, or format and automatically replace it with another label, value, or format. Use Find and Replace to ensure that all occurrences of the specified label or value are verified or edited.

Project Dana Hirsch wants to know how many weddings are booked in 2015. You will use the Find feature to review the wedding bookings in the special events workbook. Dana has also advised you that the prices that were input at 32.95 should be 34.95. You will use the Replace feature to correct these errors.

Tutorial 2.10A
Using Find and Replace

Tutorial 2.10B
Finding and Replacing Text and Formatting

1. Open **WBSpecEvents.xlsx**. Save the workbook with Save As in the ExcelS2 folder and name it **ES2-WBSpecEvents**.

2. Press Ctrl + Home to make cell A1 the active cell.

3. Click the Find & Select button in the Editing group on the HOME tab and then click *Find* at the drop-down list.

4. Type **wedding** in the *Find what* text box and then click the Find Next button.

> Notice that Excel has moved to cell C6, which has the entry *25th Wedding Anniversary*. This cell contains the search text *wedding* but you do not want to review wedding anniversary events. In the next step, you will specify that you want only cells that match the search text exactly.

5. Click the Options button in the Find and Replace dialog box, click the *Match entire cell contents* check box to insert a check mark and then click the Find Next button.

> The dialog box expands when you click the Options button to reveal find and replace options. Notice that this time, Excel bypassed the entry *50th Wedding Anniversary* in cell C9 and moved directly to cell C10, which contains the text *Wedding*.

6. Click the Find Next button.

> Excel moves the active cell to cell C16.

7. Click the Find Next button.

> Excel moves the active cell to cell C20.

8. Continue clicking the Find Next button until the active cell returns to cell C10 near the top of the worksheet.

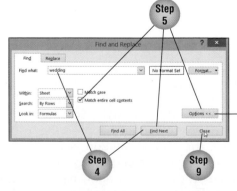

The Options >> button changes to Options << when the dialog box has been expanded to reveal the additional find and replace settings.

> Your review has determined seven weddings are booked in 2015. Although in this small worksheet you could easily have completed this calculation by quickly scanning the contents of column C, in a large worksheet with many rows and columns, the Find feature is an efficient method of moving to a specific cell. Typing a specific value into the *Find what* text box could move you to a section title or label very quickly.

9 Click the Close button to close the Find and Replace dialog box.

10 Click the Find & Select button in the Editing group and then click *Replace* at the drop-down list.

11 With *Match entire cell contents* still selected in the Find and Replace dialog box with the Replace tab selected, drag to select *wedding* in the *Find what* text box and then type **32.95**.

Step 11   Step 12

12 Press Tab to move the insertion point to the *Replace with* text box and then type **34.95**.

Step 13

13 Click the Replace All button.

> Excel searches through the entire worksheet and automatically changes all occurrences of *32.95* to *34.95*.

14 Click OK at the message that Excel has completed the search and has made four replacements.

15 Click the *Match entire cell contents* check box to clear the check mark, click the Options button to remove the expanded find and replace options, and then click the Close button to close the Find and Replace dialog box.

16 Review the entries in column H and note that no prices exist at 32.95.

Step 15

17 Save **ES2-WBSpecEvents.xlsx**.

In Addition

Replacing Formats

You can use the Replace feature to find formats and replace them with other formats or no formatting. For example, you could use Excel to find all occurrences of bold and blue font color applied to a cell and replace with bold and green font color. At the Find and Replace dialog box with the Replace tab selected, click the Options button to expand the dialog box and display Format buttons to the right of the *Find what* and *Replace with* text boxes (shown at the right). Use these buttons to specify the required format options. The Preview boxes to the left (initially display *No Format Set*) displays the formats Excel will find and replace.

Activity 2.11

Freezing Panes; Changing the Zoom

When you scroll to the right or down to view parts of a worksheet that do not fit in the current window, some column or row headings may scroll off the screen, making relating to text or values difficult. Freezing panes causes rows and columns to remain fixed when scrolling.

Magnify or reduce the worksheet display by dragging the Zoom slider bar button, clicking the Zoom In or Zoom Out buttons, or by specifying a percentage to zoom to at the Zoom dialog box. Changing the magnification does not affect printing since worksheets automatically print at 100% unless scaling options are changed.

Project

You will freeze column and row headings in the special events worksheet to facilitate scrolling and practice with various Zoom settings to view more cells within the current window.

SNAP

Tutorial 2.11
Freezing Panes and Changing the Zoom

1. With **ES2-WBSpecEvents.xlsx** open, make cell A4 the active cell.
2. Click the VIEW tab.
3. Click the Freeze Panes button [icon] in the Window group.
4. Click *Freeze Panes* at the drop-down list.

The position of the active cell before you freeze panes is important since all rows above and all columns left of the active cell are frozen. Notice you made cell A4 the active cell so that rows 1–3 are now frozen. A horizontal black line appears indicating which rows remain fixed when scrolling.

5. Press the Page Down key a few times to scroll down the worksheet.

Look at Figure 2.1 and notice rows 1 through 3 do not scroll off the screen.

FIGURE 2.1 Step 5

As you press Page Down, notice that rows 1–3 do not scroll off the screen.

Horizontal black line indicates that the rows above the line are frozen. The position of the active cell when you freeze panes determines which rows and columns are frozen.

6 Press Ctrl + Home and notice that Excel returns to cell A4 instead of cell A1 since cell A1 is frozen.

7 Click the Freeze Panes button in the Window group and then click *Unfreeze Panes*.

> The *Freeze Panes* option changes to *Unfreeze Panes* when rows or columns have been frozen.

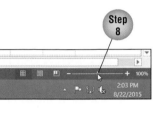

Step 7

8 Practice dragging the button on the Zoom slider bar (located at the right end of the Status bar above the system time) and watch the cells magnify and shrink as you drag right and left.

Step 8

9 Drag the slider bar button to the halfway mark on the slider bar to redisplay the worksheet at 100%.

10 Click over *100%* at the right edge of the slider bar to open the Zoom dialog box.

11 At the Zoom dialog box, click *75%* and then click OK.

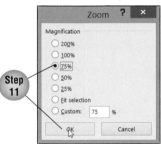

Step 11

12 Click the Zoom In button at the right side of the Zoom slider bar (displays as a plus symbol).

13 Continue to click the Zoom In button until the zoom percentage returns to 100%.

> When the worksheet is set to 100% magnification, clicking the Zoom In or Zoom Out buttons at either side of the slider bar magnifies or shrinks the display of the worksheet by 10% each time the button is clicked.

14 Save **ES2-WBSpecEvents.xlsx**.

In Brief

Freeze Panes
1. Make cell active below and right of row or column headings you want to freeze.
2. Click VIEW tab.
3. Click Freeze Panes button.
4. Click *Freeze Panes*.

Change Zoom Setting
Drag Zoom slider bar.
OR
Click Zoom In or Zoom Out buttons.
OR
Click zoom percentage value and choose magnification option at Zoom dialog box.

In Addition

Zoom to Selection

The VIEW tab contains a Zoom group with three buttons to change zoom settings. Click the Zoom button in the Zoom group to open the Zoom dialog box. This is the same dialog box that you displayed in Step 10. Click the 100% button to return the view to 100%. Select a range of cells and then click the Zoom to Selection button to cause Excel to scale the zoom setting so that the selected range fills the worksheet area.

Activity 2.12

Inserting, Moving, and Resizing Clip Art and Pictures

Microsoft Office includes a gallery of media images you can insert in a document, such as clip art, photographs, and illustrations. Use the Online Pictures button on the INSERT tab to search for and insert images at Office.com. Once an image has been inserted, it can be moved, resized, or deleted. Format an image with options at the PICTURE TOOLS FORMAT tab. A company logo or other digital picture can also be inserted into a worksheet using the Pictures button in the Illustrations group on the INSERT tab.

Project

Before printing the special events list, you decide to add a clip art image to the top right and the bistro's logo to the top left of the worksheet. After inserting the images, you will resize and move them.

Tutorial 2.12
Inserting and Modifying Images

① With **ES2-WBSpecEvents.xlsx** open, make cell A1 the active cell.

② Click the INSERT tab and then click the Online Pictures button 🖼 in the Illustrations group.

> This displays the Insert Pictures window with search boxes.

③ Click in the search box that displays to the right of the Office.com Clip Art option, type **lobster**, and then press Enter.

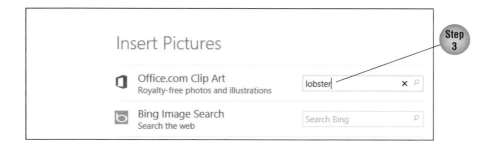

④ Double-click the image shown below. If this image is not available, choose another image related to *seafood*.

> The clip art image is inserted in the worksheet starting at cell A1.

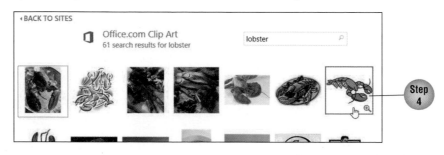

⑤ Position the pointer on the white sizing handle at the bottom right corner of the clip art image, hold down the left mouse button, and drag the pointer up and left until the image fits within the first two rows and columns as shown at the right.

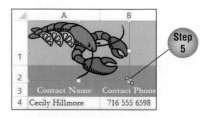

6 Move the mouse pointer over the image until the four-headed arrow move icon appears attached to the pointer, hold down the left mouse button, and then drag the image until the right edge of the clip art image is aligned at the right edge of the worksheet.

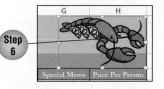

Step 6

In Brief

Insert Clip Art
1. Click INSERT tab.
2. Click Online Pictures button.
3. Search for image by keyword.
4. Double-click desired image in the window.
5. Move and/or resize as required.

Insert Picture from File
1. Click INSERT tab.
2. Click Pictures button.
3. Navigate to drive and/or folder.
4. Double-click file containing picture.
5. Move and/or size as required.

7 Click cell A1, click the INSERT tab, and then click the Pictures button 🖼 in the Illustrations group.

8 At the Insert Picture dialog box, navigate to the ExcelS2 folder on your storage medium and then double-click **TWBLogo.jpg**.

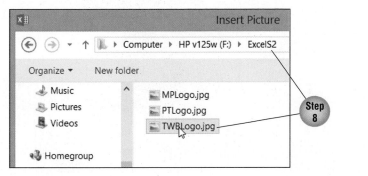

Step 8

9 Click in the *Shape Height* measurement box in the Size group on the PICTURE TOOLS FORMAT tab, type **1.07**, and then press Enter.

Step 9

10 Using the mouse, drag the picture so it is positioned as shown in the image below.

11 Click in any cell to deselect the logo image.

Steps 10-11

12 Select the range of cells A1:A2 and add *Outside Borders*. Select the range of cells A3:H36 and add *All Borders*.

13 Deselect the range.

14 Change the page orientation to landscape in the Print backstage area and then print the worksheet.

15 Save and then close **ES2-WBSpecEvents.xlsx**.

In Addition

Picture Tools

When a clip art image or picture inserted from a file is selected, the PICTURE TOOLS FORMAT tab becomes available. Customize the image using picture tools or picture styles. For example, use the crop button to cut an unwanted area from the image, or set a specific height or width measurement for the image. Buttons in the Arrange group allow you to group multiple images together, as well as control the alignment, rotation, or order of the image(s) within the worksheet. Use buttons in the Adjust group to control the brightness, contrast, and color of the image(s).

Features Summary

Feature	Ribbon Tab, Group	Button	Keyboard Shortcut
Accounting format	HOME, Number	$	
align left	HOME, Alignment		
align right	HOME, Alignment		
bold	HOME, Font	B	Ctrl + B
borders	HOME, Font		Ctrl + Shift + &
cell styles	HOME, Styles		
center	HOME, Alignment		
clear cell	HOME, Editing		
clip art	INSERT, Illustrations		
Comma format	HOME, Number	,	
copy	HOME, Clipboard		Ctrl + C
cut	HOME, Clipboard		Ctrl + X
decrease decimal	HOME, Number		
decrease indent	HOME, Alignment		
delete cell, column, or row	HOME, Cells		
fill color	HOME, Font		
find	HOME, Editing		Ctrl + F
font	HOME, Font	Calibri	
font color	HOME, Font	A	
font size	HOME, Font	11	
Format Painter	HOME, Clipboard		
freeze panes	VIEW, Window		
increase decimal	HOME, Number		
increase indent	HOME, Alignment		
insert cell, column, or row	HOME, Cells		

Feature	Ribbon Tab, Group	Button	Keyboard Shortcut
italic	HOME, Font	I	Ctrl + I
merge and center	HOME, Alignment		
middle-align	HOME, Alignment		
paste	HOME, Clipboard		Ctrl + V
picture from file	INSERT, Illustrations		
redo an action			Ctrl + Y
repeat			Ctrl + Y or F4
replace	HOME, Editing		Ctrl + H
Spelling	REVIEW, Proofing	ABC	F7
theme	PAGE LAYOUT, Themes	Aa	
theme colors	PAGE LAYOUT, Themes		
theme fonts	PAGE LAYOUT, Themes	A	
Thesaurus	REVIEW, Proofing		Shift + F7
undo an action			Ctrl + Z
zoom	VIEW, Zoom		

Knowledge Check

Completion: In the space provided at the right, indicate the correct term, command, or option.

1. Use this feature to remove everything from a cell including text and formats. _____

2. Make a cell active anywhere in this row to insert a new row between 11 and 12. _____

3. Make a cell active anywhere in this column to insert a new column between E and F. _____

4. This is the term for adjusting a column width to the length of the longest entry. _____

5. This term refers to the feature that shows the results of a format option while pointing to the option in a drop-down gallery. _____

6. By default, cells are initially set to this numeric style format. _____

7. Click this button in the Alignment group on the HOME tab to center cells vertically between the top and bottom cell boundaries. _____

8. Click this button in the Clipboard group on the HOME tab to copy the formats of the active cell. _____

9. This feature stores predefined format options. _____

10. This feature stores a set of colors, fonts, and effects that can be applied to the entire worksheet. _____

11. Make this cell active to freeze rows 1 through 5. _____

12. List two methods for changing the zoom magnification to view more cells in the current window. _____

13. Click this tab and button to search for clip art at Office.com. _____

14. Click this button in the Illustrations group to insert an image stored in a folder. _____

Skills Review

Review 1 Editing, Moving, Copying, and Clearing Cells; Performing a Spell Check; Inserting and Deleting Rows

1. Open **WBInvToNPC.xlsx** and then save the workbook in the ExcelEOS folder and name it **ES2-R-WBInvToNPC**.
2. Change the amount in cell D20 from *13.73* to *15.23*.
3. Clear the contents of cell A8.
4. Change the label in cell A21 from *Soup* to *French Onion Soup*.
5. Type new data in the cells indicated.
     E14   **PO No.**   F14   **TA-11-643**
6. Delete rows 7, 8, and 9.
7. Complete a spelling check of the worksheet. (All names are spelled correctly.)
8. Move the range of cells E7:F7 to E10:F10.
9. Copy cell A24 to cell A30.

10. Delete the rows that contain the labels *Milk* and *Donuts*.
11. Insert a new row between *Prime Rib* and *Mixed Vegetables* and then type **Seafood Pasta** in column A of the new row.
12. Save **ES2-R-WBInvToNPC.xlsx**.

Review 2 Adjusting Column Widths; Replacing Data; Moving Cells

1. With **ES2-R-WBInvToNPC.xlsx** open, adjust the width of column A to *17.00 (160 pixels)*.
2. Change the width of column C to the length of the longest entry (AutoFit).
3. Change the width of column D to *17.00 (160 pixels)* and column E to *7.00 (70 pixels)*.

4. Use the Replace feature to replace the value *32* with *36* for all occurrences.
5. Create a SUM formula in cell F33 to total cells F17 through F31.
6. Apply numeric formats as follows:
    a. Apply accounting formatting to cells F17 and F33.
    b. Apply comma formatting to cells F28 and F31.
7. Indent once the range of cells A18:A27 and A29:A30.
8. Select the range of cells D1:D3 and then change the font to 10-point Cambria bold.
9. Move the range of cells D1:D3 to F1:F3 and then align the text at the right edge of the cells.
10. Save **ES2-R-WBInvToNPC.xlsx**.

Review 3 Applying Formatting Features; Inserting a Picture

1. With **ES2-R-WBInvToNPC.xlsx** open, merge and center and then apply the Input cell style (in the *Data and Model* section) to the range of cells A17:B17 and A28:B28.
2. Merge and center cell A5 across columns A–F and then apply the Title cell style (in the *Titles and Headings* section) to cell A5.
3. Center the values in columns C and D and the labels in the range of cells C16:F16.
4. Add a top and bottom border to the range of cells A16:F16 and turn on bold formatting.
5. Add a top and double bottom border to cell F33 and turn on bold formatting.
6. Add an outside border to the range of cells A1:F36.
7. Add the fill color Green, Accent 6, Lighter 80% to cell A5.
8. Add the fill color Green, Accent 6, Lighter 60% to the range of cells A16:F16.
9. Apply the Integral theme to the worksheet.
10. Apply the Green Yellow theme colors.
11. Make cell A1 the active cell and then insert the picture file named *TWBLogo.jpg*. Change the height of the picture to 0.75 inch.
12. Save, print, and then close **ES2-R-WBInvToNPC.xlsx**. *Note: Check with your instructor if you submit your work in hard copy to see if you need to print two copies of this worksheet with one of the copies showing the cell formulas instead of the calculated results.*

Skills Assessment

Note: If you submit your work in hard copy, check with your instructor before completing these Assessments to find out if you need to print two copies of each worksheet, with one of the copies showing the cell formulas instead of the calculated results.

Assessment 1 Editing Cells; Inserting Columns; Copying Formulas; Inserting Pictures; Applying Formatting Features

1. Bobbie Sinclair of Performance Threads has started preparing a workbook that tracks the costs of costume research, design, and production for a Marquee Productions project. You have been asked to complete the workbook. Open **PTMarqCost.xlsx** and spend a few moments reviewing the worksheet Bobbie has started.
2. Save the workbook in the ExcelEOS folder and then name it **ES2-A1-PTMarqCost**.
3. Complete the worksheet using the following information:
   a. Design costs for all costumes should be *122.50* instead of *22*.
   b. Insert a new column between *Fabric* and *Total Cost* and type the column heading **Notions** in cell J9. Type the values in the range of cells J10:J16 as follows:

Henry II	101.50	John	47.85
Queen Eleanor	88.23	Geoffrey	47.85
Alias	58.40	Philip	47.85
Richard	47.85		

   c. The formula to calculate total cost for each costume is incorrect. Enter the correct formula for the first costume (cell K10) and then copy the formula to the range of cells K11:K16. *Hint: The current formula does not include the fabric and notions costs. Add the correct cells to the end of the formula.*
   d. Create a formula in cell L10 to calculate the costume fee that will multiply the total cost in cell K10 by *2* and then copy the formula to the range of cells L11:L16.
   e. Create a formula in cell M10 to calculate the profit as costume fee minus total cost and then copy the formula to the range of cells M11:M16.
   f. Format the numeric cells in an appropriate style.
   g. Change the alignment of any headings that could be improved in appearance.
   h. Merge and center the titles in cells A6 and A7 over the columns.
   i. Insert the picture file named **PTLogo.jpg** and then resize it to fit in the five rows at the top left of the worksheet.
   j. Insert a clip art image of your choosing after searching using the word *sewing* and then resize the image to fit in the five rows at the top right of the worksheet.
   k. Apply font, border, and color changes to enhance the appearance of the worksheet. Adjust column widths as needed.
4. Change the page layout to landscape orientation with the width scaled to fit 1 page. (Select *1 page* in the *Width* list box in the Scale to Fit group on the PAGE LAYOUT.)
5. Save, print, and then close **ES2-A1-PTMarqCost.xlsx**.

Assessment 2 Completing and Formatting a Worksheet

1. Camille Matsui, production assistant for Marquee Productions, has requested the invoice in advance for the custom-made costumes so that she can make sure the budget funds are allocated. Bobbie Sinclair has started the invoice and has asked you to finish it. Open **PTMarqCostInv.xlsx** and spend a few moments reviewing the invoice Bobbie has started. *Note: Completion of Assessment 1 is required to finish the invoice for this assessment.*

2. Save the workbook in the ExcelEOS folder and then name it **ES2-A2-PTMarqCostInv**.

3. Complete the invoice using the following information:
   a. Type the current date in cell G6.
   b. Refer to your electronic copy or your printout of the costumes in Assessment 1. Type the values from the *Costume Fee* column (the range of cells L10:L16) into the appropriate cells in the range of cells F15:F21.
   c. Create a formula to total the costume fees in cell F22. *Hint: Make sure the total agrees with the total costume fee on your printout from Assessment 1.*
   d. A transportation and storage container fee for each of the seven costumes is *$75.00*. Enter the appropriate formula in cell F24 that will calculate the fee for seven containers.
   e. Enter in cell F25 the delivery fee for all seven costumes as *$250.00*.
   f. Enter in cell F26 a formula that will add the total for the costume fees with the additional charges.
   g. Enter in cell F27 a formula that will calculate 13% Canadian Harmonized Sales Tax on the total in cell F26.
   h. Enter in cell F28 a formula to calculate the total invoice as the sum of cells F26 and F27.

4. Insert the picture file named **PTLogo.jpg** in cell A1 and then resize it to fit in the three rows at the top left of the worksheet.

5. Improve the appearance of the worksheet by adjusting column widths, deleting blank rows, moving cells, and/or applying formatting features that you learned in this section.

6. Save, print, and then close **ES2-A2-PTMarqCostInv.xlsx**.

Assessment 3 Performing a Spelling Check; Adjusting Column Width; Using Find and Replace; Inserting Clip Art; Applying Formatting Features

1. Sam Vestering, manager of North American Distribution for Worldwide Enterprises, has created a workbook to summarize revenues from distribution of Marquee Productions' documentary film *The Endangered Monarch Butterfly*. You have been asked to review the worksheet and make enhancements to the appearance. Begin by opening **WEMPRev.xlsx** and then reviewing the worksheet's layout, data, and formulas.
2. Save the workbook in the ExcelEOS folder and name it **ES2-A3-WEMPRev**.
3. Make the following corrections:
   a. Perform a spelling check.
   b. Adjust column widths so all data is completely visible.
   c. Change all of the venues named *Cinema House* to *Cinema Magic*.
   d. In cell A3, type **Date:** and then enter today's date in cell B3.
   e. Search for a clip art image of a monarch butterfly and then insert the image at the top right of the worksheet.
   f. Improve the appearance of the worksheet by applying formatting features you learned in this section.
4. Print the worksheet in portrait orientation with the width scaled to fit 1 page.
5. Save and then close **ES2-A3-WEMPRev.xlsx**.

Assessment 4 Finding the Select All Button

HELP

1. Use the Help feature to find out where the Select All button is located in the Excel window.
2. Open **WBInventory.xlsx** and then save the workbook in the ExcelEOS folder, naming it **ES2-A4-WBInventory**.
3. Click the Select All button and then apply italic formatting.
4. Deselect the cells and then scroll the worksheet to view the change.
5. Save, print, and then close **ES2-A4-WBInventory.xlsx**.

Assessment 5 Individual Challenge
Locating Information on Theatre Arts Programs

1. You are considering enrolling in a drama/theatre arts program at a college or university. Search the Internet for available programs in postsecondary schools in the United States and Canada. Choose three schools that interest you the most and find out as much as you can about the costs of attending these schools. Try to find information on costs beyond tuition and books, such as transportation and room and board.
2. Create a workbook that compares the costs for each of the three schools. For example, create the cost categories in column A and include three columns next to each cost category where you will enter the costs you found for each school. Total the costs for each of the schools.
3. Apply formatting features you learned in this section to the worksheet.
4. Save the workbook in the ExcelEOS folder and then name it **ES2-A5-TheatreArts**.
5. Print and then close **ES2-A5-TheatreArts.xlsx**.

Marquee Challenge

Challenge 1 Creating a Direct Wages Budget Report for a Film Shoot

1. You work with Chris Greenbaum, production manager at Marquee Productions. Chris has asked you to create the direct wages budget for the company's remote location film shoot. Create the worksheet shown in Figure 2.2. *Note: The logo is a file named MPLogo.jpg*.
2. Link the values in the *Estimated Daily Rates* table (columns I and J) to the *Daily Rate* column (column F) in the budget section.
3. Calculate the extended cost by summing the number of days for site prep, shoot, and cleanup and then multiplying by the daily rate.
4. Calculate the total in cell G16.
5. Apply formatting options as shown and then format the values in column G to an appropriate number format. Use your best judgment to determine the font, font size, column widths, borders, and fill colors.
6. Although not visible in the figure, a border should also be applied along the top (columns A–G) and left edges (rows 1–16) of the budget cells so that, when printed, the entire budget has a perimeter border.
7. Print the worksheet in landscape orientation and then save the workbook in the ExcelEOS folder naming it **ES2-C1-MPLocBudg**.
8. Close **ES2-C1-MPLocBudg.xlsx**.

FIGURE 2.2 Challenge 1

	Personnel		Site Prep Days	Shoot Days	Cleanup Days	Daily Rate	Extended Cost		Estimated Daily Rates Subject to Change	
				Direct Wages Budget						
Crew			9	32	2	1,275	$ 54,825		Crew	1,275
Cast			0	32	0	13,775	$ 440,800		Cast	13,775
Actor Assistants			0	32	0	3,250	$ 104,000		Actor Assistants	3,250
Extras			0	19	0	2,800	$ 53,200		Extras	2,800
Cleaners			9	32	5	875	$ 40,250		Cleaners	875
Security			7	32	5	3,750	$ 165,000		Security	3,750
Administration			9	32	5	1,275	$ 58,650		Administration	1,275
				Total Direct Wages Budget			$ 916,725			

Remove Location Film Shoot
July 11 to Agust 31, 2015

Challenge 2 Creating a Room Timetable

1. You are an assistant to the person who schedules classroom space in the Theatre Arts Division at Niagara Peninsula College. You have been given the room schedule for the auditorium for next semester. The division posts a printed copy of the timetable outside the auditorium door so that students know when the room is available to work on projects and rehearse for upcoming plays. You want to use Excel to create and format the timetable so that the printed copy is easy to read and has a more professional appearance.
2. Refer to the data in Figure 2.3 and then create the timetable in a new workbook. Apply formatting features learned in this section to create a colorful, easy-to-read room timetable.
3. Save the workbook in the ExcelEOS folder and name it **ES2-C2-NPCRoomSch**.
4. Print and then close **ES2-C2-NPCRoomSch.xlsx**.

FIGURE 2.3 Challenge 2

Niagara Peninsula College					
Room:	T1101		Period Covered: January 1 to April 30		
Time	Monday	Tuesday	Wednesday	Thursday	Friday
8:00 AM	SM100-01	AC215-03		MG210-01	SM240-03
9:00 AM	Prasad	McLean	LE100-03	Spelberger	Prasad
10:00 AM	LE253-03	(lab)	Das	SM355-02	SD350-04
11:00 AM	Das			Prasad	Attea
12:00 PM	SD451-01	PD250-02	Common	PD320-03	
1:00 PM	Attea	Kemper	Period	Kemper	LE310-02
2:00 PM	PD340-02	MG410-03	AC478-01	AC480-01	Das
3:00 PM	Kemper	Spelberger	Simmons	Simmons	MG210-01
4:00 PM	MG150-02	SM165-01	AC140-01	(lab)	Spelberger
5:00 PM	Spelberger	Prasad	Chou		
Use of this facility is restricted to staff and registered students only of Niagara Peninsula College. Failure to abide by this policy is considered a serious violation of the college's code of conduct.					
Note 1:	Monday through Thursday evenings, room is booked for Continuing Education department.				
Note 2:	Room is booked 8:00 AM to 5:00 PM the second Saturday of each month for the local community theatre group.				

Excel SECTION 3

Using Functions, Setting Print Options, and Adding Visual Elements

Skills

- Create formulas with absolute addresses
- Create AVERAGE, COUNT, MAX, and MIN formulas to perform statistical analysis
- Create NOW and TODAY formulas
- Create PMT formulas to calculate loan payments
- Create and use range names
- Create an IF formula to return a result based on a logical test
- Create, edit, and format a column, pie, and line chart
- Draw shapes and text boxes
- Modify and format charts
- Change page layout options for printing such as margins, horizontal and vertical centering, and scaling
- Manipulate a worksheet in Page Layout view
- Insert headers and footers

Projects Overview

Add functions, create charts, and change page layout options for a quarterly expense and revenue budget forecast; finish an invoice by entering dates and changing page layout options; calculate loan payment amounts for a patio expansion loan; calculate year-end bonuses; create charts for performance benchmarks.

Create and format charts for a grades analysis report; create a chart and apply formatting enhancements to an international student registration report.

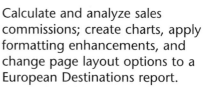

Calculate and analyze sales commissions; create charts, apply formatting enhancements, and change page layout options to a European Destinations report.

Calculate payments for an office expansion loan for two finance companies.

Create two charts that depict movie attendance statistics for a staff development workshop.

Model Answers for Projects

These model answers for the projects you complete in Section 3 provide a preview of the finished projects before you begin working and also allow you to compare your own results with these models to ensure you have created the materials accurately.

ES3-WBQtrExpBudg.xlsx is the project in Activities 3.1 and 3.2 and part of the project in Activities 3.7, 3.8, and 3.10.

The Waterfront Bistro											
Quarterly Expense Budget Forecast											
		Target Factors for Increases by Quarter									
		1.05		1.08		1.15		1.14			
	Last Year's Avg Qtr	Qtr1		Qtr2		Qtr3		Qtr4		Total	
Advertising	$ 2,150.00	$ 2,257.50	$	2,322.00	$	2,472.50	$	2,451.00	$	9,503.00	
Bank charges	500.00	525.00		540.00		575.00		570.00		2,210.00	
Cleaning	650.00	682.50		702.00		747.50		741.00		2,873.00	
Linens	1,100.00	1,155.00		1,188.00		1,265.00		1,254.00		4,862.00	
Office supplies	175.00	183.75		189.00		201.25		199.50		773.50	
Telephone	250.00	262.50		270.00		287.50		285.00		1,105.00	
Utilities	2,050.00	2,152.50		2,214.00		2,357.50		2,337.00		9,061.00	
Total		$ 7,218.75	$	7,425.00	$	7,906.25	$	7,837.50	$	30,387.50	
Average expense		$ 1,031.25	$	1,060.71	$	1,129.46	$	1,119.64	$	4,341.07	
Maximum expense		$ 2,257.50	$	2,322.00	$	2,472.50	$	2,451.00	$	9,503.00	
Minimum expense		$ 183.75	$	189.00	$	201.25	$	199.50	$	773.50	
Count of expense items		7									

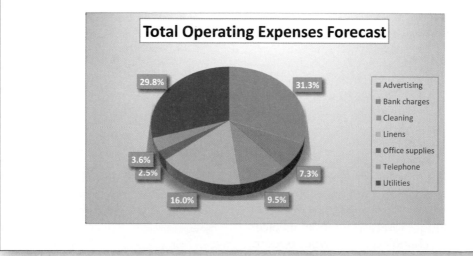

ES3-WBOverdueAccts.xlsx is the project in Activity 3.3 and part of the project in Activity 3.11.

The Waterfront Bistro

3104 Rivermist Drive
Buffalo, NY 14280
716 555 3166

Current date: 8/28/15

Overdue Accounts

Customer	Account #	Amount Due	Date	Terms	Due Date
Monroe & Associates	1232	$ 3,258.50	3/1/15	30	3/31/15
John and Susan Martin	1205	$ 4,500.00	3/15/15	15	3/30/15
Harold Streeter	1244	$ 1,755.50	3/15/15	15	3/30/15
Paulina Cardoza	1259	$ 6,400.00	4/1/15	30	5/1/15

ES3-WBPatioLoan.xlsx is the project in Activity 3.4 and part of the project in Activity 3.11.

The Waterfront Bistro

Patio Expansion Loan Analysis

	Funds Unlimited	Venture Funds Inc.	Details
Interest Rate	7.25%	8.15%	Annual rate
Term	15	12	Years for repayment
Loan Amount	420,000	420,000	Principal borrowed
Monthly Payment	($3,834.02)	($4,580.92)	Includes principal and interest

NOTE:

Both payments are calculated based on a constant interest rate and a constant payment.

Total loan payments	($690,124.34)	($659,651.81)

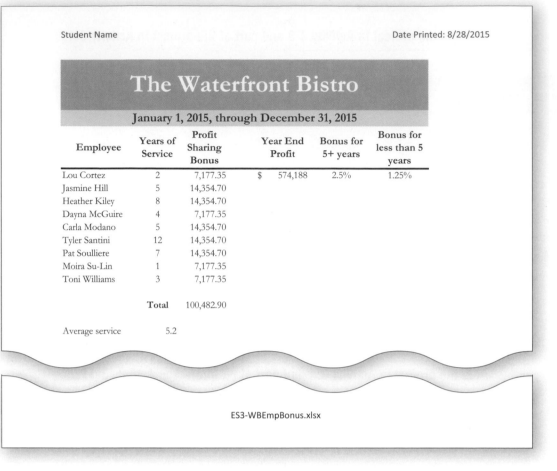

Student Name   Date Printed: 8/28/2015

The Waterfront Bistro

January 1, 2015, through December 31, 2015

Employee	Years of Service	Profit Sharing Bonus	Year End Profit	Bonus for 5+ years	Bonus for less than 5 years
Lou Cortez	2	7,177.35	$ 574,188	2.5%	1.25%
Jasmine Hill	5	14,354.70			
Heather Kiley	8	14,354.70			
Dayna McGuire	4	7,177.35			
Carla Modano	5	14,354.70			
Tyler Santini	12	14,354.70			
Pat Soulliere	7	14,354.70			
Moira Su-Lin	1	7,177.35			
Toni Williams	3	7,177.35			
Total		100,482.90			
Average service	5.2				

ES3-WBEmpBonus.xlsx

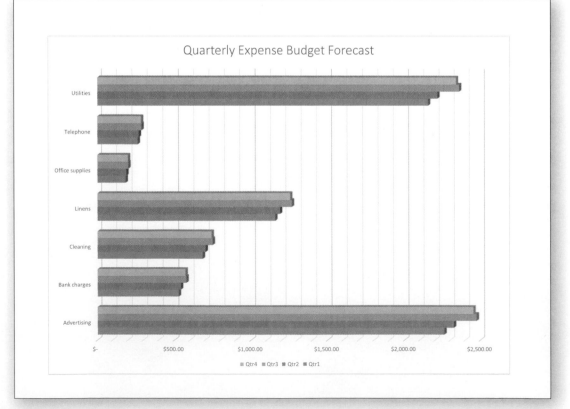

The Waterfront Bistro

Quarterly Performance Benchmarks

	Qtr1	Qtr2	Qtr3	Qtr4
Avg check per person	8.25	9.50	15.00	17.25
Avg seat turnover	2.0	1.0	1.5	2.6

National Restaurant Association Statistics

	Qtr1	Qtr2	Qtr3	Qtr4
NRA Avg check per person	10.00	12.50	11.00	14.00
NRA Avg seat turnover	1.3	1.1	1.8	2.0

A strong finish!

Qtr 4 30% above NRA!

EXCEL SECTION 3
Project Model Answers

Activity 3.1

Creating Formulas with Absolute Addressing

In the previous two sections, when you copied and pasted formulas in worksheets, the cell addresses in the destination cells changed automatically *relative* to the destination row or column. The formulas in these worksheets used **relative addressing**. Sometimes you need a cell address to remain fixed when it is copied to another location in the worksheet. To do this, the formulas must include **absolute addressing** for those cell addresses that you do not want changed. Make a cell address absolute by typing a dollar symbol ($) in front of the column letter or row number that cannot be changed. You can also use the F4 function key to toggle through variations of the address as relative, absolute, or mixed, in which either the row is absolute and the column is relative or vice versa.

Project

Worldwide Enterprises

SNAP

Tutorial 3.1
Creating Formulas with Absolute Addressing

Dana Hirsch has started a worksheet to forecast next year's expenses by quarter. Dana uses a model wherein next year's expenses are estimated based on last year's average quarter values multiplied by a factor that represents the expected increase for this year. For example, a factor of 1.05 means Dana is expecting the expense to increase by 5%. You will calculate each quarter's expense using the factors in the model Dana has started.

1. Open **WBQtrExpBudg.xlsx** and then save the workbook in the ExcelS3 folder, naming it **ES3-WBQtrExpBudg**.

2. Review the layout of the worksheet. Notice the values in D4:G4 are factors that represent the increases by quarter for next year's expenses. For example, advertising in quarter 1 is expected to increase by a factor of *1.05* (an increase of five percent).

3. Make cell D6 active. All of the Qtr1 values in column D will be created by multiplying last year's average quarter amount by the factor in cell D4. The formula will include an address that should not change when the formula is copied (D4). To create a formula with an absolute address, type **=b6*d4** and then press function key F4.

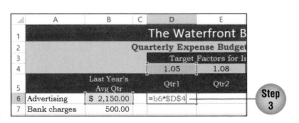

Pressing F4 causes Excel to insert dollar symbols in front of the row number and column letter immediately left of the insertion point — *d4* becomes $D$4, an absolute address. You can enter column letters in formulas in either uppercase or lowercase. Excel will convert lowercase letters to uppercase automatically when you press the Enter key after typing the formula or when pressing F4 to specify an absolute reference.

4. Press Enter.

The result *$2,257.50* is entered in cell D6. In the cell D6 formula, the first cell reference (B6) is relative and the second cell reference (D4) is absolute. This is an example of **mixed referencing** with some addresses relative and some absolute. When the formula is copied in a later step, only cell D4 remains the same.

5. With cell D7 active, type **=b7*d4** and then press Enter.

You can also type the dollar symbol in front of the column letter or row number to make an address absolute.

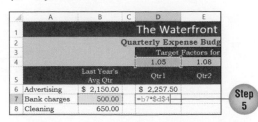

---

80 EXCEL **Section 3**

6 Make cell D7 active and then drag the fill handle down to cell D12.

7 Click cell D8 and look at the formula in the Formula bar. Notice that the first cell address (B8) was changed relative to the current row number but the second cell address ($D$4) remained the same as the original when the formula was copied.

8 Make cell E6 active, type **=b6*e4**, press the F4 function key, and then press Enter.

9 Make cell F6 active and then create the formula *=B6*$F$4* by either typing **=b6*f4** and pressing the F4 function key or by typing the dollar symbols before *f* and *4*.

In Brief

Make Cell Address Absolute
With insertion point positioned just after cell address or with cell address selected in Formula bar, press F4.
OR
Type dollar symbol immediately preceding column letter and/or row number.

10 Make cell G6 active and then create the formula *=B6*$G$4* by either typing **=b6*g4** and pressing F4 or by typing the dollar symbols before *g* and *4*.

	A	B	C	D	E	F	G
1				The Waterfront Bistro			
2				Quarterly Expense Budget Forecast			
3					Target Factors for Increases by Quarter		
4				1.05	1.08	1.15	1.14
5		Last Year's Avg Qtr		Qtr1	Qtr2	Qtr3	Qtr4
6	Advertising	$ 2,150.00		$ 2,257.50	$ 2,322.00	$ 2,472.50	$ 2,451.00
7	Bank charges	500.00		525.00	$ 540.00	$ 575.00	$ 570.00
8	Cleaning	650.00		682.50	$ 702.00	$ 747.50	$ 741.00
9	Linens	1,100.00		1,155.00	$ 1,188.00	$ 1,265.00	$ 1,254.00
10	Office supplies	175.00		183.75	$ 189.00	$ 201.25	$ 199.50
11	Telephone	250.00		262.50	$ 270.00	$ 287.50	$ 285.00
12	Utilities	2,050.00		2,152.50	$ 2,214.00	$ 2,357.50	$ 2,337.00
13							
14	Total						

Steps 8-11

11 Select E6:G6 and then drag the fill handle down to row 12.

12 Click a few cells in the copied range and verify that in each case, the cell reference with the dollar symbols remained the same when the formula was copied.

13 Make cell D14 active and then click the AutoSum button to calculate the total for column D. Click the AutoSum button a second time to accept the suggested formula *=SUM(D6:D13)*.

	B	C	D	E	F	G	H
			The Waterfront Bistro				
			Quarterly Expense Budget Forecast				
			Target Factors for Increases by Quarter			
			1.05	1.08	1.15	1.14	
	Last Year's Avg Qtr		Qtr1	Qtr2	Qtr3	Qtr4	Total
	$ 2,150.00		$ 2,257.50	$ 2,322.00	$ 2,472.50	$ 2,451.00	$ 9,503.00
	500.00		525.00	$ 540.00	$ 575.00	$ 570.00	$ 2,210.00
	650.00		682.50	$ 702.00	$ 747.50	$ 741.00	$ 2,873.00
	1,100.00		1,155.00	$ 1,188.00	$ 1,265.00	$ 1,254.00	$ 4,862.00
	175.00		183.75	$ 189.00	$ 201.25	$ 199.50	$ 773.50
	250.00		262.50	$ 270.00	$ 287.50	$ 285.00	$ 1,105.00
	2,050.00		2,152.50	$ 2,214.00	$ 2,357.50	$ 2,337.00	$ 9,061.00
			$ 7,218.75	$ 7,425.00	$ 7,906.25	$ 7,837.50	$ 30,387.50

Step 14

Step 13

Step 15

14 Make cell H6 active, click the AutoSum button, and then press Enter to accept the suggested formula *=SUM(D6:G6)*.

15 Complete the formulas in E14:H14 and H7:H12 by copying the appropriate SUM functions.

16 Select cells E7:H12 and apply the comma style format.

17 Save **ES3-WBQtrExpBudg.xlsx**.

In Addition

More about Mixed Addressing

You can instruct Excel to fix only the row number or the column letter of a cell that is copied and pasted to another location. This table shows more ways that a cell address can use absolute referencing. Pressing F4 repeatedly causes Excel to scroll through each of these variations for the selected cell address.

Example	Action
=$A$12*.01	Neither the column nor the row will change.
=$A12*.01	The column will remain fixed at column A, but the row will change.
=A$12*.01	The column will change, but the row remains fixed at row 12.
=A12*.01	Both the column and row will change.

Activity 3.2

Using Statistical Functions

Until now, you have only used the SUM function when you click the AutoSum button in the Editing group on the HOME tab. Excel includes numerous other built-in formulas that are grouped into function categories. The Statistical category contains several functions that can be used to perform statistical analysis on data, such as calculating medians, variances, frequencies, and so on.

The structure of a function formula begins with the equals sign (=), followed by the name of the function, and then the argument within parentheses. *Argument* is the term given to the values to be included in the calculation. The structure of the argument is dependent on the function being used and can include a single range of cells, multiple ranges, single cell references, or a combination thereof.

Project

Dana Hirsch has asked you to add statistics below the quarterly expenses budget forecast. Specifically, you will calculate the average, maximum, and minimum expenses, as well as the total number of expense items.

The Waterfront
B·I·S·T·R·O

SNAP

Tutorial 3.2
Using Statistical
Functions

1. With **ES3-WBQtrExpBudg.xlsx** open, type the following labels in the cells indicated.
   - A17: **Average expense**
   - A18: **Maximum expense**
   - A19: **Minimum expense**
   - A20: **Count of expense items**

2. Make cell D17 active.

   In the next steps, you will insert the AVERAGE function to determine the arithmetic mean of the expenses in column D. If an empty cell or a cell containing text is included in the argument, Excel ignores the cell when determining the result. If, however, the cell contains a zero value, it is included in the average calculation.

3. Click the AutoSum button arrow in the Editing group on the HOME tab.

4. Click *Average* at the drop-down list.

   Excel inserts the formula =AVERAGE(D14:D16) in the active cell with the suggested range highlighted. In the next step, you will drag to select the correct range and then complete the formula.

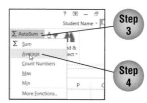

5. Position the cell pointer over cell D6, hold down the left mouse button, drag down to cell D12, and then release the left mouse button.

   Excel inserts the range *D6:D12* in the formula and the moving marquee expands to display the selected cells.

5		Last Year's Avg Qtr	Qtr1	Qtr2	
6	Advertising	$ 2,150.00	$ 2,257.50	$ 2,322.00	$ 2
7	Bank charges	500.00	525.00	540.00	
8	Cleaning	650.00	682.50	702.00	
9	Linens	1,100.00	1,155.00	1,188.00	1
10	Office supplies	175.00	183.75	189.00	
11	Telephone	250.00	262.50	270.00	
12	Utilities	2,050.00	2,152.50	2,214.00	2
13					
14	**Total**		$ 7,218.75	$ 7,425.00	$ 7
15					
16					
17	Average expense		=AVERAGE(D6:D12)		
18	Maximum expense		AVERAGE(**number1**, [number2], ...)		
19	Minimum expense				
20	Count of expense items				

In Brief

Use AVERAGE, MAX, MIN, COUNT Functions
1. Make desired cell active.
2. Click AutoSum button arrow.
3. Click desired function.
4. Type or select argument range.
5. Press Enter or click Enter button.

6 Press Enter or click the Enter button on the Formula bar.

> Excel returns the result *$1,031.25* in cell D17.

7 Make cell D18 active, click the AutoSum button arrow, and then click *Max* at the drop-down list.

> The MAX function returns the largest value in the argument.

8 Type **d6:d12** and then press Enter.

> Excel returns the result *$2,257.50* in cell D18. Typing the range into the formula is sometimes faster if you are sure of the starting and ending cell references.

5		Last Year's Avg Qtr	Qtr1	Qtr2
6	Advertising	$ 2,150.00	$ 2,257.50	$ 2,322.00
7	Bank charges	500.00	525.00	540.00
8	Cleaning	650.00	682.50	702.00
9	Linens	1,100.00	1,155.00	1,188.00
10	Office supplies	175.00	183.75	189.00
11	Telephone	250.00	262.50	270.00
12	Utilities	2,050.00	2,152.50	2,214.00
13				
14	**Total**		$ 7,218.75	$ 7,425.00
15				
16				
17	Average expense		$ 1,031.25	
18	Maximum expense		=MAX(d6:d12	
19	Minimum expense		MAX(**number1**, [number2], ...)	
20	Count of expense items			

Step 8

9 With cell D19 active, type the function **=min(d6:d12)** and then press Enter.

> MIN returns the smallest value in the argument. As soon as you type the letter *m* after the equals sign, the Formula AutoComplete feature displays a drop-down list of functions that begin with the letter typed. Formula AutoComplete helps you to write formulas by displaying function names, descriptions, and argument syntax. You can scroll the list and point to a function name to display in a ScreenTip the function's purpose. Double-click a function name in the list to enter the function into the cell.

10 With cell D20 active, type the function **=count(d6:d12)** and then press Enter.

> COUNT returns the number of cells that contain numbers or numbers that have been formatted as text and dates. Empty cells, text labels, or error values in the range are ignored.

11 Select D17:D19 and then drag the fill handle right to column H. (You are not including the COUNT formula in cell D20 since the count value (7) does not change.

> This copies the AVERAGE, MAX, and MIN formulas to columns E through H.

5		Last Year's Avg Qtr	Qtr1	Qtr2	Qtr3	Qtr4	Total
6	Advertising	$ 2,150.00	$ 2,257.50	$ 2,322.00	$ 2,472.50	$ 2,451.00	$ 9,503.00
7	Bank charges	500.00	525.00	540.00	575.00	570.00	2,210.00
8	Cleaning	650.00	682.50	702.00	747.50	741.00	2,873.00
9	Linens	1,100.00	1,155.00	1,188.00	1,265.00	1,254.00	4,862.00
10	Office supplies	175.00	183.75	189.00	201.25	199.50	773.50
11	Telephone	250.00	262.50	270.00	287.50	285.00	1,105.00
12	Utilities	2,050.00	2,152.50	2,214.00	2,357.50	2,337.00	9,061.00
13							
14	**Total**		$ 7,218.75	$ 7,425.00	$ 7,906.25	$ 7,837.50	$ 30,387.50
15							
16							
17	Average expense		$ 1,031.25	$ 1,060.71	$ 1,129.46	$ 1,119.64	$ 4,341.07
18	Maximum expense		$ 2,257.50	$ 2,322.00	$ 2,472.50	$ 2,451.00	$ 9,503.00
19	Minimum expense		$ 183.75	$ 189.00	$ 201.25	$ 199.50	$ 773.50
20	Count of expense items		7				

Step 11

12 Click in any cell to deselect D17:H19.

13 Save and then close **ES3-WBQtrExpBudg.xlsx**.

Activity 3.3

Writing Formulas with Date Functions and Dates

Excel provides the TODAY and NOW date and time functions that insert the current date or date and time in a worksheet. The advantage to using the functions rather than just typing the date and time is that the date and time are automatically updated when you open the worksheet. When you type a date in a cell, Excel stores the date as a serial number. Serial numbers in Excel begin with the number 1 (which represents January 1, 1900) and increase sequentially. Because dates are stored as numbers, they can be used in formulas. A date will appear in a cell based on how it is entered. Specify the appearance of dates in a worksheet with options at the Format Cells dialog box with the Number tab selected.

Project

Tutorial 3.3
Writing Formulas with Date Functions and Dates

An overdue accounts worksheet needs to be completed by entering the current date, formatting the dates, and calculating the account due dates. You will open the overdue accounts worksheet and experiment with the TODAY and NOW functions, change the formatting of the dates, and write a formula that determines the due date.

1. Open **WBOverdueAccts.xlsx**.

2. Save the workbook in the ExcelS3 folder and name it **ES3-WBOverdueAccts**.

3. Make cell B4 active, type **=now()**, and then press Enter.

The current date and time are inserted in cell B4. In the next steps, you will delete the date and time and then use the TODAY function to see the difference between the two date functions. Instead of typing a function (as you did in Step 3), you can insert a date and time function with the Date & Time button on the FORMULAS tab.

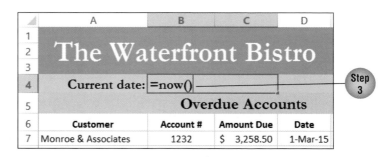

4. Make cell B4 active and then press the Delete key to delete the date and time.

5. Click the FORMULAS tab, click the Date & Time button in the Function Library group, and then click *TODAY* at the drop-down list.

6. At the Function Arguments dialog box, click OK.

The current date is inserted in the cell with the time displayed as *0:00*. Normally, the time does not display with the TODAY function; however, since the NOW function was used first, Excel retained the time format for the cell. In the next steps, you will change the formatting of the date.

7 With cell B4 the active cell, click the HOME tab, click the Number Format button arrow, and then click the *More Number Formats* option at the bottom of the drop-down list.

8 At the Format Cells dialog box, click *Date* in the *Category* list box and then double-click the fourth option in the *Type* list box (the option that displays the date as *#/##/##*).

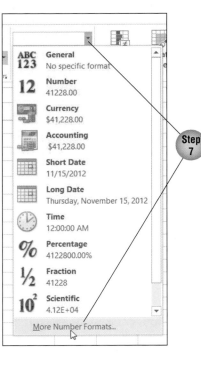

Step 8

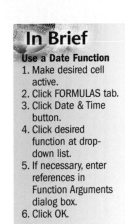

Step 7

9 Select cells D7:D10 and then apply to the cells the same date formatting you applied to cell B4.

10 Turn on the display of formulas by clicking the FORMULAS tab and then clicking the Show Formulas button in the Formula Auditing group.

> With the display of formulas turned on, the dates in cell B4 and cells D7 through D10 display as serial numbers.

11 Press Ctrl + ` to turn off the display of formulas.

> The grave symbol (`) is located to the left of the number 1 key on most keyboards.

12 Make cell F7 active and then insert a formula that calculates the date plus the days in the *Terms* column by typing **=d7+e7** and then pressing Enter.

> Excel used the date serial number in cell D7, added the number of days in the *Terms* column, and then inserted the due date in the date format.

13 Copy the formula in cell F7 down to cells F8:F10.

14 Save, print, and then close **ES3-WBOverdueAccts.xlsx**.

In Addition

TIME Function

Time values are stored as decimal numbers that represent the portion of a day starting at 0 (12:00:00 AM) and continuing up to 0.999988426 (23:59:59 PM). The format of the TIME function using the 24-hour clock is *=TIME(hour,minute,second)*. In the worksheet shown at the right, the formula *=(C2-B2)*24* is used to calculate how many hours the employee worked.

D2		× ✓ *fx*	=(C2-B2)*24	
	A	B	C	D
1		Start Time	End Time	Hours Worked
2	Lou Cortez	8:00 AM	3:30 PM	7.5

Activity 3.4

Using the Financial Function PMT

Use Excel's financial functions to calculate depreciation, interest rates, payments, terms, present values, future values, and so on. The PMT function is used to calculate a payment for a loan based on constant payments, a constant interest rate, and a set period of time. This function is useful if you want to borrow money and need to estimate the payment you would make given a specified interest rate and length of time to pay back the loan. To use the PMT function correctly, the time periods for the interest rate and the term have to be consistent. For example, if you want to calculate the monthly payment on a loan, make sure the interest rate and the number of periods are expressed in months, or convert the interest rate and time period to months within the formula. The PMT function requires three arguments: the interest rate for the loan (*Rate*), the number of payments to be made (*Nper*), and the amount of money that is borrowed (*Pv*).

Project

The Waterfront Bistro is planning a patio expansion next year. Dana Hirsch has received pre-approval from two finance companies and wants you to estimate monthly loan payments for each to help decide from which company to borrow funds.

The Waterfront B·I·S·T·R·O

SNAP

Tutorial 3.4
Using Financial Functions

1. Open **WBPatioLoan.xlsx**.

2. Save the workbook in the ExcelS3 folder and name it **ES3-WBPatioLoan**.

3. Make cell B10 active.

4. Click the FORMULAS tab and then click the Financial button in the Function Library group.

5. Scroll down the *Financial* drop-down list and then click *PMT*.

6. If necessary, drag the Function Arguments dialog box Title bar to the right of column B.

7. With the insertion point positioned in the *Rate* text box, click the mouse in cell B6 and then type **/12**.

   The interest rate in cell B6 is 7.25%, which is the annual interest rate. Typing /12 divides the annual interest rate by 12 to obtain a monthly interest rate. Since you want to calculate a payment per month, you need to ensure the time periods for all input values are the same.

8. Click in the *Nper* text box, click cell B7, and then type ***12**.

   The term in cell B7 represents the number of years that loan payments will be made. Multiplying this value times 12 payments per year represents the total number of payments to be made for the loan. Note that you have converted both the interest rate and the number of payments within the function arguments to months.

9. Click in the *Pv* text box, click cell B8, and then click OK.

   Pv stands for **present value** and represents the principal amount that is being borrowed. Excel returns the payment amount *$3,834.02* for the Funds Unlimited loan in cell B10. Payments are displayed as negative values; in this spreadsheet file, negative values are displayed in red and within parentheses. Consider loan payments as money that is subtracted from your cash balance, which helps you relate to the negative value returned in the formula cell. If you prefer, you can enter a negative value in cell B8 (-420,000) and the calculated payment displays as a positive number.

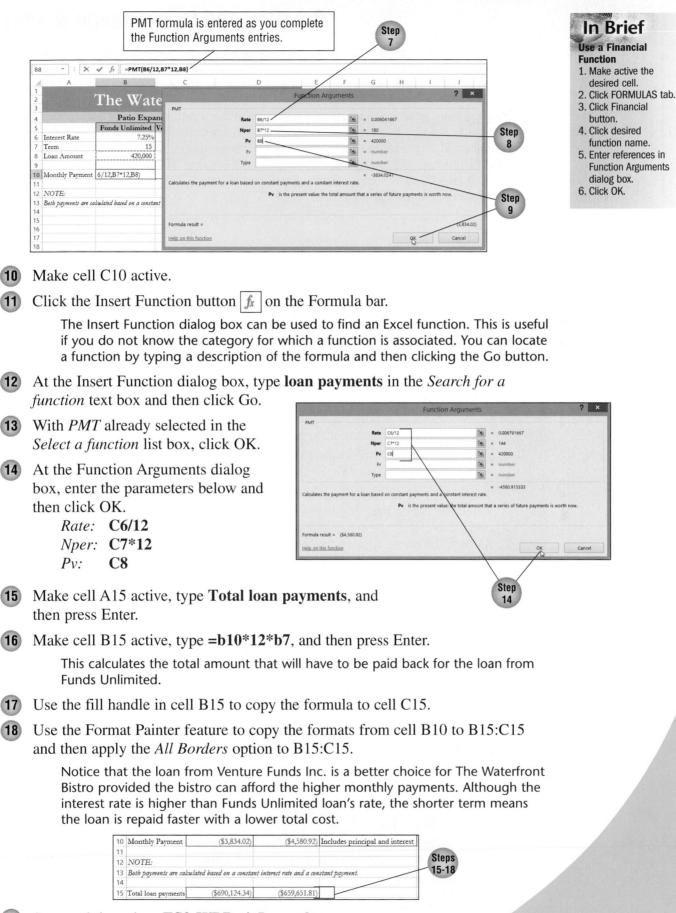

PMT formula is entered as you complete the Function Arguments entries.

Step 7

Step 8

Step 9

In Brief

Use a Financial Function
1. Make active the desired cell.
2. Click FORMULAS tab.
3. Click Financial button.
4. Click desired function name.
5. Enter references in Function Arguments dialog box.
6. Click OK.

10 Make cell C10 active.

11 Click the Insert Function button f_x on the Formula bar.

> The Insert Function dialog box can be used to find an Excel function. This is useful if you do not know the category for which a function is associated. You can locate a function by typing a description of the formula and then clicking the Go button.

12 At the Insert Function dialog box, type **loan payments** in the *Search for a function* text box and then click Go.

13 With *PMT* already selected in the *Select a function* list box, click OK.

14 At the Function Arguments dialog box, enter the parameters below and then click OK.

> Rate: **C6/12**
> Nper: **C7*12**
> Pv: **C8**

Step 14

15 Make cell A15 active, type **Total loan payments**, and then press Enter.

16 Make cell B15 active, type **=b10*12*b7**, and then press Enter.

> This calculates the total amount that will have to be paid back for the loan from Funds Unlimited.

17 Use the fill handle in cell B15 to copy the formula to cell C15.

18 Use the Format Painter feature to copy the formats from cell B10 to B15:C15 and then apply the *All Borders* option to B15:C15.

> Notice that the loan from Venture Funds Inc. is a better choice for The Waterfront Bistro provided the bistro can afford the higher monthly payments. Although the interest rate is higher than Funds Unlimited loan's rate, the shorter term means the loan is repaid faster with a lower total cost.

10	Monthly Payment	($3,834.02)	($4,580.92)	Includes principal and interest
11				
12	NOTE:			
13	*Both payments are calculated based on a constant interest rate and a constant payment.*			
14				
15	Total loan payments	($690,124.34)	($659,651.81)	

Steps 15-18

19 Save and then close **ES3-WBPatioLoan.xlsx**.

Activity 3.5

Creating and Using Range Names

Assigning a name to a cell or a range of cells allows you to reference the cell(s) by a descriptive label rather than the cell address or range address when creating formulas, printing, or when navigating a large worksheet. Referencing by name makes a formula easier to understand. For example, a formula such as *=Sales-Expenses* is readily understood. A standard formula such as *=D3-D13* requires the reader to look at the labels next to the values in the formula cells in order to grasp the formula's purpose. A range name can be a combination of letters, numbers, underscore characters, or periods up to 255 characters. The first character in a range name must be a letter, an underscore, or a back-slash (\). Spaces are not valid in a range name. To create a range name, select the desired cells and then type the name in the Name box at the left of the Formula bar.

Project

Tutorial 3.5
Naming and Using a Range

The profit-sharing bonus for the employees needs to be calculated. Dana Hirsch has started the worksheet and asked you to finish it. Since the bonus amount varies depending on the employee's years of service, you decide to begin by naming cells so that you can use names in the function to help you build the correct formula.

1 Open **WBEmpBonus.xlsx**.

2 Save the workbook in the ExcelS3 folder and name it **ES3-WBEmpBonus**.

To begin, you want to name the cells in column B *Years*. The first step in naming a range is to select the cell or group of cells to which the name will be associated.

3 Select B7:B15.

4 Point at the white box at the left end of the Formula bar (currently displays *B7* in the box) and notice the ScreenTip displays *Name Box*.

The white box at the left end of the Formula bar is called the Name box. The Name box displays the cell address of the active cell. If the active cell has been named, the name appears in the Name box. To assign a new name to a cell or selected range, click in the Name box and then type the desired name.

5 Click in the Name box, type **Years**, and then press Enter.

Notice the range name now appears in the Name box. You want to assign a name to each cell that will be referenced when you create the profit-sharing formula in the next project. In the next steps, you will assign a range name to individual cells that will be needed to calculate the profit-sharing bonus.

6 Make cell E7 active.

7 Click in the Name box, type **Profit**, and then press Enter.

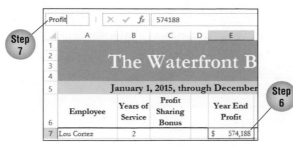

8 Make cell F7 active, click in the Name box, type **FiveAndOver**, and then press Enter.

9 Make cell G7 active, click in the Name box, type **LessThanFive**, and then press Enter.

10 Make cell A1 active and then click the down-pointing arrow at the right of the Name box.

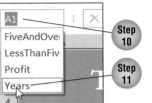

A drop-down list of range names in the current workbook appears. To move the active cell to a named cell or range, click the range name in the drop-down list.

11 Click *Years* at the drop-down list.

The range B7:B15 is selected since this is the group of cells associated with the name *Years*.

12 Make cell A19 active, type **Average service**, and then press Enter.

13 Make cell B19 active, type **=average(years)**, and then press Enter.

Notice that range names are not case sensitive when you use the name in a formula. When you type the range name *years* in the formula, notice that Excel color-codes B7:B15 to show you the cells that are being referenced in the formula.

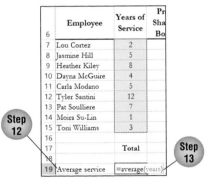

14 Format cell B19 to display only one decimal place.

15 Save **ES3-WBEmpBonus.xlsx**.

In Brief

Name a Range
1. Select cell(s).
2. Click in Name box.
3. Type desired range name.
4. Press Enter.

In Addition

Managing Range Names

To edit or delete a range name, display the Name Manager dialog box shown at the right. To do this, click the FORMULAS tab and then click the Name Manager button in the Defined Names group. The Name Manager dialog box displays the range names in the active workbook and provides buttons to edit or delete the name.

Activity 3.6

Using the Logical IF Function

The IF function returns one of two values in a cell based on a true-or-false answer to a question called a logical test. The format of an IF function is *=IF(logical_test,value_if_true,value_if_false)*. For example, assume a salesperson earns a 3% commission if sales are greater than or equal to $100,000, or a 2 percent commission for sales less than $100,000.

Assume the sales value resides in cell B4. The logical test in this example would be B4>=100000. Excel can only return a true-or-false answer when this test is performed. The commission will be calculated at either B4*3% *(value_if_true)* or B4*2% *(value_if_false)*. In this example, the IF function formula would be *=IF(B4>=100000,B4*3%,B4*2%)*.

Project

Tutorial 3.6
Using the Logical
IF Function

The catering staff participate in a profit-sharing bonus at the end of a year. The bonus amount is based on the year-end profit and the employee's years of service—2.5% for those with 5 years of service and more, and 1.25% for those employees with less than 5 years of service. Since the percentage bonus can be either one of two values, you need an IF function to calculate the bonus.

1. With **ES3-WBEmpBonus.xlsx** open, make cell C7 the active cell.

2. Click the FORMULAS tab.

3. Click the Logical button ⬚ in the Function Library group.

4. Click *IF* at the drop-down list.

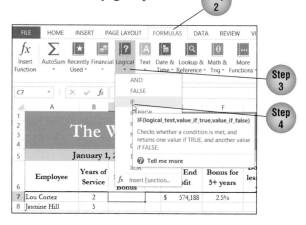

The Function Arguments dialog box for the IF statement opens. Notice the three arguments: *Logical_test, Value_if_true,* and *Value_if_false.* To begin, you want Excel to test whether the value in the years-of-service column (column B) is less than 5. This test determines whether Excel calculates the bonus using the lower percent paid to employees with fewer than five years of service or the higher percent paid to employees with five or more years of service. Recall that in the last project you created range names. In the next steps, you will see how using range names will make the IF statement much easier to create and understand.

5. With the insertion point positioned in the *Logical_test* text box, type **years<5** and then press the Tab key.

Watch the entries that appear at the right of each argument text box as you build the formula. Excel updates these entries to show you how the formula is working as you build each argument. Notice that next to the *Logical_test* text box you now see the TRUE and FALSE results Excel is calculating for each entry in the Years range.

6. With the insertion point positioned in the *Value_if_true* text box, type **profit*lessthanfive** and then press the Tab key.

If the value in cell B7 is less than 5, Excel calculates the bonus as the profit (cell E7) times 1.25% (cell G7). Another advantage to using range names is that by default, range names refer to the named cell using absolute references. Since the formula will be copied to rows 8–15, absolute references are required for those cells that reference the profit and the percents.

7 With the insertion point positioned in the *Value_if_false* text box, type **profit*fiveandover**.

> If the value in cell B7 is greater than or equal to 5, the formula calculates the profit (cell E7) times 2.5% (cell F7). Notice that below the text boxes, Excel shows the result that will be placed in the active cell *Formula result = 7177.35*. Looking at cell B7 you will note that Lou Cortez has 2 years of service so Excel is calculating Lou's bonus as $574,188 times 1.25%.

8 Click OK.

In Brief

Use an IF Function
1. Make desired cell active.
2. Click FORMULAS tab.
3. Click Logical button.
4. Click *IF*.
5. Type formula in *Logical_test* text box.
6. Type value or formula in *Value_if_true* text box.
7. Type value or formula in *Value_if_false* text box.
8. Click OK.

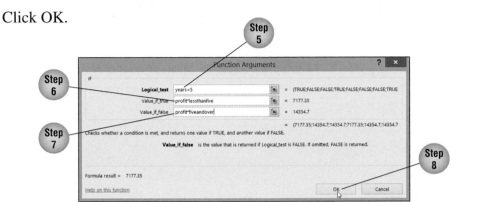

9 Drag the fill handle in cell C7 down to row 15 and then click in any cell to deselect the range.

10 Make cell C17 active, click the AutoSum button in the Function Library group, and then press Enter to calculate the total bonuses to be paid.

11 Format the values in column C in Comma style. If necessary, increase the width of column C to display the entire amounts in the column.

12 Click cell C7 and review the formula in the Formula bar that was created using the IF Function Arguments dialog box =IF(Years<5,Profit*LessThanFive,Profit*FiveAndOver).

> The formula may be easier to comprehend if you include the range names when reading it to yourself.

13 Save and then close **ES3-WBEmpBonus.xlsx**.

In Addition

More about IF Function Arguments

One advantage to creating an IF function using the Function Arguments dialog box is that the correct syntax is added automatically to the formula. For example, you did not need to worry about typing commas between arguments or the opening and closing brackets in this project. These elements are automatically added to the formula. Notice also that the range names in the completed formula are displayed in the case used when the range name is created. For example, you typed *profit*lessthanfive*, but the formula you reviewed at Step 12 displayed this entry as *Profit*LessThanFive*. When creating your range names, consider the readability of the formula and use upper- and lowercase letters to facilitate comprehension. Another alternative is to use underscores between words in a range name.

Activity 3.7

Creating a Column Chart

Numerical values are often more easily understood when presented visually in a chart. Excel includes several chart types such as column, line, pie, bar, area, scatter, and others with which you can graphically portray data. The chart can be placed in the same worksheet as the data or it can be inserted into its own sheet. To create a chart, first select the cells containing the data you want to graph and then choose the chart type. Excel graphs the data in a separate object that can be moved, resized, and formatted.

Project

Dana Hirsch has asked you to create a chart to compare the quarterly expenses in the budget forecast you completed earlier in this section.

1. Open **ES3-WBQtrExpBudg.xlsx**, select A5:A12, hold down the Ctrl key, and then select D5:G12.

   The first step in creating a chart is to select the range of cells containing the data you want to graph. Notice in the range that you are including the row labels in column A. Labels are included to provide the frame of reference for each bar, column, or other chart series. If you select multiple ranges, ensure that the data in each range has a consistent number of cells in the range.

2. Click the INSERT tab.

3. Click the Insert Column Chart button in the Charts group.

4. Click *3-D Clustered Column* at the drop-down gallery (first option in *3-D Column* section).

   Excel graphs the data in a 3-D column chart and places the chart inside an object box in the center of the worksheet.

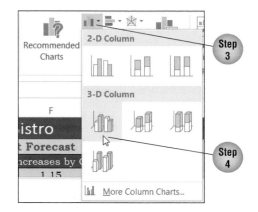

3-D column chart created at Step 4 is placed in an object box, which can be moved, resized, and formatted as needed.

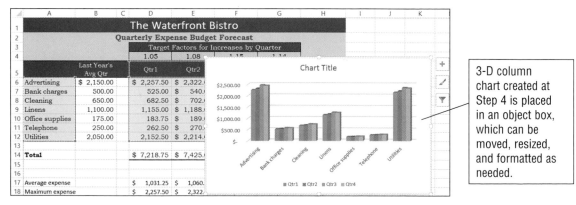

5. Click the Move Chart button in the Location group on the CHART TOOLS DESIGN tab.

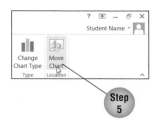

6 At the Move Chart dialog box, click the *New sheet* option.

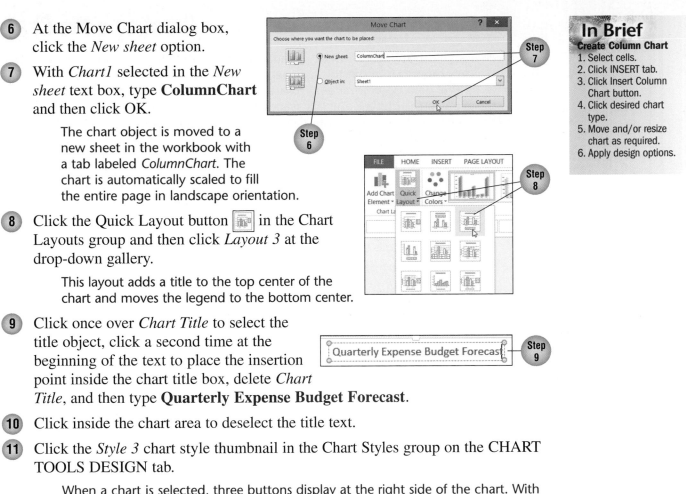

Step 7

Step 6

Step 8

7 With *Chart1* selected in the *New sheet* text box, type **ColumnChart** and then click OK.

> The chart object is moved to a new sheet in the workbook with a tab labeled *ColumnChart*. The chart is automatically scaled to fill the entire page in landscape orientation.

8 Click the Quick Layout button in the Chart Layouts group and then click *Layout 3* at the drop-down gallery.

> This layout adds a title to the top center of the chart and moves the legend to the bottom center.

9 Click once over *Chart Title* to select the title object, click a second time at the beginning of the text to place the insertion point inside the chart title box, delete *Chart Title*, and then type **Quarterly Expense Budget Forecast**.

> Quarterly Expense Budget Forecast
>
> **Step 9**

10 Click inside the chart area to deselect the title text.

11 Click the *Style 3* chart style thumbnail in the Chart Styles group on the CHART TOOLS DESIGN tab.

> When a chart is selected, three buttons display at the right side of the chart. With these buttons, you can insert or remove chart elements, apply chart styles, and edit what data points and names display in the chart.

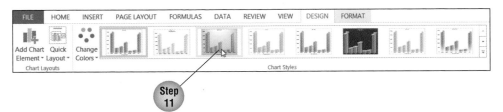

Step 11

12 Save **ES3-WBQtrExpBudg.xlsx**.

In Addition

Creating a Recommended Chart

If you are not sure what type of chart will best illustrate your data, consider letting Excel recommend a chart. To do this, select the data, click the INSERT tab, and then click the Recommended Charts button in the Charts group. This display the data in a chart in the Insert Chart dialog box. Customize the recommended chart with options in the left panel of the dialog box. Click the OK button to insert the recommended chart in the worksheet. You can also insert a recommended chart in the worksheet with the keyboard shortcut Alt+ F1.

Activity 3.8

Creating a Pie Chart

Pie charts illustrate each data point's size in proportion to the total of all items in the data source range. Each slice in the pie chart is displayed as a percentage of the whole pie. You can choose to display the percent values, the actual values used to generate the chart, or both values as data labels inside or outside the pie slices. Use a pie chart when you have only one data series you want to graph and there are no negative or zero values within the data range.

Project

Dana Hirsch has requested a second chart from the quarterly expense budget forecast worksheet that displays each expense as a proportion of the total expenses.

Tutorial 3.8
Formatting with Chart Buttons

1. With **ES3-WBQtrExpBudg.xlsx** open, click the tab labeled *Sheet1* near the bottom left corner of the window above the Status bar.

2. If necessary, click in any cell to deselect the range that was used to generate the column chart in the previous activity.

3. Select the range A5:A12, hold down the Ctrl key, and then select the range H5:H12.

4. Click the INSERT tab.

5. Click the Insert Pie or Doughnut Chart button in the Charts group.

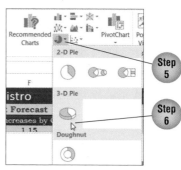

6. Click the *3-D Pie* option in the *3-D Pie* section at the drop-down gallery.

7. Point to the border of the chart object until the pointer displays with the four-headed-arrow move icon, hold down the left mouse button, and then drag the chart below the worksheet data. Position the chart approximately centered below columns A–H with the top edge in row 22.

8. With the chart selected, click the Chart Elements button that displays at the right side of the chart.

9. Point to the *Data Labels* option that displays in the drop-down list and then click the expand triangle that displays at the right side of the option.

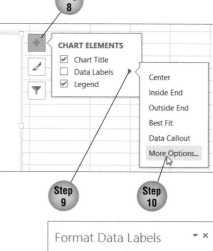

10. Click *More Options* at the side menu.

> This displays the Format Data Labels task pane at the right side of the screen.

11. At the Format Data Labels task pane, click the *Value* check box in the LABEL OPTIONS section below the *Label Contains* heading to remove the check mark and then click the *Percentage* check box to insert a check mark.

12 Scroll down the Format Data Labels task pane list box, click the expand arrow that displays to the left of *NUMBER*, click the down-pointing arrow at the right side of the *Category* option box, and then click *Percentage* at the drop-down list.

13 Select the number in the *Decimal places* text box and then type **1**.

14 Close the Format Data Labels task pane.

15 Click the Chart Styles button that displays at the right side of the chart.

16 Click the *Style 3* option at the side menu drop-down gallery.

17 Click the Chart Elements button that displays at the right side of the chart, click the expand triangle that displays at the right side of the *Data Labels* option, and then click *Outside End* at the side menu.

18 Change the chart title to **Total Operating Expenses Forecast**.

> Refer to Activity 3.7, Steps 9–10, if you need assistance with this step.

19 Click in the worksheet area outside the chart to deselect the chart.

20 Save and then close **ES3-WBQtrExpBudg.xlsx**.

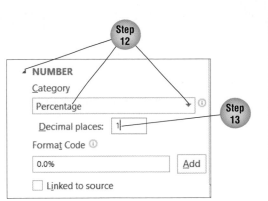

In Brief

Create Pie Chart
1. Select cells.
2. Click INSERT tab.
3. Click Insert Pie or Doughnut Chart button.
4. Click desired pie type.
5. Move and/or resize chart as required.
6. Apply design options.

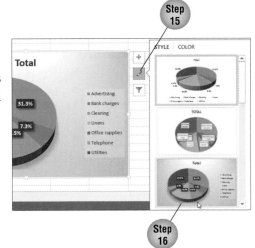

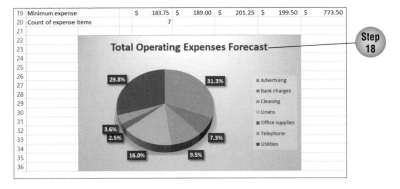

In Addition

Sparklines

A Sparklines group was added to the INSERT tab in Excel 2010. Sparklines are miniature charts that you can add to a cell. These miniature charts illustrate changes from a specified row or column of data. For example, in the worksheet shown below, the sparkline chart was created in cell F4 based on the range of values in B4:E4. Click the INSERT tab and then click the Line, Column, or Win/Loss buttons in the Sparklines group. At the Create Sparklines dialog box, select the data range that contains the values on which you want to base the chart (B4:E4), select the cell in which to draw the chart (F4), and then click OK.

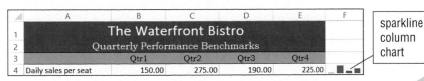

Creating a Line Chart; Drawing Shapes

A line chart shows trends and change over time at even intervals. Line charts emphasize the rate of change over time rather than the magnitude of the change. You can easily spot a trend in a line chart, look for unusual points in the data series, or even predict future values based on the line's shape and direc-tion. The Shapes button in the INSERT tab includes buttons with which you can draw lines, rectangles, basic shapes, block arrows, equation shapes, flow-chart symbols, stars and banners, and callouts. Enclosed shapes can also contain text. Draw shapes to add emphasis or insert explanatory notes in a worksheet.

Project

Dana Hirsch has created a worksheet with the bistro's performance statistics by quarter, along with the National Restaurant Association's statistics. Dana would like you to create charts in order to compare the data visually.

SNAP

Tutorial 3.9
Inserting and
Formatting a Shape

1 Open **WBPerfStats.xlsx**. Save the workbook in the ExcelS3 folder and name it **ES3-WBPerfStats**.

2 Select A3:E4, hold down the Ctrl key, and then select A8:E8.

3 Click the INSERT tab, click the Insert Line Chart button in the Charts group, and then click *Line with Markers* in the *2-D Line* section at the drop-down gallery (first column, second row).

> Notice the line chart clearly shows that the bistro performed below the association's average check per person for the first half of the year but finished the year well above the association's statistics.

4 With the CHART TOOLS DESIGN tab active, click the Quick Layout button, and then click the *Layout 12* option at the drop-down gallery (third column, fourth row).

5 Point to the border of the chart object until the pointer displays with the four-headed-arrow move icon and then drag the chart below the worksheet data approximately centered below columns A–E and with the top edge in row 11.

6 Select A3:E3, A5:E5, and A9:E9 and then create a Line chart similar to the line chart created in Steps 3 and 4.

7 Move the new line chart below the first one, leaving one blank row between the two charts.

> In the next steps, you will draw shapes and add text to the shapes to add emphasis in the two line charts.

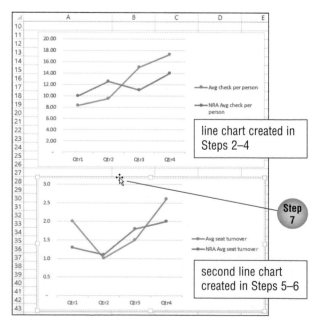

line chart created in Steps 2–4

second line chart created in Steps 5–6

8 Click the INSERT tab and then click the Shapes button in the Illustrations group.

> The Shapes drop-down list contains shape buttons grouped by category.

9 Click the *12-Point Star* shape in the *Stars and Banners* group (ninth option in first row).

> When a shape object tool has been selected, the pointer changes to a crosshairs.

10 Click in the white space above the legend in the first line chart.

> This inserts a star shape in the worksheet with default measurements of 1 inch for the height and 1 inch for the width. The shape contains eight white sizing handles around the perimeter as well as a white rotation handle and a yellow square center point. The DRAWING TOOLS FORMAT tab becomes active with options to customize the shape.

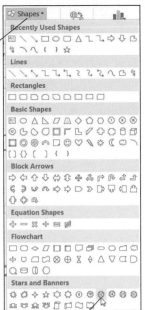

11 With the shape selected, click in the *Shape Width* measurement box, type **1.5**, and then press Enter.

12 With the shape still selected, type **A strong finish!**

> You can type text in a selected shape. You can also right-click the shape and then click *Edit Text* at the shortcut menu.

13 Select the text you just typed and then press Ctrl + E to center the text horizontally in the shape. Click the HOME tab, click the Middle Align button, change the font size to 10 points, and then apply bold formatting.

14 Position the shape inside the first line chart as shown at the right.

15 Click the INSERT tab, click the Shapes button, and then click the *Wave* shape in the *Stars and Banners* group (seventh option in second row).

16 Click in the white space above the legend in the second line chart.

17 With the shape selected, click in the *Shape Width* measurement box, type **1.5**, and then press Enter.

18 Type **Qtr 4 30% above NRA!** in the shape.

19 Select the text you just typed and then press Ctrl + E to center the text horizontally. Click the HOME tab, click the Middle Align button, change the font size to 10 points, and then and apply bold formatting.

20 Position the shape inside the second line chart as shown above.

21 Print the worksheet.

22 Save and then close **ES3-WBPerfStats.xlsx**.

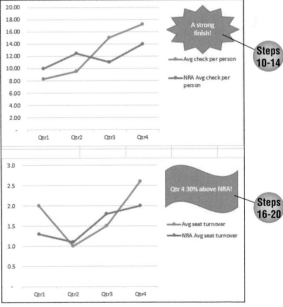

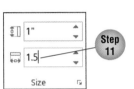

In Brief

Create Line Chart
1. Select cells.
2. Click INSERT tab.
3. Click Insert Line Chart button.
4. Click desired line type.
5. Move and/or resize chart as required.
6. Apply design options.

Draw Shape
1. Click INSERT tab.
2. Click Shapes button.
3. Click desired shape.
4. Click in worksheet or drag to create shape.
5. Move, resize, or format shape as required.

Activity
3.10

Modifying and Formatting Charts

To make changes to an existing chart, click inside a chart or chart element to display the translucent border around the perimeter of the chart object. Point to the border to move the chart or point to one of the eight sizing handles to resize the chart. When the chart is selected, the CHART TOOLS DESIGN and CHART TOOLS FORMAT tabs become available. Use these tabs to add, delete, or modify the chart or chart elements as needed.

Project You will modify the charts created for the quarterly expense budget forecast worksheet by formatting the legend, changing the font in the chart title, and changing the chart type.

SNAP

Tutorial 3.10
Changing Chart
Formatting

1. Open **ES3-WBQtrExpBudg.xlsx** and then click anywhere inside the pie chart to select the chart object.

   Once a chart is selected, two additional tabs are available—the CHART TOOLS DESIGN tab and the CHART TOOLS FORMAT tab.

2. Click inside the pie chart legend.

   Eight sizing handles appear around the legend, indicating the object is selected. You can drag the legend to another location or resize the legend using one of the handles.

3. Click the CHART TOOLS FORMAT tab.

4. Click the Shape Outline button arrow in the Shape Styles group and then click the *Light Blue* color (fourth color from the right in the *Standard Colors* section).

   This adds a thin, light-blue border around the legend.

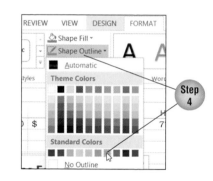

5. Click the chart title to select it, click the More button at the right side of the shape style thumbnails in the Shape Styles group, and then click the *Colored Outline - Blue, Accent 1* option (second column, first row).

6. Click inside the chart area to deselect the chart title.

7. Click inside any one of the percent values around the edge of the pie.

   This selects all seven data labels.

8. Click the Shape Fill button arrow in the Shape Styles group and then click the *Light Blue* color (fourth color from the right in the Standard Colors).

9. Click in the worksheet area outside the pie chart.

10. Click the ColumnChart tab located near the bottom left corner of the window above the Status bar and then click inside the column chart to select the chart.

11. Click the CHART TOOLS DESIGN tab and then click the Change Chart Type button in the Type group.

12 At the Change Chart Type dialog box, click *Bar* in the left pane and then click the *3-D Clustered Bar* option (fourth option toward the top of the middle pane).

13 Click OK.

14 Click the More arrow button in the Chart Styles group and then click *Style 10* in the drop-down gallery (second column, second row).

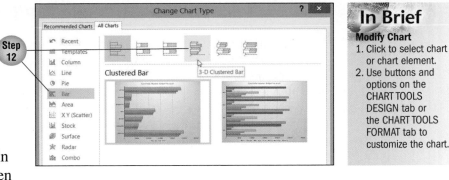

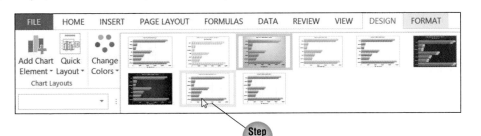

15 Print the chart.

16 Click the Sheet1 tab and then click in cell A1.

17 Click the FILE tab and then click the *Print* option.

18 Click the scaling gallery in the *Settings* category (gallery that displays *No Scaling*), click *Fit Sheet on One Page* at the drop-down list, and then click the Print button.

> Scaling a worksheet means Excel will decrease the size of print proportionately in order to fit a worksheet to the specified number of pages (in this case one page).

19 Save and then close **ES3-WBQtrExpBudg.xlsx**.

In Brief
Modify Chart
1. Click to select chart or chart element.
2. Use buttons and options on the CHART TOOLS DESIGN tab or the CHART TOOLS FORMAT tab to customize the chart.

In Addition

Chart Elements

Another method to edit a chart is to right-click a chart element to display a context-sensitive shortcut menu. For example, right-clicking the axis labels in the bar chart displays the shortcut menu shown at the right. The bottom section of the shortcut menu changes depending on the element you clicked.

Activity 3.11

Changing Page Layout Options

The PAGE LAYOUT tab contains buttons to modify the page setup and scaling options for printing purposes. You can also change print options while previewing the worksheet in the Print backstage area. The margin on a worksheet is the blank space at the top, bottom, left, and right edges of the page and the beginning of the printed text. The default margins are 0.75 inch top and bottom and 0.7 inch left and right. Smaller worksheets can be centered horizontally and/or vertically to improve the printed appearance. For larger worksheets, you can choose to shrink the text by scaling the size of printed text to force the printout to a maximum number of pages. For example, in the previous activity you scaled the quarterly expense budget forecast to print on one page.

Project

You need to print the invoice to Performance Threads completed in Activity 3.3. Prior to printing, you will adjust the margins to improve the worksheet's appearance using the Print backstage area. Dana would also like the worksheet printed with the loan analysis for the patio expansion. You will center the worksheet horizontally before printing.

The Waterfront B·I·S·T·R·O

SNAP

Tutorial 3.11
Changing Page
Layout Options

1. Open **ES3-WBOverdueAccts.xlsx**.

2. Click the FILE tab and then click the *Print* option to open the Print backstage area.

    Notice the invoice is not balanced on the page. In the next steps, you will change the margins to improve the page layout.

3. Click the margins gallery in the *Settings* category (currently displays *Normal Margins*).

4. Click *Custom Margins* at the drop-down list.

    The Page Setup dialog box opens with the Margins tab active.

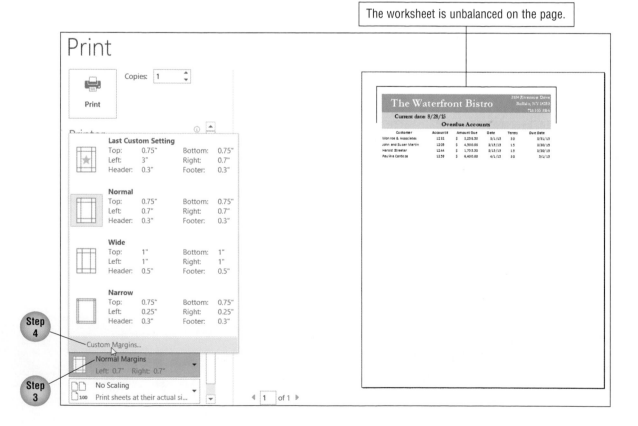

The worksheet is unbalanced on the page.

Step 4

Step 3

5 Select the current entry in the *Top* measurement box and then type **1.25**. Select the current entry in the *Left* measurement box, type **1.25**, and then click OK.

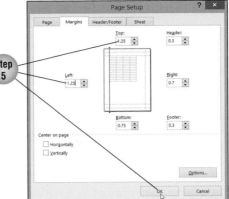

> The preview pane in the Print backstage area shows the worksheet with the new margins applied. The page layout is improved for printing.

6 Click the Print button.

7 Save and then close **ES3-WBOverdueAccts.xlsx**.

8 Open **ES3-WBPatioLoan.xlsx**.

9 Click the PAGE LAYOUT tab, click the Orientation button in the Page Setup group, and then click *Landscape*.

10 Click the Margins button in the Page Setup group and then click *Custom Margins* at the drop-down list.

> The Page Setup dialog box opens with the Margins tab active. This is another way to open the same Page Setup dialog box you accessed using the margins gallery in the Print backstage area.

11 Change the top margin to 1.25 inches.

12 Click the *Horizontally* check box in the *Center on page* section and then click OK.

> Centering the worksheet horizontally is another method you can use to ensure the worksheet prints balanced between the left and right edges of the page. You can choose both the *Horizontally* and *Vertically* check boxes to print a worksheet that is centered between both the left and right edges (horizontally), and the top and bottom edges (vertically) of the page.

13 Print the worksheet.

14 Save and then close **ES3-WBPatioLoan.xlsx**.

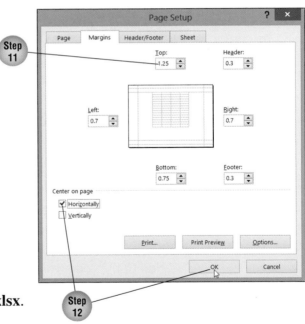

In Brief

Change Margins
1. Click PAGE LAYOUT tab.
2. Click Margins button in Page Setup group.
3. Click *Custom Margins*.
4. Change margin options as desired.
5. Click OK.
OR
1. Click FILE tab.
2. Click *Print* option.
3. Click margins gallery.
4. Click *Custom Margins*.
5. Change margin options as desired.
6. Click OK.

In Addition

Printing Column or Row Headings on Multiple Pages

Use the Print Titles button in the Page Setup group on the PAGE LAYOUT tab to define column or row headings that you want repeated at the top or left edge of each page to make the data in rows and columns in a multipage printout easier to identify.

Using Page Layout View; Inserting Headers and Footers

Page Layout view allows you to view the worksheet along with the print settings. Page Layout view also displays horizontal and vertical rulers to assist with measurements. A *header* is text that prints at the top of each worksheet and a *footer* is text that prints at the bottom of each worksheet. Excel includes pre-defined headers and footers you can select from a drop-down list or you can create your own custom header or footer text.

Project Before printing the profit-sharing bonus worksheet completed earlier, you want to add identifying information in a custom header and footer and check other print options using Page Layout view.

SNAP

Tutorial 3.12
Inserting Headers and Footers

1. Open **ES3-WBEmpBonus.xlsx**.

2. Click the Page Layout button located at the right side of the Status bar near the Zoom slider bar.

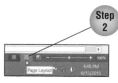

Step 2

3. If necessary, use the horizontal and vertical scroll bars to adjust the window so that the worksheet, including the white space for the top, left, and right margins, is entirely visible.

4. Hover your mouse over the text *Click to add header* near the top center of the page.

Step 4

Headers and footers are divided into three boxes. Click in the desired box and then type text or insert header and footer elements. By default, text in the left box is left-aligned, text in the center box is centered, and text in the right box is right-aligned.

5. Click in the left header box and then type your first and last names.

Step 5

6. Click in the right header box, type **Date Printed:**, and then press the spacebar once.

7. Click the Current Date button in the Header & Footer Elements group on the HEADER & FOOTER TOOLS DESIGN tab.

Excel inserts the code *&[Date]*, which causes the current date to be inserted at the location of the code when the worksheet is printed.

Step 7

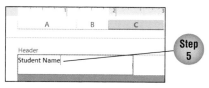

Step 6

8 Click the Go to Footer button in the Navigation group on the HEADER & FOOTER TOOLS DESIGN tab.

> The right footer box at the bottom of the page opens for editing.

Step 8

9 Click in the center footer box to open the box for editing.

Steps 9-10

10 Click the File Name button in the Header & Footer Elements group.

> Excel inserts the code *&[File]*, which causes the workbook file name to be inserted at the location of the code when the worksheet is printed.

11 Click anywhere in the worksheet area outside the footer to close the footer section.

12 Scroll to the top of the worksheet to view the header. Notice that Excel now displays the current date in place of the *&[Date]* code.

13 Look at the bottom of the worksheet and notice that the *&[File]* code now displays the workbook file name.

14 Click the PAGE LAYOUT tab.

> By default, the header and footer margin is 0.3 inch. In the next step, you will adjust the header and footer margins to provide more white space at the top and bottom of the page.

15 Click the Margins button in the Page Setup group and then click *Custom Margins* at the drop-down list. Change the margin settings as indicated below at the Page Setup dialog box with the Margins tab active:

Top:	**1**	*Header:*	**0.5**
Bottom:	**1**	*Footer:*	**0.5**
Left:	**1**		

16 Click OK to close the Page Setup dialog box.

17 Review the new margin settings in Page Layout view.

Step 17

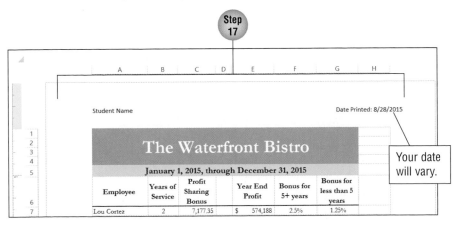

> Your date will vary.

18 Print the worksheet.

19 Click the Normal button located at the right side of the Status bar near the Zoom slider bar (immediately left of the Page Layout button).

20 Save and then close **ES3-WBEmpBonus.xlsx**.

In Brief

Insert Header or Footer
1. Switch to Page Layout view.
2. Click over *Click to add header* or *Click to add footer*.
3. Insert desired header and footer elements and/or type text in left, center, or right section.
4. Click in the worksheet area to end header or footer editing.

Features Summary

Feature	Ribbon Tab, Group	Button
change margins	PAGE LAYOUT, Page Setup OR FILE, *Print*	
create a column chart	INSERT, Charts	
create a line chart	INSERT, Charts	
create a pie chart	INSERT, Charts	
Date & Time functions	FORMULAS, Function Library	
draw a shape	INSERT, Illustrations	
Financial functions	FORMULAS, Function Library	
insert function	FORMULAS, Function Library	
insert header or footer	INSERT, Text OR Page Layout view	
Logical functions	FORMULAS, Function Library	
Page Layout view	VIEW, Workbook Views	OR
scale page width and/or height	PAGE LAYOUT, Scale to Fit OR FILE, *Print*	
Statistical functions	FORMULAS, Function Library	

Knowledge Check SNAP

Completion: In the space provided at the right, indicate the correct term, command, or option.

1. This symbol next to a column or row number means the reference is absolute.
2. AVERAGE and COUNT are two of the functions grouped in this function category.
3. This Date and Time function inserts the current date (without the time) in the active cell.
4. This financial function returns the payment for a loan based on a constant interest rate and period of time for repayment.
5. A range name is typed in this box at the left end of the Formula bar.
6. The IF function is found in this category of functions in the Function Library group.
7. This type of chart is used to illustrate each data point as a proportion of the total.

8. When a chart is selected, these two additional tabs appear. _____
9. The Shapes button is located in this group on the INSERT tab. _____
10. Page Setup options such as custom margins can be changed using the PAGE LAYOUT tab or while viewing a preview of how the worksheet will print in this area. _____
11. You can type header or footer text directly in the worksheet while viewing the worksheet in this view. _____
12. This code is inserted in the header or footer when you click the File Name button in the Header & Footer Elements group. _____

Skills Review

Review 1 Inserting Statistical, Date, and IF Functions; Creating Range Names; Changing Page Layout Options

1. Open **WBQtrRev.xlsx** and then save the workbook in the ExcelEOS folder and name it **ES3-R-WBQtrRev**.
2. Make cell B14 active and then insert a formula that finds the average of cells B4:B8.
3. Copy the formula in cell B14 to cells C14:E14.
4. Make cell B15 active and then insert a formula that finds the maximum quarterly revenue of cells B4:B8.
5. Copy the formula in cell B15 to cells C15:E15.
6. Make cell B16 active and then insert a formula that finds the minimum quarterly revenue of cells B4:B8.
7. Copy the formula in cell B16 to cells C16:E16.
8. Select cells F4:F8 and name the range *TotalRev*.
9. Make cell B18 active and then insert a formula that finds the average of the totals in the TotalRev range.
10. Make cell B20 active and then name the cell *MinTarget*.
11. Make cell B21 active and then calculate the amount under target the quarter's total revenue by entering the IF formula: **=IF(b10<mintarget,b10-mintarget,0)**.
12. Copy the IF formula in cell B21 to cells C21:E21.
13. Make cell B23 active and then format the date in the cell to display as *#/##/##*.
14. Make cell B24 active and then insert a formula that adds 350 days to the date in cell B23.
14. Change the page orientation to landscape.
15. Change the top margin to 1.5 inches and center the worksheet horizontally.
16. Display the worksheet in Page Layout view and then create a header that prints your first and last names at the left margin and the current date at the right margin.
17. Create a footer that prints the file name at the bottom center of the page.
18. Save and then print **ES3-R-WBQtrRev.xlsx**.

Review 2 Creating Charts; Drawing Shapes

1. With **ES3-R-WBQtrRev.xlsx** open, select the range A3:E8 and then create a column chart with the following options:
   a. Click the *Clustered Column* chart, the first chart option in the *2-D Column* section.
   b. Move the chart to a new sheet with the sheet label *ColumnChart*.
   c. Apply the Layout 5 quick layout.
   d. Apply the Style 6 chart style.
   e. Change the chart title to *Quarterly Revenue Budget Forecast*.
   f. Select and then delete the Axis Title box that displays rotated at the left side of the chart.
2. Print the ColumnChart sheet.
3. Make Sheet1 the active sheet, select the ranges A3:A8 and F3:F8, and then create a pie chart with the following options:
   a. Click the *Pie* option in the *2-D Pie* section.
   b. Move the chart to a new sheet with the sheet label *PieChart*.
   c. Apply the Layout 6 quick layout.
   d. Apply the Style 3 chart style.
   e. Change the chart title to *Total Revenue Budget Forecast*.
   f. Select the legend and then change the font size to 11 points.
4. With PieChart the active sheet, draw an *Up Arrow Callout* shape (last shape in second row in the *Block Arrows* group) in the pie chart with the following specifications:
   a. Select the *Up Arrow Callout* shape and then click directly below the *55%* in the Dining room pie slice.
   b. Change the height of the shape to 1.4 inches and the width to 1.6 inches.
   c. Type the text **This is a 10% increase over last year!** inside the up arrow callout shape.
   d. Position the arrow below *55%* with the tip of the arrow touching the middle of the bottom border of the *55%*.
   e. With the shape selected, click the HOME tab, click the Bold button in the Font group, and then click the Center button and the Middle Align button in the Alignment group.
5. Print the PieChart sheet.
6. Save and then close **ES3-R-WBQtrRev.xlsx**.

Skills Assessment

Note: If you submit your work in hard copy, check with your instructor before completing these Assessments to find out if you need to print two copies of each worksheet with one of the copies showing the cell formulas instead of the calculated results.

Assessment 1 Creating Statistical and IF Functions; Using Absolute References

1. Alex Torres, manager of the Toronto office for First Choice Travel, has started a workbook to calculate sales commission for the Toronto sales agents. First Choice Travel has implemented a new bonus commission based upon the number of cruises booked. Alex has asked for your help in writing the correct formulas to calculate the commission owed to the agents and analyze the results. To begin, open **FCTSalesComm.xlsx** and then save the workbook in the ExcelEOS folder, naming it **ES3-A1-FCTSalesComm**.

2. Make cell D4 active and then write an IF statement using the information in the Commission table in cells F2:G4. Write the IF statement so if the number of cruises booked is greater than 2 then multiply the total value of travel bookings by the commission percentage in G4 and if the condition is not met, then insert a zero. You will be copying the formula so cell G4 in the formula needs to be an absolute reference.
3. Copy the IF function in cell D4 to the remaining rows in column D.
4. Format the values in column D to match the formatting of the numbers in column B.
5. Enter **Average commission** in cell B20 and create a function in cell D20 to calculate the average commission paid. Enter **Maximum commission** in cell B21 and create a function in cell D21 to show the highest commission paid.
6. Change the page orientation to landscape.
7. Change the top margin to 1.25 inches and the left margin to 1.5 inches.
8. Save, print, and then close **ES3-A1-FCTSalesComm.xlsx**.

Assessment 2 Applying the PMT Function

1. You are the assistant to Sam Vestering, manager of North American Distribution for Worldwide Enterprises. Sam has entered in a workbook details on financing from two companies for an office expansion loan. Sam would like you to enter the formulas to calculate the estimated monthly loan payments and the total cost of each loan. To begin, open **WELoan.xlsx** and then save the workbook in the ExcelEOS folder, naming it **ES3-A2-WELoan**.
2. Calculate the monthly payments on the loan in cells B7 and D7.
3. Calculate the total payments required for each loan in cells B11 and D11.
4. Save, print, and then close **ES3-A2-WELoan.xlsx**.

Assessment 3 Creating Charts; Drawing Shapes

1. Cal Rubine, chair of the Theatre Arts Division at Niagara Peninsula College, has asked you to create charts from the grades analysis report to present at a divisional meeting. After reviewing the grades, you decide to create a line chart depicting the grades for all of the courses and a pie chart summarizing the total grades. To begin, open **NPCGrades.xlsx** and then save the workbook in the ExcelEOS folder, naming it **ES3-A3-NPCGrades**.
2. Create a line chart in a new sheet labeled *LineChart* that displays the number of A+ through F grades earned for all five courses. Include an appropriate chart title. You determine the line chart style, layout, and any other chart elements and formats that will make the chart easy to interpret.
3. Create a 3-D pie chart that displays the total of each grade as a percentage of 100. *Hint: Select the ranges B4:G4 and B11:G11 to create the chart*. Include an appropriate chart title and display percents around the outside of the pie slices as well as the Category names. Position the pie chart below the grades worksheet starting in row 14.
4. In the white space at the top left of the chart, draw a right-pointing block arrow pointing to the percent value above the pie slice for the F grade. Inside the block arrow type the text **Lowest failure rate since 2011!** If necessary, format the text to a smaller font to fit the text within the available space.
5. Print the worksheet centered horizontally and print the line chart.
6. Save and then close **ES3-A3-NPCGrades.xlsx**.

Assessment 4 Creating Charts; Changing Page Layout; Inserting a Footer

1. Melissa Gehring, manager of the Los Angeles office for First Choice Travel, has prepared a workbook with European destinations and current package pricing options. Melissa wants you to create two charts and improve the appearance of the worksheet before she presents it at the next staff meeting. To begin, open **FCTEurope.xlsx** and then save the workbook in the ExcelEOS folder, naming it **ES3-A4-FCTEurope**.

2. Insert a new row at the beginning of the worksheet and add the title *European Packages* merged and centered over the worksheet.

3. Increase the height of row 1 to *27.00 points (36 pixels)*.

4. Apply the Slice theme to the worksheet.

5. Apply the Title style to cell A1, the Accent2 style to the range A2:G2, and the Accent1 cell style to the range A3:G3.

6. Format the values in B4:G13 to comma style format with zero decimals.

7. Create a 3-D Clustered Bar bar chart in a new sheet labeled *14NightsChart* that graphs the standard and deluxe rates for all of the destinations for 14 nights. Add an appropriate title to the chart and make any other formatting choices you think would enhance the chart.

8. Print the 14NightsChart sheet.

9. Create a 3-D Clustered Bar bar chart in a new sheet labeled *21NightsChart* that graphs the standard and deluxe rates for all of the destinations for 21 nights. Add an appropriate title to the chart and make any other formatting choices you think would enhance the chart.

10. Print the 21NightsChart sheet.

11. Make Sheet1 the active sheet, change the page orientation to landscape, change the top margin to 1.5 inches, and center the worksheet horizontally.

12. Create a custom footer that prints your name at the left margin and the file name at the right margin.

13. Print Sheet1.

14. Save and then close **ES3-A4-FCTEurope.xlsx**.

Assessment 5 Finding Information on Chart Axis Options

1. Use the Help feature to find information on changing the vertical axis scale options in a chart. Use the text *change axis labels* as the search text.

2. Open **ES3-A4-FCTEurope.xlsx**.

3. Save the workbook in the ExcelEOS folder and name it **ES3-A5-FCTEurope**.

4. Make the 14NightsChart sheet active.

5. Using the information you learned in Help, change the value axis options so that the minimum bounds value is fixed at 1,000 and the major unit is fixed at 500. This means the value axis will start at $1,000 instead of zero and gridlines will show at every $500 interval. ***Hint: Make these changes in the Format Axis task pane with the Axis Options icon selected.***

6. Print the 14NightsChart sheet.

7. Save and then close **ES3-A5-FCTEurope.xlsx**.

Assessment 6 Individual Challenge
Social Networking Survey

1. You want to know which social networking tool and which social activity is the most popular among your friends, family, and classmates. Ask 10 to 20 friends, family, or classmates the following two questions and collect the responses in an Excel worksheet.
   a. Which of the following social networking sites do you use?

      Facebook   Instagram
      Pinterest   Twitter
   b. Which social networking activities do you do at these sites?

      Share photos   Share family updates
      Promote a blog   Share media
      Connect with people

2. Create a chart in a new sheet labeled *SocialNetSites* that displays the total users for each of the social networking sites in the first survey question. You determine the most appropriate chart type to display the survey results. Add an appropriate chart title and any other chart formatting options to enhance the chart's appearance.
3. Print the SocialNetSites sheet.
4. Create a chart in a new sheet labeled *SocialNetAct* that displays the total participants for each type of social networking activity in the second survey question. You determine the appropriate chart type to display the survey results. Add an appropriate chart title and any other chart formatting options to enhance the chart's appearance.
5. Print the SocialNetAct sheet.
6. Save the workbook and name it **ES3-A6-SocialNetSurvey**.
7. Print the worksheet with the source data for the two charts and then close **ES3-A6-SocialNetSurvey.xlsx**.

Marquee Challenge

Challenge 1 Creating Charts on Movie Attendance Statistics

1. You are working with Shannon Grey, president of Marquee Productions, on presentation materials for an upcoming staff development workshop on producing and marketing movies. As part of Shannon's research for the workshop, she compiled a workbook with statistics related to movie attendance by age group and by household income. Shannon has asked you to create two charts for the workshop based on this source data. To begin, open **MPMovieStats.xlsx** and then save the workbook in the ExcelEOS folder, naming it **ES3-C1-MPMovieStats**.

2. Using data in the workbook, create the bar chart in Figure 3.1 with the following specifications:

   a. Create a 3-D Clustered Bar chart.

   b. Move the chart to a new sheet and name the sheet *AgeChart*.

   c. Apply the Style 6 chart style.

   d. Change the font for the title to 20-point Cambria bold.

   e. Change the font for the axes (information at the left) to 12-point Cambria bold, and change the font color to White.

   f. Insert the shape with the Down Arrow Callout shape in the Block Arrows group.

   g. Make any other formatting changes so your chart looks like the chart in Figure 3.1.

3. Using data in the workbook, create the Doughnut chart in Figure 3.2 with the following specifications:

   a. Create a Doughnut chart.

   b. Move the chart to a new sheet and name the sheet *IncomeChart*.

   c. Apply the Style 3 chart style.

   d. Apply the Layout 5 chart layout.

   e. Change the font for the title to 20-point Cambria bold.

   f. Insert the shape with the 8-Point Star shape in the Stars and Banners group.

   g. Make any other formatting changes so your chart looks like the chart in Figure 3.2.

4. Save the revised workbook.

5. Print each chart and then close **ES3-C1-MPMovieStats.xlsx**.

FIGURE 3.1 Challenge 1 Bar Chart

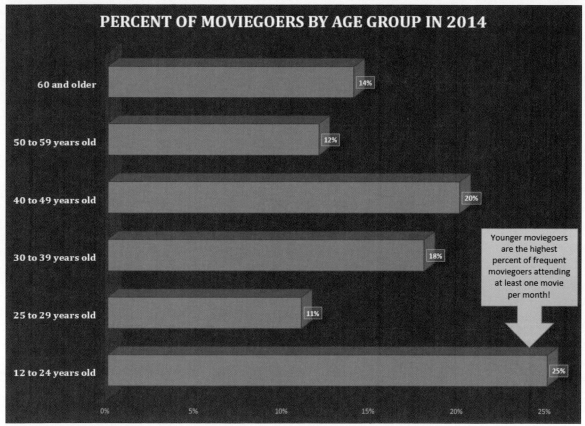

FIGURE 3.2 Challenge 1 Doughnut Chart

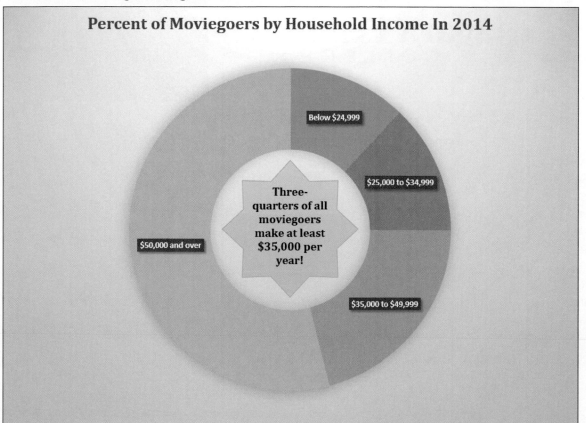

Challenge 2 Preparing an International Student Report

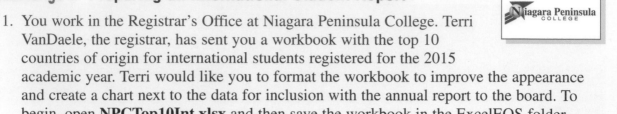

1. You work in the Registrar's Office at Niagara Peninsula College. Terri VanDaele, the registrar, has sent you a workbook with the top 10 countries of origin for international students registered for the 2015 academic year. Terri would like you to format the workbook to improve the appearance and create a chart next to the data for inclusion with the annual report to the board. To begin, open **NPCTop10Int.xlsx** and then save the workbook in the ExcelEOS folder, naming it **ES3-C2-NPCTop10Int**.
2. Using the data in the workbook, create the chart shown in Figure 3.3. Create a 2-D clustered column chart, apply the Style 4 chart style, and delete the title. Size and move the chart so it is positioned as shown in the figure.
3. Insert and position the Niagara Peninsula College logo as shown in the figure using the **NPCLogo.jpg** file.
4. Insert, move, and size the image of the students as shown in the figure. (Use the word *diversity* when searching for the image.)
5. Insert, size, and move the clip art image of the globe as shown in the figure. (Use the words *hands around globe* to find the clip art image.)
6. Make sure the workbook fits on one page. If it does not, change the page orientation to landscape.
7. Save, print, and then close **ES3-C2-NPCTop10.xlsx**.

FIGURE 3.3 Challenge 2

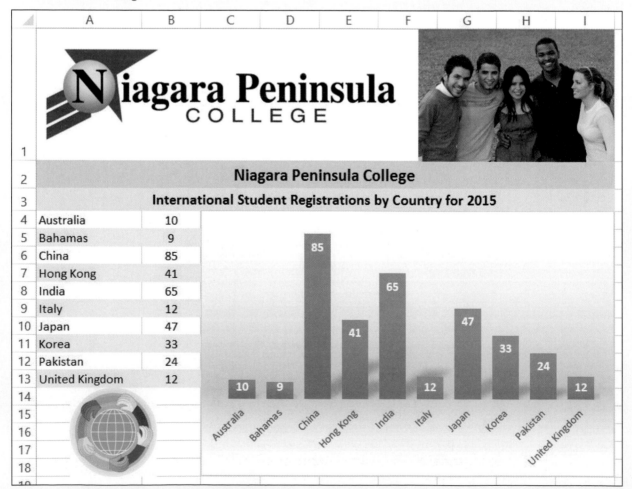

Excel SECTION 4

Working with Multiple Worksheets, Tables, and Other File Formats

Skills

- Insert, delete, and rename a worksheet
- Format worksheet tabs
- Move and copy a worksheet
- Group and ungroup worksheets
- Create 3-D references in formulas
- Link cells between worksheets
- Print multiple worksheets
- Use Page Break Preview to manipulate page breaks
- Format data as a table
- Apply table design options
- Insert rows and columns into a table
- Add a total row to a table
- Sort and filter a table by single and multiple criteria
- Insert, edit, delete, and print comments
- Create a new workbook using a template
- Save a workbook in a different file format
- Create a PDF/XPS copy of a workbook

Projects Overview

Complete the quarterly sales report and the payroll report; format, sort, filter, and insert comments in the special events section and order workbooks; create a mortgage calculator, invoice, and billing statement using templates; save the quarterly sales report in a previous version of Excel and publish the workbook in PDF format.

Create a grade summary worksheet for the Theatre Arts Co-op Internships report.

Produce a list of costumes with a final delivery date of July 9; insert comments in the production schedule section in preparation for the design team meeting; format the costume rentals report; and calculate the rental fees.

Import U.S. and Canadian distributor information from text files, combine the information into one workbook, and then format and sort the report.

Model Answers for Projects

These model answers for the projects that you complete in Section 4 provide a preview of the finished projects before you begin working and also allow you to compare your own results with these models to ensure you have created the materials accurately.

ES4-WBQtrlySales.xlsx is the project in Activities 4.1 to 4.4.

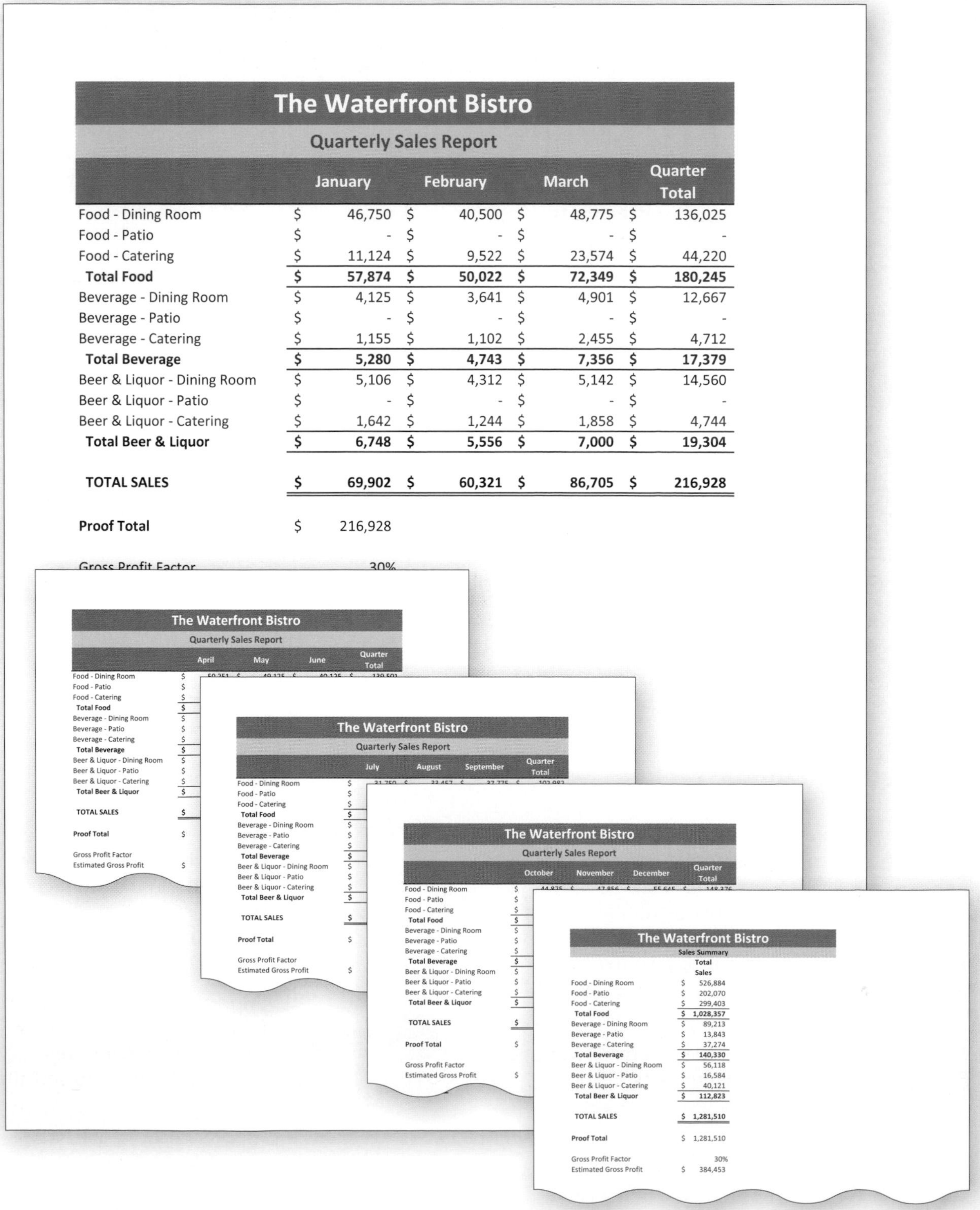

The Waterfront Bistro

Quarterly Sales Report

	January	February	March	Quarter Total
Food - Dining Room	$ 46,750	$ 40,500	$ 48,775	$ 136,025
Food - Patio	$ -	$ -	$ -	$ -
Food - Catering	$ 11,124	$ 9,522	$ 23,574	$ 44,220
Total Food	**$ 57,874**	**$ 50,022**	**$ 72,349**	**$ 180,245**
Beverage - Dining Room	$ 4,125	$ 3,641	$ 4,901	$ 12,667
Beverage - Patio	$ -	$ -	$ -	$ -
Beverage - Catering	$ 1,155	$ 1,102	$ 2,455	$ 4,712
Total Beverage	**$ 5,280**	**$ 4,743**	**$ 7,356**	**$ 17,379**
Beer & Liquor - Dining Room	$ 5,106	$ 4,312	$ 5,142	$ 14,560
Beer & Liquor - Patio	$ -	$ -	$ -	$ -
Beer & Liquor - Catering	$ 1,642	$ 1,244	$ 1,858	$ 4,744
Total Beer & Liquor	**$ 6,748**	**$ 5,556**	**$ 7,000**	**$ 19,304**
TOTAL SALES	**$ 69,902**	**$ 60,321**	**$ 86,705**	**$ 216,928**
Proof Total	$ 216,928			
Gross Profit Factor	30%			

The Waterfront Bistro

Quarterly Sales Report

	April	May	June	Quarter Total

(April–June report, values partially obscured)

The Waterfront Bistro

Quarterly Sales Report

	July	August	September	Quarter Total

(July–September report, values partially obscured)

The Waterfront Bistro

Quarterly Sales Report

	October	November	December	Quarter Total

(October–December report, values partially obscured)

The Waterfront Bistro

Sales Summary

	Total Sales
Food - Dining Room	$ 526,884
Food - Patio	$ 202,070
Food - Catering	$ 299,403
Total Food	**$ 1,028,357**
Beverage - Dining Room	$ 89,213
Beverage - Patio	$ 13,843
Beverage - Catering	$ 37,274
Total Beverage	**$ 140,330**
Beer & Liquor - Dining Room	$ 56,118
Beer & Liquor - Patio	$ 16,584
Beer & Liquor - Catering	$ 40,121
Total Beer & Liquor	**$ 112,823**
TOTAL SALES	**$ 1,281,510**
Proof Total	$ 1,281,510
Gross Profit Factor	30%
Estimated Gross Profit	$ 384,453

ES4-WBCatering.xlsx is the project in Activities 4.5 and 4.6 and part of the project in Activity 4.7.

			The Waterfront Bistro									
			Catering Contracts									
First Name	Last Name	Contact Phone	Event	Date	Room	Guests	Special Menu	Price Per Person		Contract Total	
Weston	Kressman	716 555 4219	Wedding	2/28/2015	Sunset	266	Yes	28.95	$	7,700.70
Alfonso	Ramirez	716 555 3488	Wedding	12/31/2015	Westview	160	Yes	35.95	$	5,752.00
Mario	Fontaine	716 555 1886	Engagement Party	1/20/2015	Westview	177	Yes	28.95	$	5,124.15
Zack	Doucet	716 555 3488	Wedding	6/20/2015	Sunset	168	Yes	28.95	$	4,863.60
Matteo	Limardi	716 555 9447	50th Wedding Anniversary	12/24/2015	Westview	125	Yes	35.95	$	4,493.75
Bahurai	Omkar	905 555 3411	Wedding	8/30/2015	Sunset	155	Yes	28.95	$	4,487.25
Max	Santore	905 555 3264	Wedding	4/28/2015	Sunset	157	Yes	25.95	$	4,074.15
Reed	Pavelich	716 555 2286	Wedding	7/25/2015	Starlake	110	Yes	31.95	$	3,514.50
Tao	Okinawa	716 555 1665	Wedding	12/21/2015	Westview	110	Yes	27.95	$	3,074.50
Orlando	Fagan	716 555 3694	25th Wedding Anniversary	3/10/2015	Westview	88	Yes	28.95	$	2,547.60
Omar	Hamid	716 555 8796	Engagement Party	5/8/2015	Sunset	85	Yes	28.95	$	2,460.75
Raji	Jai	716 555 6885	Baby Shower	11/6/2015	Westview	85	No	28.95	$	2,460.75
Corina	Guzman	716 555 4112	Wedding	12/22/2015	Westview	85	Yes	28.95	$	2,460.75
Elena	Alvarez	905 555 4884	Wedding	11/19/2015	Westview	112	No	21.95	$	2,458.40
Sonora	Yee	716 555 2668	Birthday Party	12/31/2015	Starlake	73	Yes	31.95	$	2,332.35
Kim	Pockovic	905 555 3698	Birthday Party	3/18/2015	Westview	62	Yes	35.95	$	2,228.90
Frances	Corriveau	716 555 3256	Birthday Party	1/23/2015	Westview	85	Yes	25.95	$	2,205.75
Elizabeth	McMaster	716 555 9442	Engagement Party	7/11/2015	Sunset	75	Yes	27.95	$	2,096.25
Percy	Bresque	716 555 1248	50th Wedding Anniversary	4/12/2015	Westview	62	Yes	32.95	$	2,042.90
Mahika	Kapoor	716 555 3669	Birthday Party	10/5/2015	Sunset	68	Yes	28.95	$	1,968.60
Nicole	Griffin	905 555 4166	25th Wedding Anniversary	6/17/2015	Starlake	54	Yes	31.95	$	1,725.30
Bogdana	Petrov	716 555 6889	Birthday Party	12/20/2015	Sunset	51	Yes	31.95	$	1,629.45
Carlotta	Balducci	716 555 9665	Birthday Party	8/22/2015	Starlake	62	Yes	25.95	$	1,608.90
Liana	Fantino	716 555 9648	25th Wedding Anniversary	11/30/2015	Sunset	54	No	28.95	$	1,563.30
Lane	Gill	416 555 3264	Business Meeting	3/29/2015	Starlake	71	No	21.95	$	1,558.45
Jesse	Golinsky	716 555 4218	Business Meeting	6/26/2015	Westview	57	No	24.95	$	1,422.15
Su-Lin	Ping	716 555 7774	Baby Shower	7/10/2015	Sunset	62	Yes	21.95	$	1,360.90
Bianca	Vargas	716 555 3884	Engagement Party	10/15/2015	Starlake	40	Yes	31.95	$	1,278.00
Walter	Szucs	905 555 6998	Birthday Party	6/10/2015	Starlake	42	No	28.95	$	1,215.90
Sofia	Delgado	716 555 8465	Birthday Party	8/10/2015	Starlake	55	No	21.95	$	1,207.25
Alfredo	Juanitez	716 555 4668	Business Meeting	7/31/2015	Westview	49	No	23.95	$	1,173.55
Franco	Costa	716 555 3345	Business Meeting	9/30/2015	Sunset	32	No	31.95	$	1,022.40
Carlo	Sanchez	905 555 6344	Business Meeting	9/10/2015	Westview	45	No	21.95	$	987.75
Dana	Russell	716 555 4965	Birthday Party	5/30/2015	Starlake	36	No	26.95	$	970.20
Mei-Yin	Zhang	716 555 2121	Business Meeting	12/1/2015	Starlake	28	Yes	31.95	$	894.60
Guido	Donato	716 555 8444	Business Meeting	10/22/2015	Westview	30	No	25.95	$	778.50
Cecily	Hillmore	716 555 6598	Business Meeting	1/15/2015	Starlake	35	No	21.95	$	768.25
Jack	Torrance	716 555 1469	Business Meeting	5/15/2015	Westview	26	No	23.95	$	622.70
Cristian	Martinez	716 555 4331	Business Meeting	12/15/2015	Starlake	18	No	31.95	$	575.10
Total						3155		28.36	$	90,710.25

The Waterfront Bistro

Catering Contracts

First Name	Last Name	Contact Phone	Event	Date	Room	Guests	Special Menu	Price Per Person		Contract Total
Nicole	Griffin	905 555 4166	25th Wedding Anniversary	6/17/2015	Starlake	54	Yes	31.95	$	1,725.30
Liana	Fantino	716 555 9648	25th Wedding Anniversary	11/30/2015	Sunset	54	No	28.95	$	1,563.30
Orlando	Fagan	716 555 3694	25th Wedding Anniversary	3/10/2015	Westview	88	Yes	28.95	$	2,547.60
Percy	Bresque	716 555 1248	50th Wedding Anniversary	4/12/2015	Westview	62	Yes	32.95	$	2,042.90
Matteo	Limardi	716 555 9447	50th Wedding Anniversary	12/24/2015	Westview	125	Yes	35.95	$	4,493.75
Su-Lin	Ping	716 555 7774	Baby Shower	7/10/2015	Sunset	62	Yes	21.95	$	1,360.90
Raji	Jai	716 555 6885	Baby Shower	11/6/2015	Westview	85	No	28.95	$	2,460.75
Dana	Russell	716 555 4965	Birthday Party	5/30/2015	Starlake	36	No	26.95	$	970.20
Walter	Szucs	905 555 6998	Birthday Party	6/10/2015	Starlake	42	No	28.95	$	1,215.90
Sofia	Delgado	716 555 8465	Birthday Party	8/10/2015	Starlake	55	No	21.95	$	1,207.25
Carlotta	Balducci	716 555 9665	Birthday Party	8/22/2015	Starlake	62	Yes	25.95	$	1,608.90
Sonora	Yee	716 555 2668	Birthday Party	12/31/2015	Starlake	73	Yes	31.95	$	2,332.35
Mahika	Kapoor	716 555 3669	Birthday Party	10/5/2015	Starlake	68	Yes	28.95	$	1,968.60
Bogdana	Petrov	716 555 6889	Birthday Party	12/20/2015	Sunset	51	Yes	31.95	$	1,629.45
Frances	Corriveau	716 555 3256	Birthday Party	1/23/2015	Westview	85	Yes	25.95	$	2,205.75
Kim	Pockovic	905 555 3698	Birthday Party	3/18/2015	Westview	62	Yes	35.95	$	2,228.90
Cecily	Hillmore	716 555 6598	Business Meeting	1/15/2015	Starlake	35	No	21.95	$	768.25
Lane	Gill	416 555 3264	Business Meeting	3/29/2015	Starlake	71	No	21.95	$	1,558.45
Mei-Yin	Zhang	716 555 2121	Business Meeting	12/1/2015	Starlake	28	Yes	31.95	$	894.60
Cristian	Martinez	716 555 4331	Business Meeting	12/15/2015	Starlake	18	No	31.95	$	575.10
Franco	Costa	716 555 3345	Business Meeting	9/30/2015	Sunset	32	No	31.95	$	1,022.40
Jack	Torrance	716 555 1469	Business Meeting	5/15/2015	Westview	26	No	23.95	$	622.70
Jesse	Golinsky	716 555 4218	Business Meeting	6/26/2015	Westview	57	No	24.95	$	1,422.15
Alfredo	Juanitez	716 555 4668	Business Meeting	7/31/2015	Westview	49	No	23.95	$	1,173.55
Carlo	Sanchez	905 555 6344	Business Meeting	9/10/2015	Westview	45	No	21.95	$	987.75
Guido	Donato	716 555 8444	Business Meeting	10/22/2015	Westview	30	No	25.95	$	778.50
Bianca	Vargas	716 555 3884	Engagement Party	10/15/2015	Starlake	40	Yes	31.95	$	1,278.00
Omar	Hamid	716 555 8796	Engagement Party	5/8/2015	Sunset	85	Yes	28.95	$	2,460.75
Elizabeth	McMaster	716 555 9442	Engagement Party	7/11/2015	Sunset	75	Yes	27.95	$	2,096.25
Mario	Fontaine	716 555 1886	Engagement Party	1/20/2015	Westview	177	Yes	28.95	$	5,124.15
Reed	Pavelich	716 555 2286	Wedding	7/25/2015	Starlake	110	Yes	31.95	$	3,514.50
Weston	Kressman	716 555 4219	Wedding	2/28/2015	Sunset	266	Yes	28.95	$	7,700.70
Max	Santore	905 555 3264	Wedding	4/28/2015	Sunset	157	Yes	25.95	$	4,074.15
Zack	Doucet	716 555 3488	Wedding	6/20/2015	Sunset	168	Yes	28.95	$	4,863.60
Bahurai	Omkar	905 555 3411	Wedding	8/30/2015	Westview	155	Yes	28.95	$	4,487.25
Elena	Alvarez	905 555 4884	Wedding	11/19/2015	Westview	112	No	21.95	$	2,458.40
Tao	Okinawa	716 555 1665	Wedding	12/21/2015	Westview	110	Yes	27.95	$	3,074.50
Corina	Guzman	716 555 4112	Wedding	12/22/2015	Westview	85	Yes	28.95	$	2,460.75
Alfonso	Ramirez	716 555 3488	Wedding	12/31/2015	Westview	160	Yes	35.95	$	5,752.00
Total						3155		28.36	$	90,710.25

ES4-WBCatering.xlsx is part of the project in Activity 4.8.

First Name	Last Name	Contact Phone	Event	Date	Room	Guests	Special Menu	Price Per Person	Contract Total
			The Waterfront Bistro						
			Catering Contracts						
Nicole	Griffin	905 555 4166	25th Wedding Anniversary	6/17/2015	Starlake	54	Yes	31.95	$ 1,725.30
Orlando	Fagan	716 555 3694	25th Wedding Anniversary	3/10/2015	Westview	88	Yes	28.95	$ 2,547.60
Percy	Bresque	716 555 1248	50th Wedding Anniversary	4/12/2015	Westview	62	Yes	32.95	$ 2,042.90
Matteo	Limardi	716 555 9447	50th Wedding Anniversary	12/24/2015	Westview	125	Yes	35.95	$ 4,493.75
Su-Lin	Ping	716 555 7774	Baby Shower	7/10/2015	Sunset	62	Yes	21.95	$ 1,360.90
Carlotta	Balducci	716 555 9665	Birthday Party	8/22/2015	Starlake	62	Yes	25.95	$ 1,608.90
Sonora	Yee	716 555 2668	Birthday Party	12/31/2015	Starlake	73	Yes	31.95	$ 2,332.35
Mahika	Kapoor	716 555 3669	Birthday Party	10/5/2015	Westview	68	Yes	28.95	$ 1,968.60
Bogdana	Petrov	716 555 6889	Birthday Party	12/20/2015	Sunset	51	Yes	31.95	$ 1,629.45
Frances	Corriveau	716 555 3256	Birthday Party	1/23/2015	Westview	85	Yes	25.95	$ 2,205.75
Kim	Pockovic	905 555 3698	Birthday Party	3/18/2015	Westview	62	Yes	35.95	$ 2,228.90
Mei-Yin	Zhang	716 555 2121	Business Meeting	12/1/2015	Starlake	28	Yes	31.95	$ 894.60
Bianca	Vargas	716 555 3884	Engagement Party	10/15/2015	Starlake	40	Yes	31.95	$ 1,278.00
Omar	Hamid	716 555 8796	Engagement Party	5/8/2015	Sunset	85	Yes	28.95	$ 2,460.75
Elizabeth	McMaster	716 555 9442	Engagement Party	7/11/2015	Sunset	75	Yes	27.95	$ 2,096.25
Mario	Fontaine	716 555 1886	Engagement Party	1/20/2015	Westview	177	Yes	28.95	$ 5,124.15
Reed	Pavelich	716 555 2286	Wedding	7/25/2015	Starlake	110	Yes	31.95	$ 3,514.50
Weston	Kressman	716 555 4219	Wedding	2/28/2015	Sunset	266	Yes	28.95	$ 7,700.70
Max	Santore	905 555 3264	Wedding	4/28/2015	Sunset	157	Yes	25.95	$ 4,074.15
Zack	Doucet	716 555 3488	Wedding	6/20/2015	Sunset	168	Yes	28.95	$ 4,863.60
Bahurai	Omkar	905 555 3411	Wedding	8/30/2015	Westview	155	Yes	28.95	$ 4,487.25
Tao	Okinawa	716 555 1665	Wedding	12/21/2015	Westview	110	Yes	27.95	$ 3,074.50
Corina	Guzman	716 555 4112	Wedding	12/22/2015	Westview	85	Yes	28.95	$ 2,460.75
Alfonso	Ramirez	716 555 3488	Wedding	12/31/2015	Westview	160	Yes	35.95	$ 5,752.00
Total						2408		29.99	$ 71,925.60

ES4-WBCatering.xlsx is part of the project in Activity 4.8.

First Name	Last Name	Contact Phone	Event	Date	Room	Guests	Special Menu	Price Per Person	Contract Total
			The Waterfront Bistro						
			Catering Contracts						
Nicole	Griffin	905 555 4166	25th Wedding Anniversary	6/17/2015	Starlake	54	Yes	31.95	$ 1,725.30
Dana	Russell	716 555 4965	Birthday Party	5/30/2015	Starlake	36	No	26.95	$ 970.20
Walter	Szucs	905 555 6998	Birthday Party	6/10/2015	Starlake	42	No	28.95	$ 1,215.90
Sofia	Delgado	716 555 8465	Birthday Party	8/10/2015	Starlake	55	No	21.95	$ 1,207.25
Carlotta	Balducci	716 555 9665	Birthday Party	8/22/2015	Starlake	62	Yes	25.95	$ 1,608.90
Sonora	Yee	716 555 2668	Birthday Party	12/31/2015	Starlake	73	Yes	31.95	$ 2,332.35
Cecily	Hillmore	716 555 6598	Business Meeting	1/15/2015	Starlake	35	No	21.95	$ 768.25
Lane	Gill	416 555 3264	Business Meeting	3/29/2015	Starlake	71	No	21.95	$ 1,558.45
Mei-Yin	Zhang	716 555 2121	Business Meeting	12/1/2015	Starlake	28	Yes	31.95	$ 894.60
Cristian	Martinez	716 555 4331	Business Meeting	12/15/2015	Starlake	18	No	31.95	$ 575.10
Bianca	Vargas	716 555 3884	Engagement Party	10/15/2015	Starlake	40	Yes	31.95	$ 1,278.00
Reed	Pavelich	716 555 2286	Wedding	7/25/2015	Starlake	110	Yes	31.95	$ 3,514.50
Total						624		28.28	$ 17,648.80

ES4-WBCatering.xlsx is part of the project in Activity 4.8.

First Name	Last Name	Contact Phone	Event	Date	Room	Guests	Special Menu	Price Per Person	Contract Total
			The Waterfront Bistro						
			Catering Contracts						
Weston	Kressman	716 555 4219	Wedding	2/28/2015	Sunset	266	Yes	28.95	$ 7,700.70
Max	Santore	905 555 3264	Wedding	4/28/2015	Sunset	157	Yes	25.95	$ 4,074.15
Zack	Doucet	716 555 3488	Wedding	6/20/2015	Sunset	168	Yes	28.95	$ 4,863.60
Total						591		27.95	$ 16,638.45

The Waterfront Bistro

Catering Contracts

First Name	Last Name	Contact Phone	Event	Date	Room	Guests	Special Menu	Price Per Person	Contract Total
Nicole	Griffin	905 555 4166	25th Wedding Anniversary	6/17/2015	Starlake	54	Yes	31.95	$ 1,725.30
Liana	Fantino	716 555 9648	25th Wedding Anniversary	11/30/2015	Sunset	54	No	28.95	$ 1,563.30
Orlando	Fagan	716 555 3694	25th Wedding Anniversary	3/10/2015	Westview	88	Yes	28.95	$ 2,547.60
Percy	Bresque	716 555 1248	50th Wedding Anniversary	4/12/2015	Westview	62	Yes	32.95	$ 2,042.90
Matteo	Limardi	716 555 9447	50th Wedding Anniversary	12/24/2015	Westview	125	Yes	35.95	$ 4,493.75
Su-Lin	Ping	716 555 7774	Baby Shower	7/10/2015	Sunset	62	Yes	21.95	$ 1,360.90
Raji	Jai	716 555 6885	Baby Shower	11/6/2015	Westview	85		28.95	$ 2,460.75
Dana	Russell	716 555 4965	Birthday Party	5/30/2015	Starlake	36		26.95	$ 970.20
Walter	Szucs	905 555 6998	Birthday Party	6/10/2015	Starlake	42		28.95	$ 1,215.90
Sofia	Delgado	716 555 8465	Birthday Party	8/10/2015	Starlake	55		21.95	$ 1,207.25
Carlotta	Balducci	716 555 9665	Birthday Party	8/22/2015	Starlake	62	Yes	25.95	$ 1,608.90
Sonora	Yee	716 555 2668	Birthday Party	12/31/2015	Starlake	73	Yes	31.95	$ 2,332.35
Mahika	Kapoor	716 555 3669	Birthday Party	10/5/2015	Sunset	68	Yes	28.95	$ 1,968.60
Bogdana	Petrov	716 555 6889	Birthday Party	12/20/2015	Sunset	51	Yes	31.95	$ 1,629.45
Frances	Corriveau	716 555 3256	Birthday Party	1/23/2015	Westview	85	Yes	25.95	$ 2,205.75
Kim	Pockovic	905 555 3698	Birthday Party	3/18/2015	Westview	62	Yes		2,228.90
Cecily	Hillmore	716 555 6598	Business Meeting	1/15/2015	Starlake	35	No		768.25
Lane	Gill	416 555 3264	Business Meeting	3/29/2015	Starlake	71	No		1,558.45
Mei-Yin	Zhang	716 555 2121	Business Meeting	12/1/2015	Starlake	28	Yes		894.60
Cristian	Martinez	716 555 4331	Business Meeting	12/15/2015	Starlake	18	No	31.95	$ 575.10
Franco	Costa	716 555 3345	Business Meeting	9/30/2015	Sunset	32	No	31.95	$ 1,022.40
Jack	Torrance	716 555 1469	Business Meeting	5/15/2015	Westview	26	No	23.95	$ 622.70
Jesse	Golinsky	716 555 4218	Business Meeting	6/26/2015	Westview	57	No	24.95	$ 1,422.15
Alfredo	Juanitez	716 555 4668	Business Meeting	7/31/2015	Westview	49	No	23.95	$ 1,173.55
Carlo	Sanchez	905 555 6344	Business Meeting	9/10/2015	Westview	45	No	21.95	$ 987.75
Guido	Donato	716 555 8444	Business Meeting	10/22/2015	Westview	30	No	25.95	$ 778.50
Bianca	Vargas	716 555 3884	Engagement Party	10/15/2015	Starlake	40	Yes	31.95	$ 1,278.00
Omar	Hamid	716 555 8796	Engagement Party	5/8/2015	Sunset	85	Yes	28.95	$ 2,460.75
Elizabeth	McMaster	716 555 9442	Engagement Party	7/11/2015	Sunset	75	Yes	27.95	$ 2,096.25
Mario	Fontaine	716 555 1886	Engagement Party	1/20/2015	Westview	177	Yes	28.95	$ 5,124.15
Reed	Pavelich	716 555 2286	Wedding	7/25/2015	Starlake	110	Yes	31.95	$ 3,514.50
Weston	Kressman	716 555 4219	Wedding	2/28/2015	Sunset	266	Yes	28.95	$ 7,700.70
Max	Santore	905 555 3264	Wedding	4/28/2015	Sunset	157	Yes	25.95	$ 4,074.15
Zack	Doucet	716 555 3488	Wedding	6/20/2015	Sunset	168	Yes	28.95	$ 4,863.60
Bahurai	Omkar	905 555 3411	Wedding	8/30/2015	Westview	155	Yes	28.95	$ 4,487.25
Elena	Alvarez	905 555 4884	Wedding	11/19/2015	Westview	112	No	21.95	$ 2,458.40
Tao	Okinawa	716 555 1665	Wedding	12/21/2015	Westview	110	Yes	27.95	$ 3,074.50
Corina	Guzman	716 555 4112	Wedding	12/22/2015	Westview	85	Yes	28.95	$ 2,460.75
Alfonso	Ramirez	716 555 3488	Wedding	12/31/2015	Westview	160	Yes	35.95	$ 5,752.00
Total						3155		28.36	$ 90,710.25

Student Name: Waiting for Frances to confirm the final number of guests.

Student Name: Remind Pierre that six guests require a diabetic menu.

ES4-WBMortgageLoan.xlsx **is the project in Activity 4.10.**

MORTGAGE LOAN CALCULATOR

inputs			key stastistics			optional inputs		
Mortgage Amount	$529,000		Monthly Loan Payment	$2,573		Loan Start Date	9/29/2012	
			Total Monthly Payments	$1,135,790				
Interest Rate	4.8%		Total Loan Payments	$823,657		Property Tax Rate	1.50%	
			Total Interest Paid	$358,944				
Duration of Loan (in months)	320		Months Reduced by Extra Payments	1		Property Tax Amount	$661	
			Total Extra Payments	$200				
Loan Amount	$464,000		Interest Saved	$513		PMI Rate	5.0%	
						PMI Amount	$1,933	

⬆ If you pay **25% more** each month, your loan duration will decrease to 215 months and your payment duration will decrease by 32.8%

#	payment date	opening balance	interest	principal	extra payments	property tax	pmi	total payments	closing balance	# remaining
1	9/29/2012	$464,000.00	$1,856.00	$717.30	$100.00	$661.25	$1,933.33	$5,267.89	$463,182.70	319
2	10/29/2012	$463,182.70	$1,852.73	$720.57	$100.00	$661.25	$1,933.33	$5,267.89	$462,362.12	318
3	11/29/2012	$462,362.12	$1,849.45	$723.85		$661.25	$1,933.33	$5,167.89	$461,638.27	317
4	12/29/2012	$461,638.27	$1,846.55	$726.75		$661.25	$1,933.33	$5,167.89	$460,911.52	316
5	1/29/2013	$460,911.52	$1,843.65	$729.66		$661.25	$1,933.33	$5,167.89	$460,181.86	315
6	2/28/2013	$460,181.86	$1,840.73	$732.58		$661.25	$1,933.33	$5,167.89	$459,449.29	314
7	3/28/2013	$459,449.29	$1,837.80	$735.51		$661.25	$1,933.33	$5,167.89	$458,713.78	313
8	4/28/2013	$458,713.78	$1,834.86	$738.45		$661.25	$1,933.33	$5,167.89	$457,975.33	312
9	5/28/2013	$457,975.33	$1,831.90	$741.40		$661.25	$1,933.33	$5,167.89	$457,233.93	311
10	6/28/2013	$457,233.93	$1,828.94	$744.37		$661.25	$1,933.33	$5,167.89	$456,489.56	310
11	7/28/2013	$456,489.56	$1,825.96	$747.35		$661.25	$1,933.33	$5,167.89	$455,742.22	309
12	8/28/2013	$455,742.22	$1,822.97	$750.33		$661.25	$1,933.33	$5,167.89	$454,991.88	308
13	9/28/2013	$454,991.88	$1,819.97	$753.34		$661.25	$1,933.33	$5,167.89	$454,238.55	307
14	10/28/2013	$454,238.55	$1,816.95	$756.35		$661.25	$1,933.33	$5,167.89	$453,482.20	306
15	11/28/2013	$453,482.20	$1,813.93	$759.37		$661.25	$1,933.33	$5,167.89	$452,722.82	305
16	12/28/2013	$452,722.82	$1,810.89	$762.41		$661.25	$1,933.33	$5,167.89	$451,960.41	304
17	1/28/2014	$451,960.41	$1,807.84	$765.46		$661.25	$1,933.33	$5,167.89	$451,194.95	303
18	2/28/2014	$451,194.95	$1,804.78	$768.52		$661.25	$1,933.33	$5,167.89	$450,426.42	302
19	3/28/2014	$450,426.42	$1,801.71	$771.60		$661.25	$1,933.33	$5,167.89	$449,654.83	301
20	4/28/2014	$449,654.83	$1,798.62	$774.68		$661.25	$1,933.33	$5,167.89	$448,880.14	300
21	5/28/2014	$448,880.14	$1,795.52	$777.78		$661.25	$1,933.33	$5,167.89	$448,102.36	299
22	6/28/2014	$448,102.36	$1,792.41	$780.89		$661.25	$1,933.33	$5,167.89	$447,321.47	298
23	7/28/2014	$447,321.47	$1,789.29	$784.02		$661.25	$1,933.33	$5,167.89	$446,537.45	297
24	8/28/2014	$446,537.45	$1,786.15	$787.15		$661.25	$1,933.33	$5,167.89	$445,750.29	296
25	9/28/2014	$445,750.29	$1,783.00	$790.30		$661.25	$1,933.33	$5,167.89	$444,959.99	295
26	10/28/2014	$444,959.99	$1,779.84	$793.46		$661.25	$1,933.33	$5,167.89	$444,166.53	294
27	11/28/2014	$444,166.53	$1,776.67	$796.64		$661.25	$1,933.33	$5,167.89	$443,369.89	293
28	12/28/2014	$443,369.89	$1,773.48	$799.82		$661.25	$1,933.33	$5,167.89	$442,570.07	292
29	1/28/2015	$442,570.07	$1,770.28	$803.02		$661.25	$1,933.33	$5,167.89	$441,767.04	291
30	2/28/2015	$441,767.04	$1,767.07	$806.24		$661.25	$1,933.33	$5,167.89	$440,960.81	290
31	3/28/2015	$440,960.81	$1,763.84	$809.46		$661.25	$1,933.33	$5,167.89	$440,151.35	289
32	4/28/2015	$440,151.35	$1,760.61	$812.70		$661.25	$1,933.33	$5,167.89	$439,338.65	288
33	5/28/2015	$439,338.65	$1,757.35	$815.95		$661.25	$1,933.33	$5,167.89	$438,522.70	287
34	6/28/2015	$438,522.70	$1,754.09	$819.21		$661.25	$1,933.33	$5,167.89	$437,703.49	286
35	7/28/2015	$437,703.49	$1,750.81	$822.49		$661.25	$1,933.33	$5,167.89	$436,881.00	285
36	8/28/2015	$436,881.00	$1,747.52	$825.78		$661.25	$1,933.33	$5,167.89	$436,055.22	284
37	9/28/2015	$436,055.22	$1,744.22	$829.08		$661.25	$1,933.33	$5,167.89	$435,226.14	283
38	10/28/2015	$435,226.14	$1,740.90	$832.40		$661.25	$1,933.33	$5,167.89	$434,393.74	282
39	11/28/2015	$434,393.74	$1,737.57	$835.73		$661.25	$1,933.33	$5,167.89	$433,558.01	281
40	12/28/2015	$433,558.01	$1,734.23	$839.07		$661.25	$1,933.33	$5,167.89	$432,718.94	280
41	1/28/2016	$432,718.94	$1,730.88	$842.43		$661.25	$1,933.33	$5,167.89	$431,876.51	279
42	2/28/2016	$431,876.51	$1,727.51	$845.80		$661.25	$1,933.33	$5,167.89	$431,030.71	278
43	3/28/2016	$431,030.71	$1,724.12	$849.18		$661.25	$1,933.33	$5,167.89	$430,181.53	277
44	4/28/2016	$430,181.53	$1,720.73	$852.58		$661.25	$1,933.33	$5,167.89	$429,328.96	276
45	5/28/2016	$429,328.96	$1,717.32	$855.99		$661.25	$1,933.33	$5,167.89	$428,472.97	275
46	6/28/2016	$428,472.97	$1,713.89	$859.41		$661.25	$1,933.33	$5,167.89	$427,613.56	274
47	7/28/2016	$427,613.56	$1,710.45	$862.85		$661.25	$1,933.33	$5,167.89	$426,750.71	273
48	8/28/2016	$426,750.71	$1,707.00	$866.30		$661.25	$1,933.33	$5,167.89	$425,884.41	272
49	9/28/2016	$425,884.41	$1,703.54	$869.77		$661.25	$1,933.33	$5,167.89	$425,014.64	271

Page 1 of 6

The Waterfront Bistro

Quarterly Sales Report

	January		February		March		Quarter Total
Food - Dining Room	$	46,750	$	40,500	$	48,775	$ 136,025
Food - Patio	$	-	$	-	$	-	$ -
Food - Catering	$	11,124	$	9,522	$	23,574	$ 44,220
Total Food	**$**	**57,874**	**$**	**50,022**	**$**	**72,349**	**$ 180,245**
Beverage - Dining Room	$	4,125	$	3,641	$	4,901	$ 12,667
Beverage - Patio	$	-	$	-	$	-	$ -
Beverage - Catering	$	1,155	$	1,102	$	2,455	$ 4,712
Total Beverage	**$**	**5,280**	**$**	**4,743**	**$**	**7,356**	**$ 17,379**
Beer & Liquor - Dining Room	$	5,106	$	4,312	$	5,142	$ 14,560
Beer & Liquor - Patio	$	-	$	-	$	-	$ -
Beer & Liquor - Catering	$	1,642	$	1,244	$	1,858	$ 4,744
Total Beer & Liquor	**$**	**6,748**	**$**	**5,556**	**$**	**7,000**	**$ 19,304**
TOTAL SALES	**$**	**69,902**	**$**	**60,321**	**$**	**86,705**	**$ 216,928**

Proof Total	$	216,928
Gross Profit Factor		30%
Estimated Gross Profit	$	65,078

EXCEL SECTION 4
Project Model Answers

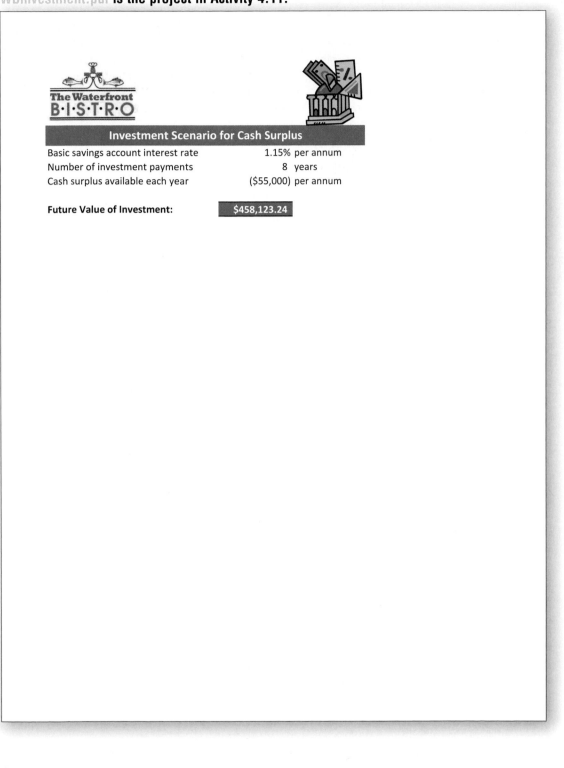

The Waterfront
B·I·S·T·R·O

Investment Scenario for Cash Surplus	
Basic savings account interest rate	1.15% per annum
Number of investment payments	8 years
Cash surplus available each year	($55,000) per annum
Future Value of Investment:	$458,123.24

Activity 4.1

Inserting, Deleting, Renaming, and Formatting Worksheet Tabs

A new workbook initially contains only one worksheet named Sheet1. Additional worksheets can be added as needed. Organizing large amounts of data by grouping related topics in individual worksheets makes the task of creating, editing, and analyzing data more manageable. For example, you could keep track of your test grades in one worksheet and assignment grades in another. A summary worksheet at the beginning or end of the workbook would be used to consolidate the test and assignment grades and calculate a final grade. By breaking down the data into smaller units, you are able to view, enter, and edit cells quickly. Format worksheet tabs using different colors to visually group related sheets.

Project

Dana Hirsch has asked you to complete the quarterly sales report workbook. To begin this project, you will insert, rename, and delete a worksheet and then organize the worksheets by applying color to the worksheet tabs.

The Waterfront B·I·S·T·R·O

SNAP

Tutorial 4.1
Inserting, Moving, Renaming, and Deleting a Worksheet

1. Open **WBQtrlySales.xlsx**.

    Two additional worksheets were added to this workbook.

2. Save the workbook in the ExcelS4 folder, naming it **ES4-WBQtrlySales**.

3. Click the Qtr2 worksheet tab and then view the worksheet.

4. Click the Sheet1 worksheet tab and then view the worksheet.

    The quarterly sales report has been organized with each quarter's sales in a separate worksheet. In the next step, you will insert a worksheet for the fourth quarter.

5. Click the New sheet button ⊕ located to the right of the Sheet1 worksheet tab.

    Clicking the New sheet button inserts a new worksheet at the end of the existing worksheets. In the next step, you will insert at the beginning of the workbook a new worksheet that will be used to summarize the sales data from the four quarters.

6. Right-click the Qtr1 worksheet tab.

    Right-clicking a worksheet tab activates the worksheet and displays the shortcut menu.

7. Click *Insert* at the shortcut menu.

8. With *Worksheet* already selected in the Insert dialog box, click OK.

    Five worksheets now exist in the workbook: Sheet3, Qtr1, Qtr2, Sheet1, and Sheet2.

9. Right-click the Sheet3 worksheet tab and then click *Rename* at the shortcut menu.

    This selects the current worksheet name in the worksheet tab.

10 Type **Summary** and then press Enter.

11 Double-click the Sheet1 worksheet tab.

> You can also rename a worksheet by double-clicking the worksheet tab.

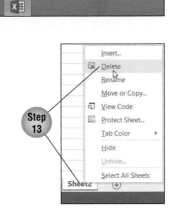

Step 10

12 Type **Qtr3** and then press Enter.

13 Right-click the Sheet2 worksheet tab and then click *Delete* at the shortcut menu.

> You can also delete the active worksheet by clicking the Delete button arrow in the Cells group on the HOME tab and then clicking *Delete Sheet* at the drop-down list. If the worksheet contains data, a message box appears warning you that data may exist in the sheet and you will have to confirm the deletion. Be careful when deleting worksheets since Undo does not restore a deleted sheet.

Step 13

14 Right-click the Summary worksheet tab to make the Summary worksheet active and display the shortcut menu.

15 Point to *Tab Color* and then click the *Dark Red* color (first option in the *Standard Colors* section).

> Changing the color of worksheet tabs can help to visually identify related worksheets or the organizational structure of the workbook.

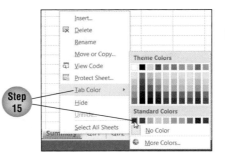

Step 15

16 Right-click the Qtr1 worksheet tab, point to *Tab Color*, and then click the *Purple* color (last option in the *Standard Colors* section).

17 Repeat Step 16 for the Qtr2 and Qtr3 worksheet tabs.

> The three worksheets containing the quarterly sales data are now organized with the same worksheet tab color (purple). The worksheet that will later contain the summary data for the entire year is differentiated by the dark red tab color.

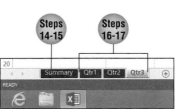

Steps 14-15   Steps 16-17

18 Save **ES4-WBQtrlySales.xlsx**.

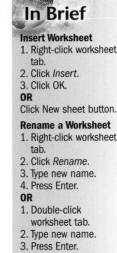
In Addition

Worksheet Tab Scrolling Buttons

The worksheet tab scrolling buttons are located at the left edge of the horizontal scroll bar as shown below. Use these buttons if there are more tabs than currently displayed. Click the Previous button to display the previous worksheet tab and click the Next button to display the next worksheet tab. To display the first worksheet tab, hold down the Ctrl key and click the Previous button. Hold down the Ctrl key and click the Next button to display the last worksheet tab. Drag the tab split box to the right or left to increase or decrease the number of worksheet tabs displayed or to change the size of the horizontal scroll bar.

tab scrolling buttons   tab split box

Activity 4.2

Moving and Copying Worksheets; Grouping and Ungrouping Worksheets

Drag a worksheet tab to move a worksheet to a different position within the workbook. Hold down the Ctrl key while dragging a worksheet tab to copy it. Exercise caution when moving or copying a worksheet since calculations may become inaccurate after the worksheet has been repositioned or copied. A workbook with multiple worksheets that all have similar column and row structures can have formatting options applied to all worksheets in one step by first grouping the worksheets.

Project

The Waterfront B·I·S·T·R·O

SNAP

Tutorial 4.2
Formatting and Printing Multiple Worksheets

Continue your work on the quarterly sales report by copying the Qtr3 worksheet, renaming the sheet, and then entering data for the fourth quarter's sales. Next, you will move the Summary sheet after the Qtr4 sheet. Finally, you will apply formatting options to all four quarters by grouping the worksheets.

1 With **ES4-WBQtrlySales.xlsx** open, make sure Qtr3 is the active sheet. Position the mouse pointer over the Qtr3 worksheet tab, hold down the left mouse button, hold down the Ctrl key, drag the pointer immediately right of the Qtr3 worksheet tab, release the mouse button, and then release the Ctrl key.

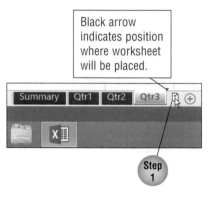

Black arrow indicates position where worksheet will be placed.

Step 1

Ctrl + dragging a worksheet tab copies a worksheet. As you drag the pointer to the right, a white page with a plus sign displays with the pointer. The copied worksheet is labeled the same as the source worksheet with *(2)* added to the end of the name.

2 Double-click the Qtr3 (2) tab, type **Qtr4**, and then press Enter.

3 With Qtr4 the active worksheet, select and delete the ranges B4:D6, B8:D10, and B12:D14 to remove the copied Qtr3 sales data, thereby preventing potential data entry errors when you add the Qtr4 sales data later.

4 Change cell B3 from *July* to *October*; cell C3 from *August* to *November*; and cell D3 from *September* to *December*.

The worksheet is now cleared of the third quarter's data. As new data is typed, the totals will automatically update. First, you will move the Summary worksheet after the four quarterly sales worksheets.

5 Click the Summary worksheet tab to make it active. Position the pointer over the Summary tab, hold down the left mouse button and drag the pointer immediately right of the Qtr4 sheet, and then release the mouse button.

Step 5

Dragging a worksheet tab moves the worksheet. As you drag the pointer to the right, a black down-pointing arrow and a white page display with the pointer, indicating the position where the worksheet will be repositioned.

6 Click the Qtr4 worksheet tab and enter the data for the fourth quarter as shown in Figure 4.1 on the following page. You do not need to type the dollar symbols, commas, or zeros after decimals since the cells are already formatted. Type a zero in the cells displayed with a dash.

FIGURE 4.1 Data for Fourth Quarter

	A	B	C	D	E
1	**The Waterfront Bistro**				
2	**Quarterly Sales Report**				
3		**October**	**November**	**December**	**Quarter Total**
4	Food - Dining Room	$ 44,875	$ 47,856	$ 55,645	$ 148,376
5	Food - Patio	$ 1,785	$ -	$ -	$ 1,785
6	Food - Catering	$ 30,254	$ 33,746	$ 65,245	$ 129,245
7	**Total Food**	$ **76,914**	$ **81,602**	$ **120,890**	$ **279,406**
8	Beverage - Dining Room	$ 41,623	$ 4,687	$ 5,642	$ 51,952
9	Beverage - Patio	$ 245	$ -	$ -	$ 245
10	Beverage - Catering	$ 3,245	$ 3,165	$ 6,452	$ 12,862
11	**Total Beverage**	$ **45,113**	$ **7,852**	$ **12,094**	$ **65,059**
12	Beer & Liquor - Dining Room	$ 3,856	$ 4,962	$ 5,179	$ 13,997
13	Beer & Liquor - Patio	$ 215	$ -	$ -	$ 215
14	Beer & Liquor - Catering	$ 3,167	$ 3,563	$ 6,538	$ 13,268
15	**Total Beer & Liquor**	$ **7,238**	$ **8,525**	$ **11,717**	$ **27,480**
16					
17	**TOTAL SALES**	$ 129,265	$ 97,979	$ 144,701	$ 371,945

(7) Click the Qtr1 worksheet tab, hold down the Shift key, and then click the Qtr4 worksheet tab.

> The four worksheets are now grouped. Notice that *[Group]* appears next to the file name in the Title bar. Any formatting options that you change apply to all four worksheets. Use the Shift key to select a group of worksheets starting with the first worksheet tab selected through to the last worksheet tab selected. Use the Ctrl key to group nonadjacent worksheets.

(8) Make cell A1 active and then apply the Green, Accent 6, Darker 25% fill color (last column, fifth row). Select cells A3 through E3 and then press F4. (This repeats the fill color formatting.) Make cell A2 active and then apply the Blue, Accent 1, Lighter 60% fill color (fifth column, third row).

(9) Right-click any of the Qtr worksheet tabs and then click *Ungroup Sheets* at the shortcut menu.

> The worksheets are no longer grouped and can be individually formatted. You can also ungroup worksheets simply by clicking one of the worksheet tabs.

Step 9

(10) Click the Qtr1 worksheet tab and view the formatting applied in Step 8. Click each of the other quarterly sales worksheets to view the same formatting.

(11) Save **ES4-WBQtrlySales.xlsx**.

In Addition

Move or Copy Dialog Box

In Steps 1 and 5 you copied and moved a worksheet by dragging the worksheet tab with the pointer. You can also use the Move or Copy dialog box (shown at the right) to move or copy worksheets within the active workbook or to another open workbook. Right-click the worksheet you want to move or copy and then click *Move or Copy* at the shortcut menu. Click the worksheet in front of which you want to place the moved or copied worksheet in the *Before* *sheet* list box and then click OK to move, or click the *Create a copy* check box and then click OK to copy. To move or copy to another open workbook, select the destination file name in the *To book* drop-down list.

Activity 4.3

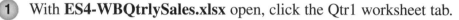

Using 3-D References

A formula that references the same cell in a range that extends over two or more worksheets is called a 3-D reference. A formula with **3-D references** is used to consolidate data from several worksheets into one worksheet. Worksheets that will use 3-D references should have the data set up the same in each worksheet. For example, if cell E4 in the Qtr1 worksheet contains the total dining room sales, then cell E4 in the remaining worksheets should contain the same value. In this project, you will create the following 3-D reference in a SUM formula: =SUM('Qtr1:Qtr4'!E4). The range *Qtr1:Qtr4* within the SUM argument is the 3-D reference that instructs Excel to add the contents of cell E4 starting in the worksheet labeled *Qtr1* and ending with the worksheet labeled *Qtr4*. The 3-D range is enclosed in single quotes and an exclamation point separates the worksheet range from the cell reference.

Project

To continue the quarterly sales report, you will copy labels from the Qtr1 worksheet to the Summary worksheet and enter 3-D formulas that reference the total sales cells in the four quarterly sales worksheets.

Tutorial 4.3
Using 3-D References

① With **ES4-WBQtrlySales.xlsx** open, click the Qtr1 worksheet tab.

② Select the range A4:A22 and then click the Copy button in the Clipboard group on the HOME tab.

③ Make the Summary worksheet active and then click in cell A4.

④ Click the Paste button arrow in the Clipboard group and then click *Keep Source Column Widths* (second option in second row) in the *Paste* section of the Paste Options gallery.

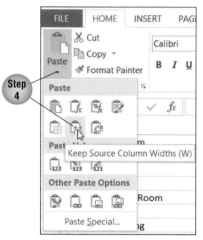

⑤ Make cell B3 active, type **Total**, press Alt + Enter, type **Sales**, and then press Enter.

⑥ Bold and center the text in cell B3.

⑦ Make the Qtr1 worksheet active, copy the text in cell A1 and then paste the text to cell A1 in the Summary worksheet.

⑧ Select A2:E2, click the Merge & Center button, type **Sales Summary**, and then press Enter.

⑨ Make cell A2 active and then apply bold formatting and the Blue, Accent 1, Lighter 60% fill color (fifth column, third row).

⑩ Change the width of column B to *12.00 (115 pixels)*.

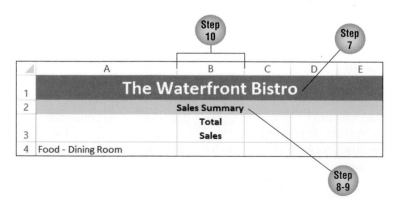

11 Save **ES4-WBQtrlySales.xlsx**.

Saving the workbook before consolidating data using 3-D references is a good idea in case you encounter difficulties when performing the consolidation. In Steps 12–15, you will enter a 3-D formula using the point-and-click method.

12 With the Summary worksheet still active, make cell B4 active.

13 Type **=sum(**.

14 Click the Qtr1 worksheet tab, hold down the Shift key, and then click the Qtr4 worksheet tab.

This groups the four quarterly sales worksheets and Qtr1 is the worksheet now displayed. Watch the Formula bar each time you click the mouse to view the formula that is being built.

15 Click in cell E4 and then press Enter.

16 Press the Up Arrow key to return the active cell back to cell B4 and then read the completed formula in the Formula bar, *=SUM('Qtr1:Qtr4'!E4)*.

Notice Excel inserted the closing bracket automatically. The result, *526884,* appears in cell B4, which is the total of the values in cell E4 in all four quarterly sales worksheets.

17 Drag the fill handle from cell B4 down through cell B15 to copy the 3-D formula to the remaining rows.

18 Make cell B17 active, type the formula **=b7+b11+b15**, and then press Enter.

19 Apply the accounting number format to B4:B17 and then decrease the decimals so that zero decimals display.

20 Deselect the range and then save **ES4-WBQtrlySales.xlsx**.

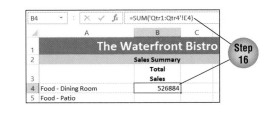

In Brief

Create Formula with 3-D Reference
1. Make desired cell active.
2. Type *=sum(*.
3. Click first worksheet tab.
4. Shift + click last worksheet tab.
5. Click cell containing data to be summed in all worksheets.
6. Press Enter.

In Addition

Using 3-D References in Dissimilar Worksheets

You can consolidate data in multiple worksheets wherein the worksheets are not structured the same. For example, assume that you want to add two salary values from two worksheets. In the first worksheet (labeled Marketing), the salary value resides in cell D6, and in the second worksheet (labeled Finance), the salary value resides in cell H12. The following formula entered into the desired cell in the summary worksheet adds the two values: =Marketing!D6+Finance!H12.

Activity 4.4

Linking Cells; Printing Multiple Worksheets

In Section 2, you learned how to use Copy and Paste to link two cells. Recall that the Paste gallery includes a Paste Link button, which establishes a link between the source and destination cell(s). You can also link cells within the same workbook or between different workbooks by entering a formula that references the source cell. If the source data changes, the cell that is linked to the source will automatically update to reflect the change. To print more than one worksheet at once, group the worksheets prior to printing, or display the Print backstage area and change the Print gallery in the Settings category to *Print Entire Workbook*.

Project

To finish the quarterly sales report, you will link to a cell in another worksheet to enter the percent of gross profit and then copy formatting to ensure consistency before setting the page layout options and printing the entire workbook.

Tutorial 4.4
Linking Data
Between Worksheets

1 With **ES4-WBQtrlySales.xlsx** open and with the Summary worksheet active, make cell B21 active.

2 Type =.

3 Click the Qtr1 worksheet tab, click in cell B21, and then press Enter.

The value *30%* displays in cell B21 in the Summary worksheet.

4 Press the Up Arrow key to return the active cell back to B21 and then look at the formula that was entered in the Formula bar from Steps 2–3.

The formula =*'Qtr1'!B21* means that the contents of cell B21 in the Summary worksheet are drawn from the contents of cell B21 in the Qtr1 worksheet. Any change made to cell B21 in Qtr1 automatically causes cell B21 in the Summary worksheet to update as well.

B21	▾	:	✕ ✓ *fx*	='Qtr1'!B21

◢	A	B
2		**Sales Summary**
3		**Total Sales**
4	Food - Dining Room	$ 526,884
5	Food - Patio	$ 136,825
6	Food - Catering	$ 364,648
7	**Total Food**	$ 1,028,357
8	Beverage - Dining Room	$ 89,213
9	Beverage - Patio	$ 13,843
10	Beverage - Catering	$ 37,274
11	**Total Beverage**	$ 140,330
12	Beer & Liquor - Dining Room	$ 56,118
13	Beer & Liquor - Patio	$ 16,584
14	Beer & Liquor - Catering	$ 40,121
15	**Total Beer & Liquor**	$ 112,823
16		
17	**TOTAL SALES**	$ 1,281,510
18		
19	**Proof Total**	
20		
21	Gross Profit Factor	30%
22	Estimated Gross Profit	

Step 4

5 Make cell B22 active, type **=b17*b21**, and then press Enter.

> Estimated Gross Profit is calculated by multiplying Total Sales (cell B17) by the Gross Profit Factor (cell B21).

6 Make cell B19 active and then type the following formula (pressing Enter after typing the formula) to check the accuracy of the total sales in cell B17:

=SUM(b4:b6)+SUM(b8:b10)+SUM(b12:b14)

> As you near completion of the quarterly sales report, in Steps 7–14 you will use the Format Painter feature to ensure formatting in the Summary worksheet is consistent with formatting in the other worksheets before you print the workbook. Recall from Section 2 that Format Painter is a feature that allows you to copy formatting attributes from one cell to other cells in the workbook.

16		
17	**TOTAL SALES**	$ 1,281,510
18		
19	**Proof Total**	=SUM(b4:b6)+SUM(b8:b10)+SUM(b12:b14)
20		
21	Gross Profit Factor	30%
22	Estimated Gross Profit	$ 384,453
23		

Step 6

Step 5

7 Click the Qtr4 worksheet tab.

8 Make cell E7 active and then double-click the Format Painter button in the Clipboard group on the HOME tab.

> Double-clicking the Format Painter button toggles on the Copy Format feature so you can paste formats multiple times. Notice that the pointer has a paint brush icon attached to it as you move the mouse over the worksheet in the next steps.

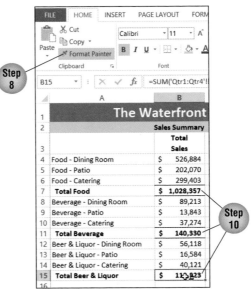

Step 8

The Waterfront
Sales Summary

	A	B
1		
2		Sales Summary
3		Total Sales
4	Food - Dining Room	$ 526,884
5	Food - Patio	$ 202,070
6	Food - Catering	$ 299,403
7	**Total Food**	**$ 1,028,357**
8	Beverage - Dining Room	$ 89,213
9	Beverage - Patio	$ 13,843
10	Beverage - Catering	$ 37,274
11	**Total Beverage**	**$ 140,330**
12	Beer & Liquor - Dining Room	$ 56,118
13	Beer & Liquor - Patio	$ 16,584
14	Beer & Liquor - Catering	$ 40,121
15	**Total Beer & Liquor**	**$ 112,823**
16		

Step 10

9 Click the Summary worksheet tab.

10 Click in cell B7, click in cell B11, and then click in cell B15.

11 Click the Format Painter button to turn off the feature.

12 Click the Qtr4 worksheet tab.

13 Make cell E17 active and then click the Format Painter button.

14 Click the Summary worksheet tab and then click in cell B17.

> Single-clicking the Format Painter turns on the feature only for the next mouse click. Notice the feature has been automatically turned off after clicking in cell B17.

continues

15 Click the Qtr1 worksheet tab, hold down the Shift key, and then click the Summary worksheet tab.

> All of the worksheets are now grouped. In the next step, you will create a footer, which will be applied to each worksheet because they are grouped.

16 Click the INSERT tab and then click the Header & Footer button in the Text group.

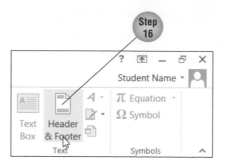

17 Click the Go to Footer button in the Navigation group on the HEADER & FOOTER TOOLS DESIGN tab.

18 With the insertion point positioned in the center text box in the footer section, click the Sheet Name button in the Header & Footer Elements group on the HEADER & FOOTER TOOLS DESIGN tab.

> Excel inserts the code *&[Tab]* in the footer, which will be replaced with the worksheet name when the worksheet is viewed in Page Layout view or printed.

19 Click in the worksheet area outside the footer area.

20 Click the FILE tab and then click the *Print* option.

21 Since all of the worksheets were grouped when you opened the Print backstage area, notice the page navigation in the print preview area indicates that five pages will print.

22 Click the Next Page button ▶ four times, viewing each preview page.

23 Click the Print button.

In Brief

Link Worksheet
1. Make destination cell active.
2. Type =.
3. Click worksheet tab for source cell.
4. Click source cell.
5. Press Enter.

Print Multiple Worksheets
1. Click first worksheet tab.
2. Shift + click last worksheet tab.
3. Click FILE tab.
4. Click *Print* option.
5. Click Print button.

Step 23

Step 22

24 Click the VIEW tab and then click the Normal button ▦ in the Workbook Views group.

25 Right-click any of the grouped worksheet tabs and then click *Ungroup Sheets* at the shortcut menu.

26 Save and then close **ES4-WBQtrlySales.xlsx**.

In Addition

Hiding a Worksheet in a Workbook

In a workbook containing multiple worksheets, you can hide a worksheet that may contain sensitive data or data you do not want to display or print with the workbook. To hide a worksheet in a workbook, click the Format button in the Cells group on the HOME tab, point to *Hide & Unhide*, and then click *Hide Sheet*. You can also hide a worksheet by right-clicking a worksheet tab and then clicking the *Hide* option at the shortcut menu.

To make a hidden worksheet visible, click the Format button in the Cells group, point to *Hide & Unhide*, and then click *Unhide Sheet*, or right-click a worksheet tab and then click *Unhide* at the shortcut menu. At the Unhide dialog box that displays, double-click the name of the hidden worksheet you want to display.

Activity 4.5

Using Page Break Preview

A page break displays in the worksheet as a dashed line along cell borders between columns or rows. Excel inserts the page breaks automatically based on the margin settings, page orientation, and paper size. You can adjust the page break positions if you do not like where the page break has occurred. Display the worksheet in Page Break Preview to view the worksheet with page numbers behind the cells indicating the number of pages required to print the entire worksheet and a blue dashed line indicating page break locations. Unused cells outside the printing area are grayed out but still accessible if you want to add additional data. Adjust the page breaks by dragging the blue dashed line to the preferred location. Excel automatically adjusts scaling options to accommodate the cells within the revised page break location.

Project

In the next few projects, you will be working with a catering contract summary. As your first task, you will view the worksheet in Page Break Preview to make adjustments to page layout options and page break locations.

SNAP

Tutorial 4.5
Using Page Break Preview

1. Open **WBCatering.xlsx**.

2. Save the workbook in the ExcelS4 folder and name it **ES4-WBCatering**.

3. Spend a moment reviewing the column headings and the data stored in the worksheet.

4. Click the VIEW tab and then click the Page Break Preview button ▦ in the Workbook Views group.

    In Page Break Preview, page breaks are shown as dashed or solid blue lines. A dashed line indicates an automatic page break inserted by Excel. A solid blue line indicates a manual page break. You can adjust a page break by dragging the blue line to the desired position.

    Step 4

5. Notice that two pages are required to print the worksheet with the current page layout settings. Click the PAGE LAYOUT tab, click the Orientation button in the Page Setup group, and then click *Landscape* at the drop-down list.

Your screen may vary from the one shown, depending on your display settings and monitor size.

	First Name	Last Name	Contact Pho	Event	Date	Room	Guests	Special M	Price Per P
	The Waterfront Bistro								
	Catering Contracts								
4	Cecily	Hillmore	716 555 6598	Business Meeting	1/15/2015	Starlake	35	No	21.95
5	Mario	Fontaine	716 555 1886	Engagement Party	1/20/2015	Westview	177	Yes	28.95
6	Frances	Corriveau	716 555 3256	Birthday Party	1/23/2015	Westview	85	Yes	25.95
7	Weston	Kressman	716 555 4219	Wedding	2/28/2015	Sunset	266	Yes	28.95
8	Orlando	Fagan	716 555 3694	25th Wedding Anniver	3/10/2015	Westview	88	Yes	28.95
9	Kim	Pockovic	905 555 3698	Birthday Party	3/18/2015	Westview	62	Yes	35.95
10	Lane	Gill	416 555 3264	Business Meeting	3/29/2015	Starlake	71	No	21.95
11	Percy	Bresque	716 555 1248	50th Wedding Anniver	4/12/2015	Westview	62	Yes	32.95
12	Max	Santore	905 555 3264	Wedding	4/28/2015	Sunset	157	Yes	25.95
13	Omar	Hamid	716 555 8796	Engagement Party	5/8/2015	Sunset	85	Yes	28.95
14	Jack	Torrance	716 555 1469	Business Meeting	5/15/2015	Westview	26	No	23.95
15	Dana	Russell	716 555 4955	Birthday Party	5/30/2015	Starlake	36	No	26.95
16	Walter	Szucs	905 555 6998	Birthday Party	6/10/2015	Starlake	42	No	28.95
17	Nicole	Griffin	905 555 4168	25th Wedding Anniver	6/17/2015	Starlake	54	Yes	31.95
18	Zack	Doucet	716 555 3488	Wedding	6/20/2015	Sunset	168	Yes	28.95
19	Jesse	Golinsky	716 555 4218	Business Meeting	6/26/2015	Westview	57	No	24.95
20	Su-Lin	Ping	716 555 7774	Baby Shower	7/10/2015	Sunset	62	Yes	21.95
21	Elizabeth	McMaster	716 555 9442	Engagement Party	7/11/2015	Sunset	75	Yes	27.95
22	Reed	Pavelich	716 555 2286	Wedding	7/25/2015	Starlake	110	Yes	31.95
23	Alfredo	Juanitez	716 555 4668	Business Meeting	7/31/2015	Westview	49	No	23.95
24	Sofia	Delgado	716 555 8465	Birthday Party	8/10/2015	Starlake	55	No	21.95
25	Carlotta	Balducci	716 555 9665	Birthday Party	8/22/2015	Starlake	62	Yes	25.95
26	Bahurai	Omkar	905 555 3411	Wedding	8/30/2015	Westview	155	Yes	28.95
27	Carlo	Sanchez	905 555 6344	Business Meeting	9/10/2015	Westview	45	No	21.95
28	Franco	Costa	716 555 3345	Business Meeting	9/30/2015	Sunset	32	No	31.95
29	Mahika	Kapoor	716 555 3669	Birthday Party	10/5/2015	Sunset	68	Yes	28.95
30	Bianca	Vargas	716 555 3884	Engagement Party	10/19/2015	Starlake	40	Yes	31.95
31	Guido	Donato	716 555 8444	Business Meeting	10/22/2015	Westview	30	No	25.95
32	Raji	Jai	716 555 6885	Baby Shower	11/6/2015	Westview	85	No	28.95
33	Elena	Alvarez	905 555 4884	Wedding	11/19/2015	Westview	112	No	21.95
34	Liana	Fantino	716 555 9648	25th Wedding Anniver	11/30/2015	Sunset	54	No	28.95
35	Mei-Yin	Zhang	716 555 2121	Business Meeting	12/1/2015	Starlake	28	Yes	31.95
36	Cristian	Martinez	716 555 4331	Business Meeting	12/15/2015	Starlake	18	No	31.95
37	Bogdana	Petrov	716 555 6889	Birthday Party	12/20/2015	Sunset	51	Yes	31.95
38	Tao	Okinawa	716 555 1665	Wedding	12/21/2015	Westview	110	Yes	27.95
39	Corina	Guzman	716 555 4112	Wedding	12/22/2015	Westview	85	Yes	28.95
40	Matteo	Limardi	905 555 9447	50th Wedding Anniver	12/24/2015	Westview	125	Yes	35.95
41	Alfonso	Ramirez	716 555 3488	Wedding	12/31/2015	Westview	160	Yes	35.95

The worksheet requires more pages to print when the orientation is changed to landscape at Step 5.

6 Scroll the worksheet to view the changes to the page breaks in landscape orientation. Notice that the worksheet now requires more pages to print.

In Brief

Page Break Preview
1. Click VIEW tab.
2. Click Page Break Preview.
OR
Click Page Break Preview button on Status bar.

7 Look at the number in the *Scale* measurement box in the Scale to Fit group on the PAGE LAYOUT tab and notice that the current value is *100%*.

> In Steps 8–10, you will adjust the position of the page breaks and then see how the scaling percentage is automatically adjusted to accommodate more cells printed in the page.

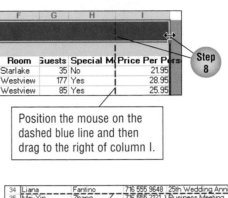

8 Position the mouse pointer on the blue dashed line between columns H and I until the pointer displays as a left- and right-pointing arrow, drag the mouse to the right of column I, and then release the mouse.

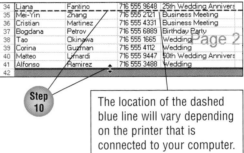

Position the mouse on the dashed blue line and then drag to the right of column I.

9 View the bottom of the worksheet. Notice that a few lines have been moved to page 2.

10 Position the mouse pointer on the dashed blue line between rows near the bottom of the worksheet until the pointer displays as an up- and down-pointing arrow, and then drag the dashed line below row 41.

> Notice that the entire worksheet now fits on one page. When you drag an automatic page break to a new location, the page break changes to a solid blue line indicating the break is a manual page break.

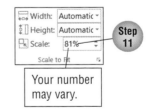

The location of the dashed blue line will vary depending on the printer that is connected to your computer.

11 Look at the revised value in the *Scale* measurement box in the Scale to Fit group and notice that the value has been reduced from 100%.

> Excel automatically adjusts the scaling percent downward when you adjust a break page that causes more cells to print on the page.

Your number may vary.

12 Click the VIEW tab and then click the Normal button in the Workbook Views group.

13 Save **ES4-WBCatering.xlsx**.

In Addition

Inserting or Removing a Page Break in Normal View

Page breaks generally do not appear in Normal view until you have displayed the worksheet in the Print backstage area. Dashed lines appear between column or row borders to indicate automatic page breaks. To insert a manual page break in Normal view, position the active cell in the row below or the column to the right of which you want the page break to occur, click the PAGE LAYOUT tab, click the Breaks button ⊞ in the Page Setup group, and then click *Insert Page Break* at the drop-down list (shown at the right).

Activity 4.6

Formatting Data as a Table; Applying Table Design Options

Create a table in Excel to manage data independently from other cells in the worksheet or to filter and sort a list. A worksheet can contain more than one range formatted as a table. By default, filter arrows appear in the first row of the table and a border surrounds the table range with a sizing arrow at the bottom right corner. Excel includes a variety of predefined table styles to apply professional quality formatting features to the range within a table. The TABLE TOOLS DESIGN tab becomes available when a range of cells is defined as a table.

Project

You will format the catering contract list as a table, add a record to the list, and create a new calculated column to extend the catering contract amounts. Finally, you will add a total row to the bottom of the table to sum the catering contracts.

Tutorial 4.6A
Formatting Data as a Table

Tutorial 4.6B
Adding Rows to a Table

1. With **ES4-WBCatering.xlsx** open, select the range A3:I41.

2. Click the HOME tab and then click the Format as Table button in the Styles group.

3. Click *Table Style Medium 17* (third column, third row in the *Medium* section) at the drop-down gallery.

> Excel includes several predefined table styles grouped into *Light*, *Medium*, and *Dark* categories with which you can add color, borders, and shading formats to cells within the table. In addition, you can create your own custom table style saved with the current workbook. The table styles shown in the drop-down gallery are dependent on the worksheet's current theme.

4. At the Format As Table dialog box, with *=$A$3:$I$41* selected in the *Where is the data for your table?* text box, click OK.

> Excel applies the table style formats to the range, displays filter arrows in the first row of the table, and adds a border to the table, including a sizing handle to the bottom right cell.

5. Click in any cell to deselect the range.

> In the next step, you will add a new record to the table.

6. Make cell A42 active and then type text in the cells in the new row in the columns indicated. Press Enter after typing the price per person.

First Name	**Sonora**
Last Name	**Yee**
Contact Phone	**716 555 2668**
Event	**Birthday Party**
Date	**12/31/2015**

Room	Starlake
Guests	73
Special Menu	Yes
Price Per Person	31.95

In Brief

Format Table
1. Select cell range.
2. Click Format as Table button.
3. Click desired table style.
4. Click OK.

Add Total Row
1. Click TABLE TOOLS DESIGN tab.
2. Click *Total Row* check box.
3. If necessary, choose desired function in numeric columns.

Since you typed data in the row immediately below the table, Excel automatically expands the table to include the new row and applies the table style formats. You can also insert a new row by pressing Tab at the last cell in the table to insert a new blank row below and then type the data.

| 41 | Alfonso | Ramirez | 716 555 3488 | Wedding | 12/31/2015 | Westview | 160 | Yes | 35.95 |
| 42 | Sonora | Yee | 716 555 2668 | Birthday Party | 12/31/2015 | Starlake | 73 | Yes | 31.95 |

Step 6

⑦ Make cell J3 active, type **Contract Total**, and then press Enter.

Typing new data in a column immediately right of the table also automatically expands the table list range.

⑧ With cell J4 active, type the formula **=g4*i4** and then press Enter.

Typing a formula in a table column causes Excel to automatically categorize the column as a calculated column and duplicate the formula in the remainder of the table.

J
Contract Total ▼
$ 768.25
$ 5,124.15
$ 2,205.75
$ 7,700.70
$ 2,547.60
$ 2,228.90
$ 1,558.45
$ 2,042.90
$ 4,074.15
$ 2,460.75
$ 622.70
$ 970.20
$ 1,215.90
$ 1,725.30
$ 4,863.60
$ 1,422.15
$ 1,360.90
$ 2,096.25

Step 9

⑨ Select J4:J42, apply the accounting number format, and then change the column width to *16.00 (151 pixels)*.

⑩ Deselect the range by clicking a cell in the table.

⑪ Click the TABLE TOOLS DESIGN tab and then click the *Total Row* check box in the Table Style Options group to insert a check mark.

Excel adds the word *Total* in the leftmost cell in the row below the table and sums the cells in column J.

Step 11

TABLE TOOLS
DESIGN
☑ Header Row ☐ First Column ☑ Filter Button
☐ Total Row ☐ Last Column
☑ Banded Rows ☐ Banded Columns
Table Style Options

⑫ Make cell G43 active, click the list arrow that appears, and then click *Sum* at the pop-up list.

⑬ Make cell I43 active, click the list arrow that appears, and then click *Average* at the pop-up list.

12/22/2015	Westview	85	Yes	28.95	$ 2,460.75
12/24/2015	Westview	125	Yes	35.95	$ 4,493.75
12/31/2015	Westview	160	Yes	35.95	$ 5,752.00
12/31/2015	Starlake	73	Yes	31.95	$ 2,332.35
		3155		28.36	$ 90,710.25

Step 12   Steps 13-14

⑭ Decrease the decimals in cell I43 to two decimal places.

⑮ Select A1:J1 and then click the Merge & Center button in the Alignment group on the HOME tab to remove the merging of columns A through I.

⑯ With A1:J1 still selected, click the Merge & Center button a second time to merge columns A through J.

⑰ Correct the centering of the title in row 2 by completing steps similar to those in Steps 15–16.

⑱ Save **ES4-WBCatering.xlsx**.

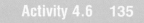

Activity 4.7

Sorting a Table by Single and Multiple Criteria

In Section 1 you learned to sort a payroll worksheet alphabetically by last names. To sort rows in a table by single or multiple criteria involves the same process as the one used in Section 1. To sort by a single column, click in any cell in the column by which you wish to sort and then use the *Sort A to Z* or *Sort Z to A* options at the Sort & Filter drop-down list. To group the rows first by one column and then sort the rows within each group by another column, open the Sort dialog box. You can continue to group and sort by multiple criteria as needed.

Project

You decide to print the catering data sorted in descending order by the contract total. Next, you want a printout of the catering list grouped first by the event, then by room, and then by date.

The Waterfront B·I·S·T·R·O

SNAP

Tutorial 4.7
Using the Sort Feature in Tables

1 With **ES4-WBCatering.xlsx** open, click any cell in column J within the table range.

2 Click the Sort & Filter button in the Editing group on the HOME tab.

3 Click *Sort Largest to Smallest* at the drop-down list.

> The table is rearranged in descending order by contract total with the highest contract amount at the top of the list. Excel displays a down-pointing black arrow in the filter arrow button to indicate that the table is ordered by the *Contract Total* column.

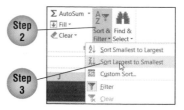

4 Select H4:I43 and center the cells within the range.

5 Deselect the range and then click the VIEW tab.

6 Display the worksheet in Page Break Preview and adjust the page breaks so that the worksheet fits on one page.

7 Print the worksheet.

8 Display the worksheet in Normal view, click any cell within the table range, and then click the HOME tab.

9 Click the Sort & Filter button and then click *Custom Sort* at the drop-down list.

10 At the Sort dialog box, click the down-pointing arrow at the right of *Sort by* option box in the *Column* section (currently reads *Contract Total*) and then click *Event* at the drop-down list.

11 Click the down-pointing arrow at the right of the option box in the *Order* section (currently reads *Z to A*) and then click *A to Z* at the drop-down list.

12 Click the Add Level button in the Sort dialog box.

13 Click the down-pointing arrow at the right of *Then by* option box in the *Column* section and then click *Room* at the drop-down list.

> The default entries of *Values* for *Sort On* and *A to Z* for *Order* are correct since you want the cells sorted by the room names in ascending order.

14 Click the Add Level button.

15 Click the down-pointing arrow at the right of the second *Then by* option box in the *Column* section and then click *Date* at the drop-down list.

> The default entries of *Values* for *Sort On* and *Oldest to Newest* for *Order* are correct since you want to sort the dates in ascending order.

16 Click OK to perform the sort.

In Brief

Sort Table by Single Column
1. Click in any row within column by which to sort.
2. Click the Sort & Filter button.
3. Click *Sort A to Z*, or *Sort Smallest to Largest*, or *Sort Z to A*, or *Sort Largest to Smallest*.

Sort Table by Multiple Columns
1. Click Sort & Filter button.
2. Click *Custom Sort*.
3. Select first column to sort by.
4. Select sort order.
5. Click Add Level.
6. Repeat Steps 3–5 for each sort column.
7. Click OK.

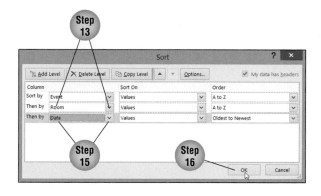

17 Examine the sorted worksheet and compare your results with the partial worksheet shown below. Notice the rows are grouped and sorted first by event starting with *25th Wedding Anniversary*. Within each event group, the rows are next arranged by room, and then within each room group, the rows are arranged by date.

	First Name	Last Name	Contact Phone	Event	Date	Room	Gue	Special Menu	Price Per Person	Contract Total
				The Waterfront Bistro						
				Catering Contracts						
4	Nicole	Griffin	905 555 4166	25th Wedding Anniversary	6/17/2015	Starlake	54	Yes	31.95	$ 1,725.30
5	Liana	Fantino	716 555 9648	25th Wedding Anniversary	11/30/2015	Sunset	54	No	28.95	$ 1,563.30
6	Orlando	Fagan	716 555 3694	25th Wedding Anniversary	3/10/2015	Westview	88	Yes	28.95	$ 2,547.60
7	Percy	Bresque	716 555 1248	50th Wedding Anniversary	4/12/2015	Westview	62	Yes	32.95	$ 2,042.90
8	Matteo	Limardi	716 555 9447	50th Wedding Anniversary	12/24/2015	Westview	125	Yes	35.95	$ 4,493.75
9	Su-Lin	Ping	716 555 7774	Baby Shower	7/10/2015	Sunset	62	Yes	21.95	$ 1,360.90
10	Raji	Jai	716 555 6885	Baby Shower	11/6/2015	Westview	85	No	28.95	$ 2,460.75
11	Dana	Russell	716 555 4965	Birthday Party	5/30/2015	Starlake	36	No	26.95	$ 970.20
12	Walter	Szucs	905 555 6998	Birthday Party	6/10/2015	Starlake	42	No	28.95	$ 1,215.90
13	Sofia	Delgado	716 555 8465	Birthday Party	8/10/2015	Starlake	55	No	21.95	$ 1,207.25
14	Carlotta	Balducci	716 555 9665	Birthday Party	8/22/2015	Starlake	62	Yes	25.95	$ 1,608.90
15	Sonora	Yee	716 555 2668	Birthday Party	12/31/2015	Starlake	73	Yes	31.95	$ 2,332.35
16	Mahika	Kapoor	716 555 3669	Birthday Party	10/5/2015	Sunset	68	Yes	28.95	$ 1,968.60
17	Bogdana	Petrov	716 555 6889	Birthday Party	12/20/2015	Sunset	51	Yes	31.95	$ 1,629.45
18	Frances	Corriveau	716 555 3256	Birthday Party	1/23/2015	Westview	85	Yes	25.95	$ 2,205.75
19	Kim	Pockovic	905 555 3698	Birthday Party	3/18/2015	Westview	62	Yes	35.95	$ 2,228.90
20	Cecily	Hillmore	716 555 6598	Business Meeting	1/15/2015	Starlake	35	No	21.95	$ 768.25
21	Lane	Gill	416 555 3264	Business Meeting	3/29/2015	Starlake	71	No	21.95	$ 1,558.45

 18 Print the worksheet.

19 Save **ES4-WBCatering.xlsx**.

In Addition

More about Sorting

By default, Excel sorts the data in a column alphanumerically. Alphanumeric sorting arranges rows with entries that begin with symbols first, then numbers, then letters. Notice in the catering events workbook that the events beginning with numbers, such as *25th Wedding Anniversary* and *50th Wedding Anniversary*, are the first rows in the sorted worksheet.

Activity 4.8

A *filter* is used to display only certain records within the table that meet specified criteria. The records that do not meet the filter criteria are temporarily hidden from view. Using a filter, you can view and/or print a subset of rows within a table. For example, you might want to print a list of catering events that have been booked into a certain room. Once you have printed the list, removing the filter redisplays all of the rows. Excel displays filter arrows in the first row of the table with which you specify the filter criteria.

Project

Tutorial 4.8
Filtering a Table

To prepare for an upcoming meeting with the executive chef, Dana has asked for a printout of the catering events that require a special menu. Another printout of the events booked into the Starlake Room is needed for planning staff requirements. Finally, Dana wants a printed list of the weddings booked into the Sunset Room.

1 With **ES4-WBCatering.xlsx** open, click the filter arrow button ▼ next to the label *Special Menu* in cell H3.

> Filter a table by selecting the criterion from a drop-down list. For each column in the table, a filter arrow button appears. Excel looks in the active column and includes in the filter drop-down list each unique field value that exists within the column. In addition, the entries *Sort A to Z, Sort Z to A,* and *Sort by Color* appear at the top of the list.

2 Click the check box next to *No* in the drop-down list to remove the check mark.

> Clearing a check mark for a check box instructs Excel to hide those rows within the table that match the check box entry. Since the only other entry in the column is *Yes*, the criterion for the filter is to display only those rows within the table that have the text entry *Yes* in column H.

Step 2

Step 3

3 Click OK.

> Excel hides any records that have a value other than *Yes* in the column as shown below. The row numbers of the matching items that were found are displayed in blue and a filter icon appears in the filter arrow button in cell H3 to indicate H is the column that was used to filter the rows. The Status bar also shows the message that 24 of 39 records were found. A filtered worksheet can be edited, formatted, charted, or printed.

4 Print the filtered worksheet.

Filter icon indicates the column used to filter the table.

3	First Name	Last Name	Contact Phone	Event	Date	Room	Gue	Special Menu
4	Nicole	Griffin	905 555 4166	25th Wedding Anniversary	6/17/2015	Starlake	54	Yes
6	Orlando	Fagan	716 555 3694	25th Wedding Anniversary	3/10/2015	Westview	88	Yes
7	Percy	Bresque	716 555 1248	50th Wedding Anniversary	4/12/2015	Westview	62	Yes
8	Matteo	Limardi	716 555 9447	50th Wedding Anniversary	12/24/2015	Westview	125	Yes
9	Su-Lin	Ping	716 555 7774	Baby Shower	7/10/2015	Sunset	62	Yes
14	Carlotta	Balducci	716 555 9665	Birthday Party	8/22/2015	Starlake	62	Yes
15	Sonora	Yee	716 555 2668	Birthday Party	12/31/2015	Starlake	73	Yes
16	Mahika	Kapoor	716 555 3669	Birthday Party	10/5/2015	Sunset	68	Yes
17	Bogdana	Petrov	716 555 6889	Birthday Party	12/20/2015	Sunset	51	Yes
18	Frances	Corriveau	716 555 3256	Birthday Party	1/23/2015	Westview	85	Yes
19	Kim	Pockovic	905 555 3698	Birthday Party	3/18/2015	Westview	62	Yes
22	Mei-Yin	Zhang	716 555 2121	Business Meeting	12/1/2015	Starlake	28	Yes
30	Bianca	Vargas	716 555 3884	Engagement Party	10/15/2015	Starlake	40	Yes
31	Omar	Hamid	716 555 8796	Engagement Party	5/8/2015	Sunset	85	Yes
32	Elizabeth	McMaster	716 555 9442	Engagement Party	7/11/2015	Sunset	75	Yes
33	Mario	Fontaine	716 555 1886	Engagement Party	1/20/2015	Westview	177	Yes
34	Reed	Pavelich	716 555 2286	Wedding	7/25/2015	Starlake	110	Yes
35	Weston	Kressman	716 555 4219	Wedding	2/28/2015	Sunset	266	Yes
36	Max	Santore	905 555 3264	Wedding	4/28/2015	Sunset	157	Yes
37	Zack	Doucet	716 555 3488	Wedding	6/20/2015	Sunset	168	Yes
38	Bahurai	Omkar	905 555 3411	Wedding	8/30/2015	Westview	155	Yes
40	Tao	Okinawa	716 555 1665	Wedding	12/21/2015	Westview	110	Yes
41	Corina	Guzman	716 555 4112	Wedding	12/22/2015	Westview	85	Yes
42	Alfonso	Ramirez	716 555 3488	Wedding	12/31/2015	Westview	160	Yes
43	Total						2408	

Excel hides rows that do not meet the criterion. Matching row numbers are displayed in blue.

(5) Point to the filter icon in the filter arrow button in cell H3 and notice the filter criterion that displays in the ScreenTip.

(6) Click the filter arrow button in cell H3.

(7) Click *Clear Filter From "Special Menu"* at the filter drop-down list.

> All rows within the table are restored to view.

(8) Click the filter arrow button in cell F3.

(9) Clear the check marks in the *Westview* and *Sunset* check boxes at the drop-down list and then click OK.

> Only the catering events for which Starlake is the specified room are displayed.

(10) Print the filtered worksheet.

(11) Click the filter arrow button in cell F3.

(12) Click the (*Select All*) check box to insert a check mark and then click OK.

> Choosing the (*Select All*) check box is another method to redisplay the entire table. In the next steps, you will filter by the event and then filter the subset of rows again to further refine a report.

(13) Click the filter arrow button in cell D3.

(14) Click the (*Select All*) check box to clear the check marks from all check boxes in the drop-down list, click the *Wedding* check box to insert a check mark and then click OK.

(15) Click the filter arrow button in cell F3.

(16) Clear the check mark from the *Starlake* and the *Westview* check boxes and then click OK.

In Brief

Filter Table
1. Click desired filter arrow button.
2. Clear check boxes for items you do not want to view.
3. Click OK.

Remove Filter
1. Click desired filter arrow button.
2. Click *Clear Filter From (column title)*.

3	First Name	Last Name	Contact Phone	Event	Date	Room
4	Nicole	Griffin	905 555 4166	25th Wedding Anniversary	6/17/2015	Starlake
11	Dana	Russell	716 555 4965	Birthday Party	5/30/2015	Starlake
12	Walter	Szucs	905 555 6998	Birthday Party	6/10/2015	Starlake
13	Sofia	Delgado	716 555 8465	Birthday Party	8/10/2015	Starlake
14	Carlotta	Balducci	716 555 9665	Birthday Party	8/22/2015	Starlake
15	Sonora	Yee	716 555 2668	Birthday Party	12/31/2015	Starlake
20	Cecily	Hillmore	716 555 6598	Business Meeting	1/15/2015	Starlake
21	Lane	Gill	416 555 3264	Business Meeting	3/29/2015	Starlake
22	Mei-Yin	Zhang	716 555 2121	Business Meeting	12/1/2015	Starlake
23	Cristian	Martinez	716 555 4331	Business Meeting	12/15/2015	Starlake
30	Bianca	Vargas	716 555 3884	Engagement Party	10/15/2015	Starlake
34	Reed	Pavelich	716 555 2286	Wedding	7/25/2015	Starlake
43	Total					

table filtered by *Starlake* in Step 9

table filtered first by Wedding *Event* and then by Sunset *Room* in Steps 13–16

3	First Name	Last Name	Contact Phone	Event	Date	Room
35	Weston	Kressman	716 555 4219	Wedding	2/28/2015	Sunset
36	Max	Santore	905 555 3264	Wedding	4/28/2015	Sunset
37	Zack	Doucet	716 555 3488	Wedding	6/20/2015	Sunset
43	Total					

(17) Print the filtered worksheet.

(18) Redisplay all records for both filtered columns.

(19) Save **ES4-WBCatering.xlsx**.

In Addition

Filtering Data Not Formatted as a Table

Data in a worksheet that has not been formatted as a table can also be filtered using techniques similar to those you learned in this activity. Select the range of cells that you wish to filter, click the Sort & Filter button in the Editing group on the HOME tab, and then click *Filter* at the drop-down list. Excel adds filter arrows in each column of the first row of the selected range.

Activity 4.9

Inserting, Editing, Deleting, and Printing Comments

A *comment* is a pop-up box containing text that displays when the cell pointer is positioned over a cell with an attached comment. A diagonal red triangle in the upper right corner of the cell alerts the reader that a comment exists. The REVIEW tab contains buttons to insert and delete comments, show or hide all comment boxes, and scroll through comments within a worksheet. Use comments to provide instructions, ask questions or add other explanatory text to a cell.

Project

Tutorial 4.9
Inserting and Editing Comments

Dana Hirsch has given you two notes and a reminder that should be inserted into the appropriate event information in the catering contracts workbook.

1 With **ES4-WBCatering.xlsx** open, make cell G10 active.

2 Click the REVIEW tab.

3 Click the New Comment button in the Comments group.

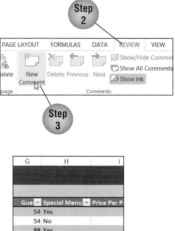

> A comment box displays anchored to the active cell with the user's name inserted in bold text at the top of the box. In worksheets accessed by multiple people, the name helps the reader identify the person who made the comment.

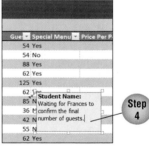

4 Type **Waiting for Frances to confirm the final number of guests.**

5 Click in the worksheet outside the comment box.

> A diagonal red triangle appears in the upper right corner of cell G10, indicating that a comment exists for the cell.

6 Right-click in cell H19 and then click *Insert Comment* at the shortcut menu.

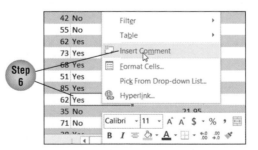

7 Type **Remind Pierre that five guests require a diabetic menu.**

8 Click in the worksheet outside the comment box.

9 Hover the cell pointer over cell G10.

> Hovering the cell pointer over a cell that contains a comment causes the comment box to pop up.

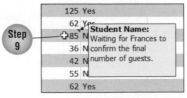

10 Click in cell I24, click the New Comment button in the Comments group, type **Signed contract not yet received. Follow up in two weeks.**, and then click in the worksheet outside the comment box.

11 Right-click in cell H19 and then click *Edit Comment* at the shortcut menu.

12 Move the insertion point and insert and delete text as needed to change the comment text from *five* to *six* guests require a diabetic menu.

Steps 11

13 Click in the worksheet outside the comment box and then press Ctrl + Home to make cell A1 active.

14 Click the Next button 📄 in the Comments group.

> Excel opens the comment box in cell G10.

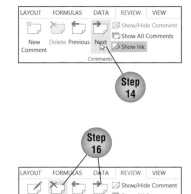

Step 14

15 Click the Next button to move to the next comment box in cell H19.

16 Click the Next button to move to the third comment box and then click the Delete button 📄 in the Comments group.

> By default, comments do not print with the worksheet. In the next steps, you will print the worksheet with the comment text displayed next to the cells.

Step 16

17 Click the Show All Comments 🗗 button in the Comments group.

18 Click the PAGE LAYOUT tab.

19 Click the Page Setup group dialog box launcher 🖿 located at the bottom right corner of the Page Setup group.

Step 19

20 Click the Sheet tab at the Page Setup dialog box, click the down-pointing arrow next to the *Comments* option box in the *Print* section, click *As displayed on sheet*, and then click OK.

21 Print the worksheet.

22 Click the REVIEW tab and then click the Show All Comments button to remove the display of the comment boxes.

23 Save and then close **ES4-WBCatering.xlsx**.

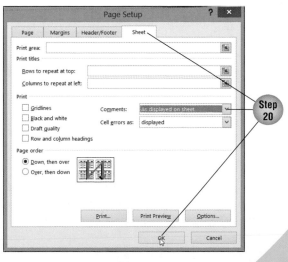

Step 20

Creating a Workbook from a Template

Excel includes worksheets that are formatted and have text and formulas created for specific uses such as creating budgets, inventories, mortgage loan calculators, sales reports, and financial state-ments. These preformatted worksheets are called *templates*. Templates can be customized and saved with a new name to reflect individual company data. Templates are available at the New backstage area and can be downloaded from Office.com.

Project

SNAP

Tutorial 4.10
Using Templates

Dana Hirsch is considering expanding the catering services offered by The Waterfront Bistro and is interested in purchasing an additional property. She has asked you to find a mortgage loan calculator template and determine the payments for various loan and interest amounts.

1 Click the FILE tab and then click the *New* option.

2 At the New backstage area, search for mortgage loan calculator templates by clicking in the search text box (displays with *Search online templates*), typing **mortgage loan calculator**, and then pressing Enter.

3 Click the mortgage loan calculator template shown at the right.

4 Read the information that displays about the template and then click the Create button.

5 Look at the template and notice the type of information required and the way the data is arranged on the page. Save the workbook in the ExcelS4 folder and name it **ES4-WBMortgageLoan**.

6 The first property Dana Hirsch is interested in is priced at $375,000. She wants you to calculate the loan with a $50,000 down payment and an interest rate of 5.5%. Click the amount *$300,000* in the template, type **375000** as the mortgage amount, and then press Enter.

7 Type **5.5** as the interest rate and then press Enter twice.

8 Type **325000** as the loan amount and then press Enter.

Notice the information that displays about the loan, such as the monthly payments, total amount of loan payments, and the interest paid.

9 The template contains a formula for determining the change in total months and payment duration if loan payments increase by 10%. Notice the information that displays with a darker gray background in the template. Click in the cell containing *10% more*. Click the down-pointing arrow that displays at the right side of the cell and then click *25% more* at the drop-down list.

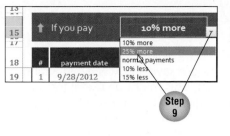

Step 9

In Brief

Create Workbook from Template
1. Click FILE tab.
2. Click *New* option.
3. Click in search text box.
4. Type search text.
5. Press Enter.
6. Click desired template.
7. Click Create button.

Notice the information that displays to the right of *25% more* indicating the decrease in months and duration of the loan if payments are increased by 25%.

10 Print the first page of the worksheet. To do this, click the FILE tab and then click the *Print* option. At the Print backstage area, click in the first text box to the right of *Pages* in the *Settings* category, type **1**, and then press the Tab key. Type **1** in the second text box (after the word *to*) and then click the Print button.

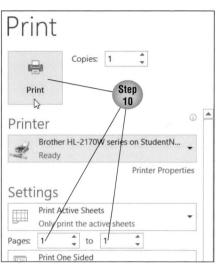

Step 10

11 Dana has located another property that is priced at $529,000. She wants you to calculate the loan with a $65,000 down payment and an interest rate of 4.8%. Click in the cell containing $375,000, type **529000** and then press Enter. Type **4.8** as the interest rate and then press Enter twice. Type **464000** as the loan amount and then press Enter.

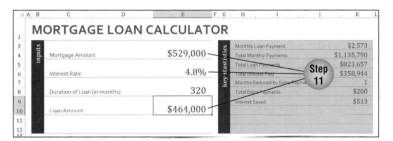

Step 11

12 Print only the first page of the worksheet.

13 Save and then close **ES4-WBMortgageLoan.xlsx**.

In Addition

Pinning a Template

If you use a template on a regular basis, consider pinning the template to the New backstage area. To do this, hover your mouse over the template and then click the gray left-pointing stick pin (*Pin to list*) that displays to the right of the template name. To unpin a template, click the down-pointing stick pin (*Unpin from list*).

Activity 4.11

Saving a Workbook in a Different Format; Creating a PDF/XPS Copy of a Workbook

You can save an Excel file in a different file format. This might be useful for saving a file in an earlier version of Excel, as a template, or in the OpenDocument format. Save files in a different format with options at the Export backstage area. In this backstage area, you can also save an Excel file in the PDF or XPS format. A **Portable Document Format (PDF)** is a file format that preserves fonts, formatting, and images in a printer-friendly version that looks the same on most computers. The recipient of a PDF file does not have to have the Excel application on his or her computer to open, read, or print the file. A PDF file can be opened in various applications including Windows 8 Reader and Adobe Reader if Adobe Reader is installed on the computer. Adobe Reader is available free of charge for download from Adobe's website. Exchanging PDF files has become a popular method for collaborating with others since compatibility does not become an issue and each person keeps his or her original Excel file intact. The **XML Paper Specification (XPS)** format is a fixed-layout format with all formatting preserved (similar to PDF) that was developed by Microsoft.

Project

The Waterfront B·I·S·T·R·O

SNAP

Tutorial 4.11
Saving a Workbook in a Different File Format

Dana needs to send the quarterly sales report workbook to a colleague using Excel 2003 and has asked you to save the workbook in the Excel 97-2003 Workbook (*.xls) format. She has also asked you to send an investment workbook to the bistro's financial advisor. You decide to send her a PDF copy of the investment workbook since you want to keep the original workbook with the formulas intact.

1. Open **WBQtrlySales.xlsx**.

   In the next steps, you will save the workbook in the Excel 97-2003 file format.

2. Click the FILE tab and then click the *Export* option.

3. At the Export backstage area, click the *Change File Type* option.

4. Click the *Excel 97-2003 Workbook (*.xls)* option in the *Change File Type* section and then click the Save As button.

5. At the Save As dialog box with **WBQtrlySales.xls** in the *File name* text box and *Excel 97-2003 Workbook (*.xls)* selected in the *Save as type* option box, click the Save button.

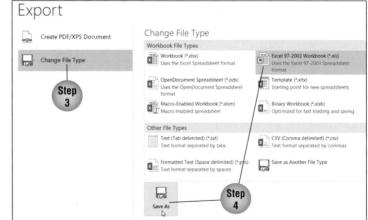

6. At the Microsoft Excel - Compatibility Checker dialog box that displays, click the Continue button.

7. Close **WBQtrlySales.xls**.

8. Open **WBInvestment.xlsx**.

   In the next steps, you will create a PDF copy of the workbook.

9 Click the FILE tab and then click the *Export* option.

10 At the Export backstage area, click the Create PDF/XPS button in the *Create a PDF/XPS Document* section.

Need Help?

Adobe Reader not installed on your computer? Go to www.adobe.com and click the Adobe Reader button (generally located in the Download section) to download and install the free program.

11 At the Publish as PDF or XPS dialog box, with *WBInvestment.pdf* entered in the *File name* text box and with the *Save as type* already set to *PDF (*.pdf)*, make sure the *Open file after publishing* check box contains a check mark (if not, click the option), and then click the Publish button.

> The worksheet is converted to the PDF file format and the published file opens in an Adobe Reader window.

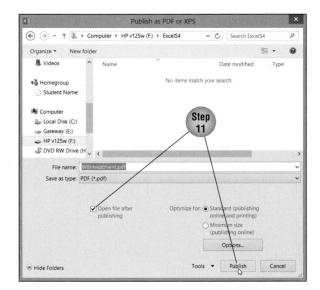

12 Print the document from the Adobe Reader window by pressing Ctrl + P to display the Print dialog box and then clicking the Print button.

13 Close the Adobe Reader window.

14 At the Excel window, close **WBInvestment.xlsx**.

In Addition

Saving a File in XPS Format

Save a file in XPS format in the same manner as saving a file in PDF format. Click the FILE tab and then click the *Export* option. At the Export backstage area, click the Create PDF/XPS button. At the Publish as PDF or XPS dialog box, click the *Save as type* option, click *XPS Document (*.xps)* at the drop-down list, and then click the Publish button. To open an XPS file, open the File Explorer in Windows 8, navigate to the folder containing the file, and then double-click the file. This opens the file in the Windows Viewer. To close the file in the Windows Viewer, position the mouse pointer at the top of the screen (displays as a hand), drag down to the bottom of the screen, and then release the mouse button. You can also open the file in the XPS Viewer by right-clicking the file name in File Explorer, pointing to *Open with* at the shortcut menu, and then clicking *XPS Viewer*.

Save Workbook in Excel 97-2003 (*.xls) File Format
1. Click FILE tab.
2. Click *Export* option.
3. Click *Change File Type* option.
4. Click *Excel 97-2003 Workbook (*.xls)*.
5. Click Save As button.
6. Type file name.
7. Click Save button.
8. Click Continue button.

Create PDF Copy of a Worksheet
1. Click FILE tab.
2. Click *Export* option.
3. Click *Create PDF/XPS Document*.
4. Click *Create a PDF/XPS*.
5. Type file name.
6. Click Publish button.

Features Summary

Feature	Ribbon Tab, Group	Button	FILE Tab Option	Keyboard Shortcut
delete comment	REVIEW, Comments			
delete worksheet	HOME, Cells			
edit comment	REVIEW, Comments			
filter table	HOME, Editing			
format sheet tab	HOME, Cells			
format table	HOME, Styles			
insert comment	REVIEW, Comments			Shift + F2
insert worksheet	HOME, Cells			Shift + F11
move or copy worksheet	HOME, Cells			
page break preview	VIEW, Workbook Views			
print comments	PAGE LAYOUT, Page Setup			
rename worksheet	HOME, Cells			
save in different file format			*Export* OR *Save As*	F12
show all comments	REVIEW, Comments			
sort	HOME, Editing			
templates			*New*	

Knowledge Check SNAP

Completion: In the space provided at the right, indicate the correct term, command, or option.

1. Click this button, located to the right of the worksheet tab(s), to insert a new worksheet in the workbook. _____

2. Perform this action with the mouse while pointing at a worksheet tab to change the worksheet name. _____

3. Perform this action with multiple worksheets to apply the same formatting options to all worksheets in one operation. _____

4. Hold down this key while dragging a worksheet tab to copy the worksheet. _____

5. The formula =SUM('Jan:Jun'!G4) includes this type of reference. _____

6. Link cells between worksheets by entering a formula or by copying and then pasting with this button in the Paste gallery. _____

7. Page breaks are displayed as dashed or solid blue lines in this view. _____

8. Click this button in the Styles group on the HOME tab to define an area of a worksheet as an independent range that can be formatted and managed separately from the rest of the worksheet. _____

9. Select this option from the Sort & Filter list to open a dialog box in which to define more than one sort column. _____

10. This term refers to temporarily hiding rows that do not meet a specified criterion. _____

11. Use this feature to type additional information about a cell that appears in a pop-up box when the cell pointer is positioned over the cell. _____

12. Predesigned formatted worksheets that have labels and formulas created for specific uses can be accessed at this backstage area. _____

13. This is the default file extension for Excel workbooks. _____

14. This type of file requires the Adobe Reader program to view. _____

Skills Review

Review 1 Managing and Formatting Worksheets; Using 3-D References; Printing Multiple Worksheets

1. Open **WBPayroll.xlsx** and then save the workbook in the ExcelEOS folder and name it **ES4-R-WBPayroll**.

2. Delete the Week4 worksheet.

3. Copy the Week3 worksheet and position the new worksheet after Week3.

4. Rename the Week3 (2) worksheet as Week4.

5. Make the Week4 worksheet active and then edit the following cells:
    Change cell C11 from *0* to *8*.
    Change cell G11 from *9* to *0*.
    Change cell I14 from *6* to *9*.

6. Apply the Dark Blue tab color to the Week1 through Week4 worksheet tabs and the Dark Red tab color to the Summary worksheet tab.

7. With the Summary worksheet active, create a SUM formula with a 3-D reference in cell C6 that sums the hours for Lou Cortez for all four weeks.

8. Drag the fill handle from cell C6 to cell C14.

9. Make the Week1 worksheet active. In cell K6, enter the formula **=if(j6>40,j6-40,0)**, drag the fill handle from cell K6 to cell K14, and then calculate the total in cell K15. (This IF statement says that if the amount in cell J6 is greater than 40, subtract the amount in the cell from 40 and return the result. If the amount is less than 40, the formula will insert a zero in the cell.) *Note: A green error flag may appear in cell J15 if error checking is turned on for the computer you are using. You can ignore this inconsistent formula error, which Excel has flagged as a potential error. The error alert occurs because the SUM function in column K is adding the cells above while the SUM function in column J adds the cells left.*

10. In cell L6, type the formula **=(j6*b17)+(k6*b17*.5)**, drag the fill handle from cell L6 to cell L14 and then calculate the total in cell L15. If necessary, increase the width of column

L to display all cell entries. (The formula multiplies the total number of hours by the pay rate in cell B17 and then adds that amount to the number of overtime hours multiplied by the pay rate in cell B17 multiplied by 0.5 since overtime pay is one-and-a-half times the pay rate.)

11. Copy and paste the formulas in columns K and L to complete the *Overtime Hours* and *Gross Pay* column entries for Week2–Week4.

12. Make the Summary worksheet active and then enter the 3-D reference formulas in cell D6 and cell E6 to sum the overtime hours and gross pay for Lou Cortez from all four worksheets.

13. Copy the 3-D formulas in cells D6:E6 and paste to D7:E14.

14. Calculate the totals in C15:E15 and then apply the Accounting format to the cells in the *Gross Pay* column.

15. Group and print all five worksheets. ***Note: If you submit your work in hard copy, check with your instructor to see if you need to print two copies of the worksheets with one of the copies showing the cell formulas instead of the calculated results.***

16. Save and then close **ES4-R-WBPayroll.xlsx**.

Review 2 Formatting a Table; Sorting; Filtering; Inserting and Printing Comments

1. Open **WBJuneOrders.xlsx** and then save the workbook in the ExcelEOS folder and name it **ES4-R-WBJuneOrders**.

2. Select cells A3:E41 and then format the range as a table using the Table Style Medium 3 table style (first row, third column in *Medium* section).

3. Make cell A42 active and then type the following text in the columns indicated. Press the Enter key after typing the amount.

    Item: **Allspice**   *Unit Price*: **39.59**
    Supplier: **Chapman Wholesale Foods**   *Amount:* **1**
    Unit: **case**

4. Make cell F3 active, type **Total**, and then press Enter.

5. With cell F4 active, type the formula **=d4*e4** and then press Enter.

6. Click the TABLE TOOLS DESIGN tab and then click the *Total Row* check box.

7. Adjust the width of column F to display the entire amount in cell F43.

8. Filter the table to display only those items purchased from Chapman Wholesale Foods.

9. Print the filtered worksheet.

10. Redisplay all rows in the table.

11. Sort the table first by *Supplier* and then by *Item* with both levels in *A to Z* order.

12. Add a comment to cell C14 with the text **Dana, please check with JL Enterprises to determine if they sell carrots in 50 pound bags.**

13. Add a comment to cell D18 with the text **Dana, I think we should negotiate with Sven to reduce this price.**

14. Show all comments in the worksheet and set comments to print *As displayed on sheet*.

15. Save and then print **ES4-R-WBJuneOrders.xlsx**.

16. Save the workbook in the PDF file format and specify that you want the file to open after publishing.

17. Print and then close the **ES4-R-WBJuneOrders.pdf** file.

18. Close **ES4-R-WBJuneOrders.xlsx**.

Review 3 Creating a Workbook Using a Template

1. Display the New backstage area, type **billing statement** in the search text box, and then press Enter. Download the billing statement template as shown in Figure 4.2.
2. Enter data into the template as shown in Figure 4.2.
3. Save the workbook in the ExcelEOS folder and name it **ES4-R-PTStmntAug31**.
4. Print and then close **ES4-R-PTStmntAug31.xlsx**.

FIGURE 4.2 Review 3

The Waterfront Bistro

3104 Rivermist Drive

Buffalo, NY 14280

Phone: (716) 555-3166

Fax: (716) 555-3190

E-mail: accounts@wfbistro.emcp.net

Statement

Statement #:	101	**Bill To:** Bobbie Sinclair
Date:	Current Date	Performance Threads
Customer ID: PT-Sinclair		4011 Bridgewater Street
		Niagara Falls, ON L2E 2T6
		CANADA

Date ▾	Type ▾	Invoice # ▾	Description ▾	Amount ▾	Payment ▾	Balance ▾
8/10/2015	Dir Mtg	2462	Catering Services	$ 726.60		$ 726.60
					Total	$ 726.60

Reminder: Please include the statement number on your check.

Terms: Balance due in 30 days.

REMITTANCE

Customer Name:	Performance Threads
Customer ID:	PT-Sinclair
Statement #:	101
Date:	Current Date
Amount Due:	$726.60
Amount Enclosed:	

Skills Assessment

Assessment 1 Inserting, Deleting, and Renaming Worksheets; Linking Worksheets

1. You are the assistant to Cal Rubine, chair of the Theatre Arts Division at Niagara Peninsula College. The co-op consultant has entered grades for the internships at Marquee Productions and Performance Threads into separate worksheets in the same workbook. You need to create a worksheet to summarize the data. To begin, open **NPCInternGrades.xlsx** and then save the workbook in the ExcelEOS folder, naming it **ES4-A1-NPCInternGrades**.

2. Insert a new worksheet before the MarqueeProductions worksheet and rename the worksheet *GradeSummary*.
3. Delete Sheet3.
4. Complete the GradeSummary worksheet by completing the following tasks:
   a. Copy cells A3:B7 in MarqueeProductions to A3:B7 in GradeSummary, keeping the source column widths.
   b. Copy A4:B8 in PerformanceThreads to A8:B12 in GradeSummary.
   c. Copy G3:H3 in MarqueeProductions to C3:D3 in GradeSummary, keeping the source column widths.
   d. Link the cells in columns C and D of the GradeSummary worksheet to the corresponding grades and dates in MarqueeProductions and PerformanceThreads.
   e. Copy the title and subtitle in rows 1 and 2 from MarqueeProductions to GradeSummary. Change the font size of rows 1 and 2 in GradeSummary to 12-point and then adjust the merge and center to columns A–D. Change the fill color in E1:H2 to *No Fill*.
   f. Center the grades in column C.
5. Group the three worksheets and then change the page orientation to landscape.
6. Change the left margin for the GradeSummary worksheet only to 3 inches.
7. Save, print all three worksheets, and then close **ES4-A1-NPCInternGrades.xlsx**.

Assessment 2 Formatting a Table; Filtering; Sorting; Saving a Workbook in the Excel 97-2003 Format

1. Bobbie Sinclair, business manager at Performance Threads, needs a list of costumes for Marquee Productions that have a final delivery date of July 9. You decide to format the list as a table and use sorting and filtering features to do this task. To begin, open **PTMarqueeSch.xlsx** and then save the workbook in the ExcelEOS folder, naming it **ES4-A2-PTMarqueeSch**.
2. Select cells A10:H17 and then format the range as a table using Table Style Light 15 (first option in third row of *Light* section).
3. Filter the table to show only those costumes with a final delivery date of July 9. *Note: Since Start Date and End Date are repeated as column headings in the table, Excel adds numbers after the first occurrences to make each column heading unique*.
4. Sort the filtered list by costume from A to Z.
5. Change the scaling option to fit the worksheet on one page and then print the filtered and sorted list.
6. Redisplay all rows in the table.
7. Sort the table first by the final delivery date from oldest to newest and then by costume from A to Z.
8. Save and then print **ES4-A2-PTMarqueeSch.xlsx**.
9. You need to send the workbook to a colleague using Excel 2003. Save the workbook in the Excel 97-2003 (*.xls) format with the same name.
10. Close **ES4-A2-PTMarqueeSch.xls**.

Assessment 3 Inserting and Printing Comments

1. The costume design team at Performance Threads is meeting at the end of the week to discuss the production schedule for the Marquee Productions project. In preparation for this meeting, Bobbie Sinclair has asked you to review the schedule and send a copy with your comments inserted. To begin, open **PTMarqueeSch.xlsx** and then save the workbook in the ExcelEOS folder, naming it **ES4-A3-PTMarqueeSch**.
2. Make cell D11 active and then type the following comment:
   Sue has not completed the research. Design may not be able to start June 10.
3. Make cell D15 active and then type the following comment:
   These dates may need adjustment due to overlapping projects.
4. Show all comments.
5. Turn on printing of comments *As displayed on sheet*.
6. Save, print, and then close **ES4-A3-PTMarqueeSch.xlsx**.

Assessment 4 Formatting Columns and Formatting a Table; Saving a Workbook in PDF File Format

1. Open **PTRentalCost.xlsx** and then save the workbook in the ExcelEOS folder and name it **ES4-A4-PTRentalCost**.
2. Select cells A3:F43 and then format the range as a table using the Table Style Light 9 table style (second column, second row in the *Light* section).
3. Type **Total Due** in cell G3 and then press Enter.
4. With cell G4 active, type the formula **=f4*c4**.
5. Insert a total row at the bottom of the table.
6. Adjust the width of column G so the entire total amount displays in cell G44.
7. Merge and center the title *Performance Threads* across columns A through G.
8. Merge and center the subtitle *Costume Rentals* across columns A through G.
9. Display the worksheet in Page Break Preview, adjust the page break so all data fits on one page, and then return the view to Normal.
10. Save and then print **ES4-A4-PTRentalCost.xlsx**.
11. Save the workbook in the PDF file format in the ExcelEOS folder and indicate that you want the file to open when published.
12. Print and then close the **ES4-A4-PTRentalCost.pdf** file.
13. Close **ES4-A4-PTRentalCost.xlsx**.

Assessment 5 Finding Information on File Formats Not Supported by Excel 2013

1. Use Excel Help to search for information on file formats not supported in Excel 2013.
2. Create a table in a new worksheet that provides the file format, the extension, and any identifier information. ***Note: Copying and pasting information from the Excel Help window or a Microsoft website is not acceptable.***
3. Apply a table style to the table.
4. Make sure the information is easy to read and understand.
5. Make sure the table will fit on one page when printed.

HELP

6. Save the workbook in the ExcelEOS folder and name it **ES4-A5-FileFormats**.
7. Print and then close **ES4-A5-FileFormats.xlsx**.

Assessment 6 Individual Challenge   Smartphone Shopping

1. After graduation, your goal is to work independently as a consultant in your field of study. You plan to travel frequently in North America and Europe. You want to purchase a smartphone to use while traveling for conference calling, emailing, web browsing, text messaging, and modifying Office documents. Research the latest product offerings for Smartphones on the Internet.

2. Select three phones from three different manufacturers for your short-list comparison. Create a worksheet for analyzing the three smartphones, organizing the information in a table so that the main features are categorized in the leftmost column with each phone's specification for that feature next to each category. Make sure each smartphone's name or manufacturer is identified at the top of the respective columns. In the last row of the table, insert the estimated cost for each smartphone.

3. Based on your perception of the best value, select one of the phones as your recommendation and insert a comment in the phone's cost cell indicating your choice.

4. Add clip art or other enhancements to improve the worksheet's appearance.

5. Save the workbook in the ExcelEOS folder and name it **ES4-A6-Smartphones**.

6. Print the worksheet in landscape orientation scaled to fit on one page and with the comment cell printed as displayed on the sheet.

7. Save and then close **ES4-A6-Smartphones.xlsx**.

Marquee Challenge

Challenge 1 Creating a Sales Invoice by Downloading a Template

1. Dana Hirsch of The Waterfront Bistro has asked you to find and download a professionally designed sales invoice template and then use the template to create an invoice to be sent to First Choice Travel for catering their business meeting.

2. Open the New backstage area, type **sales invoice blue gradient design** in the search text box and then press Enter. Download the template named *Sales invoice (Blue Gradient design)* to your computer. If you cannot find the template shown in Figure 4.3, download another suitable template for a sales invoice.

3. Complete the customer invoice using information found in Figure 4.3.

4. To insert the logo, select the logo container object, click the INSERT tab, and then click the Pictures button in the Illustrations group. At the Insert Picture dialog box, navigate to the ExcelS4 folder on your storage medium and then double-click the file named **TWBLogo.jpg**. Move and resize the logo image as shown in Figure 4.3.

5. Delete the unused rows between the billing address and the body of the invoice.

6. Delete the unused rows between the last line item and the subtotal row.

7. Format the *QTY* column as shown in Figure 4.3.

8. Type **The Waterfront Bistro** next to *Make all checks payable to* near the bottom of the invoice.

9. Save the invoice in the ExcelEOS folder and name it **ES4-C1-WBInvFCT**.

10. Print and then close **ES4-C1-WBInvFCT.xlsx**.

FIGURE 4.3 Challenge 1

INVOICE

The Waterfront
B·I·S·T·R·O

The Waterfront Bistro

3103 Rivermist Drive
Buffalo, NY 14280
P: 716.555.3166 F: 716.555.3190
www.emcp.net/wfbistro

INVOICE NO.   2463
DATE   August 31, 2015
CUSTOMER ID   FCT-Torres

TO   Alex Torres
First Choice Travel
4277 Yonge Street
Toronto, ON M4P 2E6
416.555.9834

SHIP TO   2100 Victoria Street
Niagara-on-the-Lake, ON L0S 1J0

QTY	ITEM #	DESCRIPTION	UNIT PRICE	DISCOUNT	LINE TOTAL
16		Lunches	$ 18.23		$ 291.68
16		Desserts	5.31		84.96
16		Beverages	1.87		29.92
1		Delivery and setup	65.00		65.00
			TOTAL DISCOUNT		
				SUBTOTAL	$ 471.56
				SALES TAX	9%
				TOTAL	$ 514.00

Challenge 2 Importing, Formatting and Sorting a Distributor List

1. Sam Vestering, manager of North American Distribution at Worldwide Enterprises, has provided you with two text files exported from the corporate head office computer. One file contains a list of U.S. distributors and the other contains a list of Canadian distributors. Sam would like a one-page list of all distributors.
2. In Excel, display the Open dialog box with ExcelS4 the active folder, and then change the file type option (located to the right of the File name text box) to *All Files (*.*)*. Double-click **WEUSDistributors.txt** and follow the steps in the Text Import Wizard. You only need to make a change in Step 2 of the wizard, and that is to change the delimiter to a comma.
3. Open the file named **WECdnDistributors.txt** and follow the steps in the Text Import Wizard.
4. Move or copy the data from one of the worksheets to the bottom of the other worksheet.
5. Widen columns as necessary and then delete the second address and email address columns.
6. Add the logo, title, and column labels above the data as shown in Figure 4.4. Use the Pictures button in the Illustrations group on the INSERT tab to insert the logo file named **WELogo.jpg**.
7. Format the data as a table. Use your best judgment to determine the table style, column widths, and other formatting options to apply to the table as shown in Figure 4.4.
8. Look closely at Figure 4.4 to determine the sort order and then custom sort the table. *Hint: The table is sorted by three levels*.

9. Save the worksheet as an Excel file in the *Workbook (*xlsx)* file format in the ExcelEOS folder and name the file **ES4-C2-WEDistributors**. *Hint: Display the Export backstage area, click the* **Change File Type** *option, and then choose the correct file type.*
10. Change to the landscape orientation.
11. Display the worksheet in Page Break Preview, adjust the page break to ensure that the data fits on one page, and then return to Normal view.
12. Save, print, and then close **ES4-C2-WEDistributors.xlsx**.
13. Close all other open workbooks without saving changes.

FIGURE 4.4 Challenge 2

Worldwide Enterprises		North American Distributor List					
Name	Mailing Address	City	State	Zip Code	Telephone	Fax	
Olympic Cinemas	P. O. Box 1439	Calgary	AB	T2C 3P7	403-555-4587	403-555-4589	
LaVista Cinemas	111 Vista Road	Phoenix	AZ	86355-6014	602-555-6231	602-555-6233	
West Coast Movies	P. O. Box 298	Vancouver	BC	V6Y 1N9	604-555-3548	604-555-3549	
Marquee Movies	1011 South Alameda Street	Los Angeles	CA	90045	612-555-2398	612-555-2377	
Sunfest Cinemas	341 South Fourth Avenue	Tampa	FL	33562	813-555-3185	813-555-3177	
Liberty Cinemas	P. O. Box 998	Atlanta	GA	73125	404-555-8113	404-555-2349	
O'Shea Movies	59 Erie	Oak Park	IL	60302	312-555-7719	312-555-7381	
Midtown Moviehouse	1033 Commercial Street	Emporia	KS	66801	316-555-7013	316-555-7022	
All Nite Cinemas	2188 3rd Street	Louisville	KY	40201	502-555-4238	502-555-4240	
Eastown Movie House	P. O. Box 722	Cambridge	MA	2142	413-555-0981	413-555-0226	
Riverview Cinemas	1011-848 Sheppard Street	Winnipeg	MB	R2P 0N6	204-555-6538	204-555-6533	
New Age Movies	73 Killarney Road	Moncton	NB	E1B 2Z9	506-555-8376	506-555-8377	
EastCoast Cinemas	62 Mountbatten Drive	St.John's	NF	A1A 3X9	709-555-8349	709-555-8366	
Hillman Cinemas	55 Kemble Avenue	Baking Ridge	NJ	7920	201-555-1147	201-555-1143	
Seaboard Movie House Inc.	P. O. Box 1005	Dartmouth	NS	B2V 1Y8	902-555-3948	902-555-3950	
Northern Reach Movies	P. O. Box 34	Yellowknife	NW	X1A 2N9	867-555-6314	867-555-6316	
Mainstream Movies	P. O. Box 33	Buffalo	NY	14601	212-555-3269	212-555-3270	
Victory Cinemas	12119 South 23rd	Buffalo	NY	14288	212-555-8746	212-555-8748	
Waterfront Cinemas	P. O. Box 3255	New York	NY	14288	212-555-3845	212-555-3947	
Westview Movies	1112 Broadway	New York	NY	10119	212-555-4875	212-555-4877	
Mooretown Movies	P. O. Box 11	Dublin	OH	43107	614-555-8134	614-555-8339	
Millennium Movies	4126 Yonge Street	Toronto	ON	M2P 2B8	416-555-9335	416-555-9338	
Redwood Cinemas	P. O. Box 112F	Portland	OR	97466-3359	503-555-8641	503-555-8633	
Wellington 10	1203 Tenth Southwest	Philadelphia	PA	19178	215-555-9045	215-555-9048	
Waterdown Cinemas	575 Notre Dame Street	Summerside	PE	C1N 1T8	902-555-8374	902-555-8376	
MountainView Movies	5417 Royal Mount Avenue	Montreal	PQ	H4P 1H8	514-555-3584	514-555-3585	
Danforth Cinemas	P. O. Box 22	Columbia	SC	29201	803-555-3487	803-555-3421	
Plains Cinema House	P. O. Box 209	Regina	SK	S4S 5Y9	306-555-1247	305-555-1248	
Century Cinemas	3687 Avenue K	Arlington	TX	76013	817-555-2116	817-555-2119	

Integrating Programs
Word and Excel

Skills

- Copy and paste Word data into an Excel worksheet
- Link an Excel worksheet with a Word document
- Update linked data
- View linked data as an icon
- Link an Excel chart with a Word document
- Embed an Excel worksheet into a Word document
- Edit an embedded worksheet

Projects Overview

Copy data in a Word document on costume research, design, and sewing hours for employees into an Excel worksheet. Copy data in an Excel worksheet on employee payroll and then link the data to a Word document. Update the payroll hours for the employees for the next week. Copy employee payroll data in an Excel worksheet to a Word document and then update the data in Word.

Link a chart containing sales commissions for agents with a Word document and then update the sales commissions to reflect a higher percentage.

Copy Word data on student scores into an Excel worksheet. Copy an Excel chart containing data on student areas of emphasis in the Theatre Arts Division into a Word document and then update the chart in Excel.

Copy data in an Excel worksheet on theatre company revenues into a Word document and then update the data in Word.

Model Answers for Projects

These model answers for the projects you complete in this section provide a preview of the finished projects before you begin working and also allow you to compare your own results with these models to ensure you have created the materials accurately.

Int1-PTExcelJuneHrs.xlsx is the project in Activity 1.1.

Employee	Research	Design	Sewing	Total
Scott Bercini	3	8	14	25
Terri Cantrell	5	10	18	33
Paul Gottlieb	2	7	10	19
Tae Jeong	6	12	20	38
Total	16	37	62	115

Int1-PTWordOctPay.docx is the project in Activity 1.2 and part of the project in Activity 1.3.

Proudly serving the entertainment industry for over 20 years!

Employee Payroll

Week of October 12, 2015:

Employee	Hours	Pay Rate		Total	
Rosa Levens	20.0	$	14.65	$	293.00
Scott Bercini	40.0	$	15.10	$	604.00
Tae Jeong	25.5	$	12.40	$	316.20
Terri Cantrell	15.0	$	12.00	$	180.00
Paul Gottlieb	40.0	$	16.00	$	640.00

4011 Bridgewater Street ✂ Niagara Falls, ON L2E 2T6 ✂ (905) 555-2971

Int1-PTExcelOctPay.xlsx is part of the project in Activity 1.3.

Performance Threads

Employee Payroll, Week of October 12

Employee	Hours	Pay Rate		Total	
Rosa Levens	20.0	$	14.65	$	293.00
Scott Bercini	40.0	$	15.10	$	604.00
Tae Jeong	25.5	$	12.40	$	316.20
Terri Cantrell	15.0	$	12.00	$	180.00
Paul Gottlieb	40.0	$	16.00	$	640.00

Int1-FCTWordSalesCom.docx is part of the project in Activity 1.4.

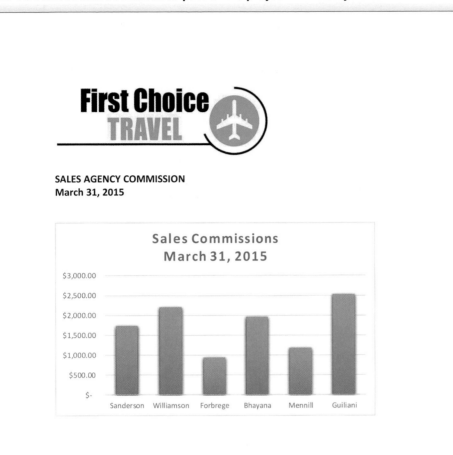

SALES AGENCY COMMISSION
March 31, 2015

Int1-FCTExcelSalesCom.xlsx is part of the project in Activity 1.4.

Int1-PTWordNovPay.docx **is the project in Activity 1.5.**

Performance Threads

Proudly serving the entertainment industry for over 20 years!

Employee Payroll

Week of November 9, 2015:

Employee	Hours	Pay Rate		Total	
Rosa Levens	40.0	$	14.65	$	586.00
Scott Bercini	40.0	$	15.10	$	604.00
Tae Jeong	40.0	$	12.40	$	496.00
Terri Cantrell	40.0	$	11.75	$	470.00
Paul Gottlieb	40.0	$	16.00	$	640.00
Total				$	2,796.00

4011 Bridgewater Street ✂ Niagara Falls, ON L2E 2T6 ✂ (905) 555-2971

Activity 1.1

Copying and Pasting Word Data into an Excel Worksheet

Microsoft Office is a suite that allows integration, which is the combining of data from two or more programs into one document. Integration can occur by copying and pasting data between programs. The program containing the data to be copied is called the **source** program and the program where the data is pasted is called the **destination** program. For example, you can copy data from a Word document into an Excel worksheet. Copy and paste data between programs in the same manner as you would copy and paste data within a program.

Project You have been handed a Word document containing data on costume research, design, and sewing hours, and you need to copy the data to an Excel worksheet.

Performance Threads

1. Open Word and then open **PTWordJuneHrs.docx**.

2. Open Excel and then open **PTExcelJuneHrs.xlsx**.

3. Save the workbook with Save As and name it **Int1-PTExcelJuneHrs**.

4. Click the Word button on the Taskbar.

5. Select the five lines of text in columns, as shown below.

6. Click the Copy button 🗐 in the Clipboard group on the HOME tab.

7. Click the Excel button on the Taskbar.

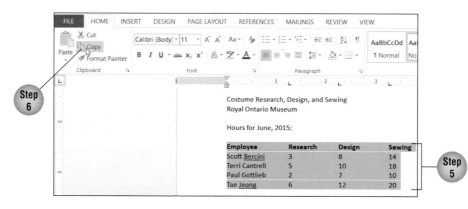

8. Make sure cell A2 is active and then click the Paste button 🗐 in the Clipboard group.

9. Click in cell E2 to deselect the text and then double-click the gray column boundary line between columns A and B.

> This increases the width of column A so the names display.

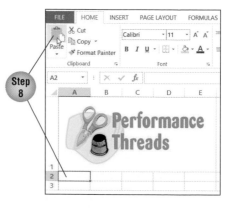

10 With cell E2 active, click the Bold button **B** and then type **Total**.

11 Make cell E3 active, click the AutoSum button **Σ** in the Editing group on the HOME tab, and then press Enter.

> This inserts a formula that calculates the total number of hours for Scott Bercini.

12 Copy the formula in cell E3 down to cells E4 through E6.

13 Make cell A7 active, click the Bold button, and then type **Total**.

14 Make cell B7 active, click the AutoSum button in the Editing group, and then press Enter.

> This inserts a formula that calculates the total number of research hours.

15 Copy the formula in cell B7 to cells C7 through E7.

16 Select cells A2 through E7.

17 Click the Format as Table button 🖌 in the Styles group on the HOME tab and then click *Table Style Light 12* (fifth column, second row in the *Light* section).

18 At the Format As Table dialog box, click OK.

19 Remove the filtering arrows that display in cells A2 through E2. To do this, click the HOME tab, click the Sort & Filter button ⏷ in the Editing group, and then click *Filter* at the drop-down list.

20 Make any other changes needed to improve the visual display of the data in cells A2 through E7.

21 Save, print, and then close **Int1-PTExcelJuneHrs.xlsx**.

22 Click the Word button on the Taskbar.

23 Close **PTWordJuneHrs.docx**.

In Brief

Copy Data from One Program to Another
1. Open desired programs and documents.
2. Select data in source program.
3. Click Copy button.
4. Click button on Taskbar representing destination program.
5. Click Paste button.

In Addition

Cycling between Open Programs

Cycle through open programs by clicking the button on the Taskbar representing the desired program. You can also cycle through open programs by pressing Alt + Tab. Pressing Alt + Tab causes a window to display. Continue holding down the Alt key and pressing the Tab key until the desired program icon is selected by a border in the window and then release the Tab key and the Alt key.

Activity 1.2

Linking an Excel Worksheet with a Word Document

In the previous activity, you copied data from a Word document and pasted it into an Excel worksheet. If you continuously update the data in the Word document, you would need to copy and paste the data each time into the Excel worksheet. If you update data on a regular basis that is copied to other programs, consider copying and linking the data. When data is linked, the data exists in the source program but not as separate data in the destination program. The destination program contains only a code that identifies the name and location of the source program and the location in the document. Since the data is located only in the source program, changes made to the data in the source program are reflected in the destination program. Office updates a link automatically whenever you open the destination program or you edit the linked data in the destination program.

Project Copy data in an Excel worksheet on employee payroll for Performance Threads and then link the data to a Word document.

1. With Word the active program, open **PTWordOctPay.docx**.

2. Save the document with Save As and name it **Int1-PTWordOctPay**.

3. Make Excel the active program and then open **PTExcelOctPay.xlsx**.

4. Save the workbook with Save As and name it **Int1-PTExcelOctPay**.

5. Link the data in cells in the worksheet into the Word document by selecting cells A3 through D8.

6. Click the Copy button in the Clipboard group on the HOME tab.

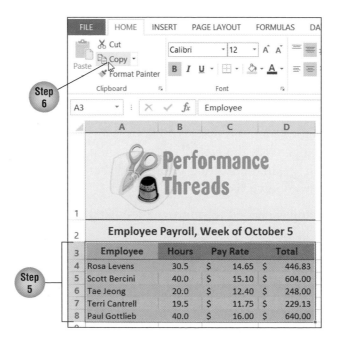

7. Click the Word button on the Taskbar.

8. Press Ctrl + End to move the insertion point to the end of the document (the insertion point is positioned a double space below *Week of October 5, 2015:*).

In Brief

Link Data between Programs
1. Open desired programs and documents.
2. Select data in source program.
3. Click Copy button.
4. Click button on Taskbar representing destination program.
5. Click Paste button arrow.
6. Click *Paste Special*.
7. Click object in *As* list box.
8. Click *Paste link*.
9. Click OK.

9 Click the Paste button arrow and then click *Paste Special* at the drop-down list.

10 At the Paste Special dialog box, click *Microsoft Excel Worksheet Object* in the *As* list box.

11 Click the *Paste link* option located at the left side of the dialog box.

12 Click OK to close the dialog box.

13 Save, print, and then close **Int1-PTWordOctPay.docx**.

The table gridlines do not print.

14 Click the Excel button on the Taskbar.

15 Press the Esc key on the keyboard to remove the moving marquee around cells A3 through D8 and then click cell A3 to make it active.

16 Close **Int1-PTExcelOctPay.xlsx**.

In Addition

Linking Data within a Program

Linking does not have to be between two different programs—you can link data between files in the same program. For example, you can create an object in a Word document such as a table or chart and then link the object with another Word document (or several Word documents). If you make a change to the object in the original document, the linked object in the other document (or documents) is automatically updated.

Activity 1.3

Updating Linked Data; Viewing a Link

The advantage of linking data over copying data is that editing the data in the source program will automatically update the data in the destination program. To edit linked data, open the document in the source program, make the desired edits, and then save the document. The next time you open the document in the destination program, the data is updated. The display of the linked data in the destination program can be changed to an icon. The icon represents the document and program to which the object is linked.

Project

Update the payroll hours for the employees of Performance Threads in the Excel worksheet for the week of October 12, 2015.

Performance Threads

1. With Excel the active program, open **Int1-PTExcelOctPay.xlsx**.

2. Make cell B4 active and then change the number to *20.0*.

   Cells D4 through D8 contain a formula that multiplies the number in the cell in column B with the number in the cell in column C.

3. Make cell B6 active and then change the number to *25.5*.

   When you make cell B6 active, the result of the formula in cell D6 is updated to reflect the change you made to the number in cell B6.

4. Make cell B7 active and then change the number to *15.0*.

5. Make cell C7 active and then change the pay rate to *12.00*.

6. Double-click cell A2 and then change the date from *October 5* to *October 12*.

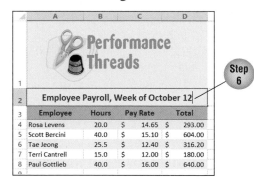

Step 6

	A	B	C	D
1	Performance Threads			
2	Employee Payroll, Week of October 12			
3	Employee	Hours	Pay Rate	Total
4	Rosa Levens	20.0	$ 14.65	$ 293.00
5	Scott Bercini	40.0	$ 15.10	$ 604.00
6	Tae Jeong	25.5	$ 12.40	$ 316.20
7	Terri Cantrell	15.0	$ 12.00	$ 180.00
8	Paul Gottlieb	40.0	$ 16.00	$ 640.00

7. Save, print, and then close **Int1-PTExcelOctPay.xlsx**.

8. Make Word the active program and then open **Int1-PTWordOctPay.docx**.

9. At the message asking if you want to update the document, click Yes.

   The document opens and is automatically updated to reflect the changes you made in **Int1-PTExcelOctPay.xlsx**.

10. Change the date above the table from *October 5* to *October 12*.

Step 10

Employee Payroll

Week of October 12, 2015:

Employee	Hours	Pay Rate	Total
Rosa Levens	20.0	$ 14.65	$ 293.00
Scott Bercini	40.0	$ 15.10	$ 604.00
Tae Jeong	25.5	$ 12.40	$ 316.20
Terri Cantrell	15.0	$ 12.00	$ 180.00
Paul Gottlieb	40.0	$ 16.00	$ 640.00

11 Save and then print **Int1-PTWordOctPay.docx**.

12 Display the linked table as an icon. Begin by right-clicking in the table, pointing to *Linked Worksheet Object*, and then clicking *Convert*.

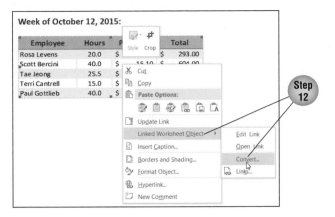

13 At the Convert dialog box, click the *Display as icon* check box to insert a check mark and then click OK.

Notice how the table changes to an icon representing the linked document.

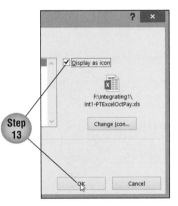

14 Print **Int1-PTWordOctPay.docx**.

15 Make sure the linked object icon is still selected and then redisplay the table. To begin, right-click the icon, point to *Linked Worksheet Object*, and then click *Convert*.

16 At the Convert dialog box, click the *Display as icon* check box to remove the check mark and then click OK.

17 Save and then close **Int1-PTWordOctPay.docx**.

In Brief

Update Linked Data
1. Open document in source program.
2. Make desired edits.
3. Save and close document.
4. Open document in destination program.
5. Click Yes to update links.
6. Save and close document.

Display Linked Object as an Icon
1. Select object.
2. Right-click in object.
3. Point to *Linked Worksheet Object* and then click *Convert*.
4. At Convert dialog box, click *Display as icon* check box.
5. Click OK.

In Addition

Breaking a Link

The link between an object in the destination and source programs can be broken. To break a link, right-click on the object, point to *Linked Worksheet Object*, and then click *Links*. At the Links dialog box, click the Break Link button. At the question asking if you are sure you want to break the link, click the Yes button.

Activity 1.4

Linking an Excel Chart with a Word Document

While a worksheet does an adequate job of representing data, you can present some data more visually by charting the data. A chart is a visual representation of numeric data and, like a worksheet, can be linked to a document in another program. Link a chart in the same manner as you would link a worksheet.

Project Link a chart containing sales commissions for agents of First Choice Travel with a Word document. Change the sales commission in the worksheet chart from 3% to 4%.

First Choice TRAVEL

1. Make Word the active program and then open **FCTWordSalesCom.docx**.

2. Save the document with Save As and name it **Int1-FCTWordSalesCom**.

3. Make Excel the active program and then open **FCTExcelSalesCom.xlsx**.

4. Save the workbook with Save As and name it **Int1-FCTExcelSalesCom**.

5. Click once in the chart area to select it. (A border displays around the chart.)

   Make sure you do not select a specific chart element.

6. Click the Copy button in the Clipboard group on the HOME tab.

7. Click the Word button on the Taskbar.

8. Press Ctrl + End to move the insertion point to the end of the document.

9. Link the chart by clicking the Paste button arrow and then clicking *Paste Special* at the drop-down list.

10. At the Paste Special dialog box, click *Microsoft Excel Chart Object* in the *As* list box, click the *Paste link* option, and then click OK.

11. Save, print, and then close **Int1-FCTWordSalesCom.docx**.

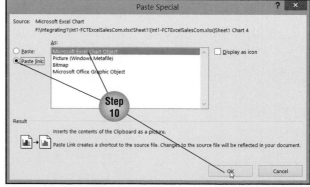

12 Click the Excel button on the Taskbar.

13 The chart is based on a sales commission of 3%. Change the formula so it calculates a sales commission of 4% by double-clicking in cell C3 and then changing *0.03* in the formula to *0.04*.

14 Press the Enter key.

> Pressing Enter displays the result of the formula calculating commissions at 4%.

15 Make cell C3 active and then copy the new formula down to cells C4 through C8.

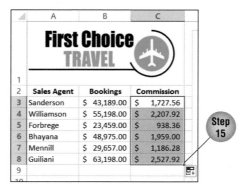

16 Save and then close **Int1-FCTExcelSalesCom.xlsx**.

17 Click the Word button on the Taskbar and then open the **Int1-FCTWordSalesCom.docx** document.

18 At the message asking if you want to update the document, click Yes.

> Notice the change in the amounts in the chart. If your chart does not update, click the chart to select it and then press the F9 function key.

19 Save, print, and then close **Int1-FCTWordSalesCom.docx**.

In Addition

Customizing a Link

By default, a linked object is updated automatically and a linked object can be edited. You can change these defaults with options at the Links dialog box. Display this dialog box by right-clicking the linked object, pointing to *Linked Worksheet Object*, and then clicking *Links*. At the Links dialog box, click the *Manual update* option if you want to control when to update linked data. With the *Manual* update option selected, update linked objects by clicking the Update Now button at the right side of the Links dialog box. If you do not want a linked object updated, click the *Locked* check box in the Links dialog box to insert a check mark.

You can copy an object between documents in a program, link an object, or embed an object. A linked object resides in the source program but not as a separate object in the destination program. An embedded object resides in the document in the source program as well as the destination program. If a change is made to an embedded object at the source program, the change is not made to the object in the destination program. Since an embedded object is not automatically updated, as is a linked object, the only advantage to embedding rather than simply copying and pasting is that you can edit an embedded object in the destination program using the tools of the source program.

Project

Copy data in an Excel worksheet on employee payroll for Performance Threads and then embed the data in a Word document. Update the payroll hours for the week of November 9 in the embedded Excel worksheet.

Performance Threads

1. With Word the active program, open **PTWordNovPay.docx**.

2. Save the document with Save As and name it **Int1-PTWordNovPay**.

3. Make Excel the active program and then open **PTExcelNovPay.xlsx**.

4. Save the workbook with Save As and name it **Int1-PTExcelNovPay**.

5. Embed cells into the Word document by selecting cells A3 through D8.

6. Click the Copy button in the Clipboard group on the HOME tab.

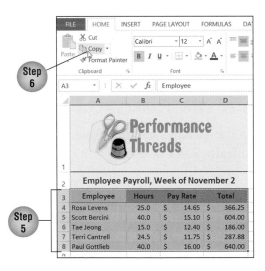

7. Click the Word button on the Taskbar.

8. Press Ctrl + End to move the insertion point to the end of the document (the insertion point is positioned a double space below *Week of November 2, 2015:*).

9. Click the Paste button arrow and then click *Paste Special* at the drop-down list.

10 At the Paste Special dialog box, click *Microsoft Excel Worksheet Object* in the *As* list box.

Paste Special dialog box

Step
10

In Brief

Embed Data
1. Open desired programs and documents.
2. Select data in source program.
3. Click Copy button.
4. Click button on Taskbar representing destination program.
5. Click Paste button arrow, *Paste Special*.
6. Click object in *As* list box.
7. Click OK.

Edit Embedded Object
1. In source program, double-click embedded object.
2. Make desired edits.
3. Click outside object.

11 Click OK.

12 Save and print **Int1-PTWordNovPay.docx**.

13 Click the Excel button on the Taskbar.

14 Press the Esc key to remove the moving marquee around cells A3 through D8.

15 Click in cell A2 to make it active and then close **Int1-PTExcelNovPay.xlsx**.

16 Click the Word button on the Taskbar.

17 Change the date above the table from *November 2* to *November 9*.

18 Position the arrow pointer anywhere in the worksheet and then double-click the left mouse button.

> In a few moments, the worksheet displays surrounded by column and row designations and the Excel tabs.

19 To produce the ordered costumes on time, the part-time employees worked a full 40 hours for the week of November 9. Make cell B4 active and then change the number to *40*.

20 Make cell B6 active and then change the number to *40*.

21 Make cell B7 active and then change the number to *40*.

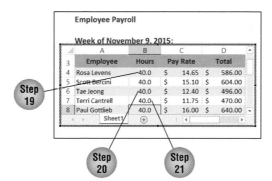

22 Bobbie Sinclair, the business manager, wants to know the payroll total for the week of November 9 to determine the impact it has on the monthly budget. Add a new row to the table by making cell A8 active and then pressing the Down Arrow key.

23 With cell A9 active, type **Total**.

24 Make cell D9 active and then click the AutoSum button in the Editing group.

25 Make sure the sum of cells D4 through D8 displays in cell D9 and then press the Enter key.

continues

26 Increase the height of the worksheet by one row by positioning the arrow pointer on the bottom middle black sizing square until the pointer turns into an up-and-down-pointing arrow. Hold down the left mouse button, drag down one row, and then release the mouse button.

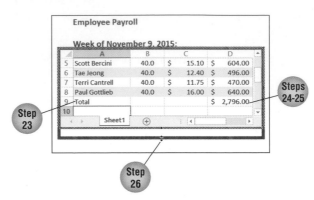

27 Using the arrow keys on the keyboard, make cell A3 active and position cell A3 in the upper left corner of the worksheet. (This will display all cells in the worksheet containing data.)

28 Click outside the worksheet to deselect it.

29 Save, print, and then close **Int1-PTWordNovPay.docx**.

> The gridlines do not print.

In Addition

Inserting an Embedded Object from an Existing File

You embedded an Excel worksheet in a Word document using the Copy button and options at the Paste Special dialog box. Another method is available for embedding an object from an existing file. In the destination program document, position the insertion point where you want the object embedded and then click the Object button in the Text group. At the Object dialog box, click the Create from File tab. At the Object dialog box with the Create from File tab selected, type the desired file name in the *File name* text box or click the Browse button and then select the desired file from the appropriate folder. At the Object dialog box, make sure the *Link to file* check box does not contain a check mark and then click OK.

Troubleshooting Linking and Embedding Problems

If you double-click a linked or embedded object and a message appears telling you that the source file or source program cannot be opened, consider the following troubleshooting options. Check to make sure that the source program is installed on your computer. If the source program is not installed, convert the object to the file format of a program that is installed. Try closing other programs to free memory and make sure you have enough memory to run the source program. Check to make sure the source program does not have any dialog boxes open and, if it is a linked object, check to make sure someone else is not working in the source file.

Skills Review

Review 1 Copying and Pasting Data

1. Create a new folder on your storage medium and name it **IntegratingEOS**.
2. With Word the active program, open **NPCWordScores.docx**.
3. Make Excel the active program and then open **NPCExcelScores.xlsx**.
4. Save the workbook in the IntegratingEOS folder and name it **Int1-R-NPCExcelScores**.
5. Click the Word button on the Taskbar.
6. Select the nine lines of text in columns (the line beginning *Student* through the line beginning *Yiu, Terry*) and then click the Copy button in the Clipboard group on the HOME tab.
7. Click the Excel button on the Taskbar.
8. With cell A5 active, paste the text into the worksheet.
9. Select cells A5 through A13, click the Delete button arrow in the Cells group on the HOME tab, click *Delete Cells*, and then click OK at the Delete dialog box.
10. Increase the width of column A by double-clicking the gray column boundary line between columns A and B.
11. Select cells B6 through D13 and then click once on the Increase Decimal button in the Number group on the HOME tab. (This displays two numbers after the decimal point.)
12. Type the word **Average** in cell E5.
13. Make cell E6 active. Insert a formula that averages the numbers in cells B6 through D6.
14. Copy the formula in cell E6 down to cells E7 through E13.
15. With cells E6 through E13 selected, change the font to 12-point Cambria.
16. Select cells B6 through E13, click the Center button in the Alignment group on the HOME tab, and then deselect the cells.
17. Save, print, and then close **Int1-R-NPCExcelScores.xlsx**.
18. Click the Word button on the Taskbar and then close the **NPCWordScores.docx** document.

Review 2 Linking an Object and Editing a Linked Object

1. With Word the active program, open **NPCWordEnroll.docx**.
2. Save the document in the IntegratingEOS folder and name it **Int1-R-NPCWordEnroll**.
3. Make Excel the active program and then open the workbook named **NPCExcelChart.xlsx**.
4. Save the workbook in the IntegratingEOS folder and name it **Int1-R-NPCExcelChart**.
5. Link the chart to the Word document **Int1-R-NPCWordEnroll.docx** a triple space below the *Student Enrollment* subtitle. (Make sure you use the Paste Special dialog box.)
6. Select the chart and then center it by clicking the Center button in the Paragraph group on the HOME tab.
7. Save, print, and close **Int1-R-NPCWordEnroll.docx**.
8. Click the Excel button on the Taskbar.
9. Click outside the chart to deselect it.
10. Print **Int1-R-NPCExcelChart.xlsx** in landscape orientation.

11. With **Int1-R-NPCExcelChart.xlsx** open, make the following changes to the data in the specified cells:

    A2:   Change *Fall Term* to *Spring Term*.
    B4:   Change *75* to *98*.
    B5:   Change *30* to *25*.
    B6:   Change *15* to *23*.
    B7:   Change *38* to *52*.
    B8:   Change *25* to *10*.

12. Make cell A2 active.
13. Save, print in landscape orientation, and then close **Int1-R-NPCExcelChart.xlsx**.
14. Make Word the active program and then open **Int1-R-NPCWordEnroll.docx**. (At the message asking if you want to update the document, click Yes.)
15. Save, print, and then close **Int1-R-NPCWordEnroll.docx**.

Review 3 Embedding an Object

1. With Word the active program, open **WERevMemo.docx**.
2. Save the document in the IntegratingEOS folder and name it **Int1-R-WERevMemo**.
3. Make Excel the active program and then open **WEExcelRev.xlsx**.
4. Embed the data in cells A2 through D8 to the Word document **Int1-R-WERevMemo.docx** a double space below the paragraph of text in the body of the memo.
5. Save and then print **Int1-R-WERevMemo.docx**.
6. Click the Excel button on the Taskbar, close the **WEExcelRev.xlsx** workbook without saving it, and then close Excel.
7. With **Int1-R-WERevMemo.docx** open, double-click the worksheet and then make the following changes to the data in the specified cells:

    A2:   Change *July Revenues* to *August Revenues*.
    B4:   Change *1,356,000* to *1,575,000*.
    B5:   Change *2,450,000* to *2,375,000*.
    B6:   Change *1,635,000* to *1,750,000*.
    B7:   Change *950,000* to *1,100,000*.
    B8:   Change *1,050,000* to *1,255,000*.

8. Move the insertion point up to cell A2 and then click outside the worksheet to deselect it.
9. In the memo document, change the date from *August 14, 2015* to *September 2, 2015*, and change the subject from *July Revenues* to *August Revenues*.
10. Save, print, close **Int1-R-WERevMemo.docx**, and then close Word.